Studies in Modern History

General Editor: **J. C. D. Clark**, Joyce and Elizabeth Hall Distinguished Professor of British History, University of Kansas

Titles include:

Lisa Steffen
TREASON AND NATIONAL IDENTITY
Defining a British State, 1608–1820

Lynne Taylor
BETWEEN RESISTANCE AND COLLABORATION
Popular Protest in Northern France, 1940–45

Studies in Modern History
Series Standing Order ISBN 0–333–79328–5
(*outside North America only*)

You can receive future titles in this series as they are published by placing a standing order.
Please contact your bookseller or, in case of difficulty, write to us at the address below with
your name and address, the title of the series and the ISBN quoted above.

Customer Services Department, Macmillan Distribution Ltd, Houndmills, Basingstoke,
Hampshire RG21 6XS, England

Jewish Immigrant Entrepreneurship in New York and London 1880–1914

Enterprise and Culture

Andrew Godley
Lecturer in Economics
University of Reading

palgrave

First published 2001 by
PALGRAVE
Houndmills, Basingstoke, Hampshire RG21 6XS and
175 Fifth Avenue, New York, N. Y. 10010
Companies and representatives throughout the world

PALGRAVE is the new global academic imprint of
St. Martin's Press LLC Scholarly and Reference Division and
Palgrave Publishers Ltd (formerly Macmillan Press Ltd).

ISBN 0–333–96045–9

This book is printed on paper suitable for recycling and
made from fully managed and sustained forest sources.

A catalogue record for this book is available
from the British Library.

Library of Congress Cataloging-in-Publication Data
Godley, Andrew, 1963–
    Jewish immigrant entrepreneurship in New York and London,
    1880–1914 : enterprise and culture / Andrew Godley.
        p. cm.
    Includes bibliographical references and index.
    ISBN 0–333–96045–9
    1. Jewish businesspeople—New York (State)—New York–
    –History. 2. Jewish businesspeople—England—London—History.
    3. Immigrants—New York (State)—New York—History.
    4. Immigrants—England—London—History. 5. Entrepreneurship–
    –History. 6. Corporate culture—United States—History.
    7. Corporate culture—Great Britain—History. I. Title.
    HC108.N7 G63 2001
    338'.04'08992407471—dc21
                                                        2001021622

10   9   8   7   6   5   4   3   2   1
10   09 08 07 06 05 04 03 02 01

Printed and bound in Great Britain by
Antony Rowe Ltd, Chippenham, Wiltshire

To Dorothy

Contents

List of Tables and Figures

Tables

ix

Figures

Preface and Acknowledgements

My aim in writing this book was to see if it was possible to analyse the effects of cultural differences in economic history. Despite many attempts, it must be confessed that to date this has been a frustrating field, with many well-known difficulties (rehearsed here in Chapter 1). Perhaps the book's most novel contribution therefore is the use of a control population – a group of people with a common culture in two different locations (the United States and Britain) – to test for the economic effects of assimilating British and American cultural values. In this social science experiment, the East European Jewish immigrants in New York and London represent that control population. And so, while they are the book's subjects, the result is not primarily Jewish history. Jewish historians may, nevertheless, find one or two topics of interest here.

No economic historian is ever surprised that historical statistics are incomplete and imperfect for whatever task is at hand. The extent of the statistical poverty of any analysis of the Jews in Britain and America is still shocking nevertheless. Without quantitative estimates of Jewish immigration or social mobility, especially for those in Britain, this study would have remained stillborn. Thankfully, however, and with the generous cooperation of the Board of Deputies of British Jews, the Chief Rabbi's Office, the Federation of Synagogues and the United Synagogue, as well as the secretaries of many London synagogues, I was able to construct various statistical series from the occupational and other information contained on Jewish marriage records. Particular credit needs to be given to David Massil and Marlena Schmool of the Board of Deputies and Charles Tucker from the Chief Rabbi's Office.

Constructing the various data sets has taken rather longer than originally anticipated! This was originally my PhD thesis, and my supervisor, Paul Johnson, of the London School of Economics, did warn me that I was being a little ambitious! I am deeply thankful that, nevertheless, he encouraged me to continue; something that, I fear, would be far less likely to happen in today's climate.

Others at the LSE, Reading and elsewhere to whom I am particularly indebted include Mark Casson, Stanley Chapman, Barry Chiswick, Peter Earle, David Feldman, Lloyd Gartner, Les Hannah, Katrina Honeyman, Eddie Hunt, Eric Jones, Geoff Jones, Anne Kershen, Thomas Kessner, Avner Offer, Harold Pollins, Bill Rubinstein, Barry Supple and Robert

Whaples, as well as many, many others whose comments and questions at seminars and conferences have helped to shape and hone the argument. To all these interested colleagues and critics, I offer my thanks. And throughout this long, drawn-out episode, my wife has admired my stamina, speculated on the nature of obsession, defended my progress and not once even hinted that the end-product would be anything other than immensely important. How can I do anything other than dedicate the book to her? Yet the simple truth is that whatever the book contains it fades into sheer insignificance beside her.

ANDREW GODLEY

Part I
Enterprise and Culture

1
Culture and Economic Behaviour

This is a book about culture and economic behaviour. For a professional economic historian, this is an unusual combination. Economists (and following them, economic historians), after all, have studiously avoided including culture in their understanding of human behaviour. This scholar is nevertheless convinced that culture matters in economics. Culture influences economic outcomes: it is in part responsible for the material standard of living enjoyed by people around the world; there are, in other words, good cultures and bad. In attaining prosperity and driving down poverty, some values help, some hinder. While this is often claimed, it is far less often specified. Exactly how culture influences some (surely not all) economic outcomes is rarely addressed by social scientists.

The difficulties of incorporating culture into any analysis based on methodological individualism are well known. How can culture be specified when it is yet to be satisfactorily defined? How can it be quantified if it remains vague and unclassifiable? Far better, retort the economists, to continue modelling value-free behaviour. But economics needs culture.

Economics without culture explains lots of the little stories of development, but falls short in the big story. On the basis of innovations in technology, developments in trade and reductions in transaction costs, economic historians are, broadly speaking, able to account for the rise of the West. But without culture we have only a vague idea of why the industrial revolution occurred in Britain rather than elsewhere, or of how industrialisation was transmitted to some nations and not others in the decades since. Culture is a fundamentally important component in understanding global economic development.[1]

The difficulty about including culture in any systematic analysis is not that most economists think it irrelevant; it is rather that the

3

assumption of individual rationality at the heart of economic theory precludes any easy inclusion. Under similar circumstances, economic theory essentially predicts that people behave the same.[2]

Many readers may find this perverse. After all, casual observation among academics and non-academics alike suggests that cultural differences between nations are acute. Travel guidebooks tell us how to behave, international businessmen are briefed on successful negotiating styles, universities hold special orientation sessions for foreign students. Anyone content with ignoring cultural differences, we might think, has simply never left home.

Reassuringly for believers in the power of casual observation, social scientists across the spectrum increasingly agree. A mass of empirical studies have spawned new sub-fields in management studies, social psychology and sociology. Since Hofstede's landmark volume, *Culture's Consequences*, was published in 1980, the tide of related studies has flowed ever higher.[3] Among sociologists there has been a near-universal rejection of the traditional consensus of behavioural convergence on a Weberian 'rationality', in favour of one of culture's 'embeddedness' in all societies, shaping and governing all social interaction. Cultural variations in concepts as diverse yet fundamental as property rights, equality, group membership and so on have now been firmly accepted within the broad social science canon. Different values lead to different behaviour, including economic behaviour.[4]

This divergence between one group of social scientists, for whom culture is core, and the economists, who cannot use it, is surely undesirable. Moreover, the apparent reluctance among mainstream economists to incorporate culture more rigorously is surprising. After all, it does not require a particularly close reading of current research in many of its branches to see that many leading economists believe in its importance. It is rather that they don't know what to do with it.

Akerloff has suggested that cultural differences influence international variations in levels of unemployment, Atkinson has mused on whether they are related to varying levels of inequality throughout the western world, Muellbauer (among many) has emphasised the importance of subjective factors in forming consumer expectations, Sowell has stressed the relationship between culture and entrepreneurship and Casson has modeled its role in firm performance.[5] Finance experts may disagree, but beyond the supply side (entrepreneurship and the corporate sector), the demand side (consumer behaviour) and welfare implications (unemployment and inequality), economics is actually a pretty limited subject. Culture's importance in economic behaviour ought, in other words, not to be a particularly controversial issue nowadays. The difficulty, of course, is to know how to go beyond vague allusions to social norms to being able to incorporate culture and custom in mainstream economic theory.

While some approaches have used game theory to model cultural variations in behaviour, and some approaches have tried to understand better the institutional links between cultural values and economic outcomes, perhaps the most important recent contribution has been Ekkehart Schlicht's *On Custom in the Economy*. Schlicht's foundation is rooted in the observation from social psychology that individuals derive emotional satisfaction from aligning their behaviour with social norms. This is then grafted onto an otherwise conventional economic analysis to probe the role of property rights, law and division of labour within the firm.[6]

While this modelling is both eminently laudable and sensible, in fact, and in order to give added momentum to further work in this area, what is first required is a simple empirical proof of the impact of culture on economic behaviour. That is what this book aims to provide. Before describing the social science experiment that has been designed to provide this proof, some words about the economics of culture are in order.

The economics of culture

Economics is interested primarily in how scarce goods and services are allocated. In principle, there are an infinite variety of regimes for allocating goods and services, but the most efficient system yet devised by human civilisation for the allocation of most goods and services is called a market. As long as there exists sufficient freedom to participate, a moderate respect for property rights, and a reasonable amount of available information, individuals will buy, barter and truck. Markets, by definition, are then human institutions and so, at least in part, culturally determined, and have been for several millennia.[7] The most important cultural values for economic prosperity are materialism, trust, teamwork and entrepreneurship.

Materialism

Markets are efficient because they largely solve the coordination problem of allocating scarce goods and services to their best uses. Among any group of people, some will have stronger preferences than others for any given good. Their higher valuation will lead to a willingness to pay a higher price for it. In the bidding process, those who value items most highly will end up consuming them. Goods therefore go to those who value them most and, in this sense, goods and services are supplied to those who will put them to their best (most highly valued) use. Markets are therefore efficient.

For communities to benefit from this efficiency, certain cultural values supporting the creation and development of markets must be in palce. Prime among them is a form of materialism that views human life and experience as detached from the surrounding material world. Without this it is surely unlikely that the related concepts of property rights and their transferability would ever develop. In the absence of transferable property rights, trade would never be able to supersede war as the leading form of human exchange.

Trust

Where goods and services are allocated outside the market, perhaps within firms or governments, culture may also be important. This is because there are costs associated with coordinating supply and demand. These transaction costs can be very high; in complex and specialised transactions, for instance, that require a sequence of obligations and promises to be honoured from several parties. Members of high-trust cultures can coordinate these complex transactions more efficiently than those with low-trust cultures, whether within a firm, a market or whatever, because in cultures where cheating is rife, transactions will break down as one or other party cheats. High-trust cultures, by contrast, continue to trade. When endemic in society and over time, cheating leads to stunted economic growth and reduced prosperity. Trust reduces transaction costs and so increases material wealth.[8]

Teamwork

Cultural values associated with detached materialism on the one hand and trustworthiness on the other are therefore important to economic development. Economically successful cultures also promote cooperation among the members of the social group. In a fallen world there will always be disasters. Cooperation is important because a collective response to any unforeseen shock is more efficient than the sum of individual responses.[9]

Entrepreneurship

If materialism, teamwork and trust provide the ground for efficient solutions to complex economic problems, innovation is the seed of growth. Cultural values that promote innovation and entrepreneurship must tolerate at the very least individual experimentation. Successful experimentation depends on the encouragement of reflection on past experience and the development of forms of scientific rationality.

While prosperity may therefore be especially associated with materialism, teamwork, trust and entrepreneurship, this subset of values hardly encompasses culture. Capturing the sum of the world's values, customs and beliefs is, however, not only beyond the scope of this book but is probably unimportant. This is because some values are more influential than others. For instance, it is not especially obvious how some religious practices facilitate wealth creation; circumcision, for example, or the observation of feast days, or religious worship in general. Contrast this with the thriftiness and ensuing capital accumulation seen in some religions and it is obvious that some customs are more important than others.[10] For the purposes of studying its relationship with economic outcomes, culture *in toto* can be discarded and attention focused on isolating one or more of the core values alone.

Before fixing on our chosen cultural value, one further facet of the economic analysis of culture needs highlighting, namely conformity. Conformity is not the same as culture, nor any specific cultural value. It is not the same as cooperation, for example, with which it might be confused. Rather, conformity is the degree to which a social group behaves in accordance with any given cultural value or custom. Take Hofstede's widely accepted indices of cultural values. Here some national cultures emphasise, say, cooperation more than others – Sweden compared with the UK, for example. What this statement actually means is that, according to the results from multiple questionnaires, the average Swedish response rated cooperation more highly than the average British.

Conformity therefore indicates not the mean cultural values but their dispersion around these averages. Knowing what conformity is in any given national culture is important because mean scores alone are not particularly helpful. Consider the relationship between class and culture, for instance. If class influences culture, then the distribution of the scores for any given cultural value among the population may be far from the normal bell-shaped curve. If working- and middle-class values have ever been antipathetic (a consensual view among British social historians), then a bimodal distribution would be more likely, in which case, the mean would be fairly meaningless. High conformity therefore implies that a high proportion of the population behaves in accordance with the custom or value, low conformity that only a small proportion follow the herd.

For the long-term survival of core cultural values such as teamwork and trust, conformity must be fairly high. However, complete conformity is surely far short of being optimal. The gains from innovation and arbitrage require some tolerance for and an openness to new ideas, whether they emerge from inside or outside the social group.

Culture, then, is best seen as an ever-changing series of trade-offs between openness and trust, innovation and teamwork, and so on, in response to environmental change. Should returns to innovation and openness increase (perhaps through the adoption of new technology), for instance, then teamwork and trust may diminish. Should returns to cooperation increase (perhaps because of the threat of war), then teamwork and trust will increase.[11]

The underlying concepts for an economic analysis of culture are now in place, for both the core cultural values themselves and the degree of conformity to them must be captured. The core cultural values are the key variables and here, as elsewhere, their quantitative manifestation will be their averages, but knowing the degree of conformity, their standard deviation, is also essential to any analysis. With culture and conformity, the route to establishing a credible social science experiment is now open. One of the core values needs to be selected and a method of measuring the chosen value and its conformity across nations must be derived. Armed with newly derived measures of cultural differences, old observations of economic behaviour can be revisited and, one hopes, more fully explained.

There are many episodes in history where the efflorescence of culture may have sparked economic change. Deirdre McCloskey, for example, has recently suggested that the surge in British eighteenth-century inventiveness was a cultural phenomenon, with profound economic consequences for the Industrial Revolution.[12]

In fact, the impact of culture has been a common thread throughout the writing of economic history since Weber's assertion that Calvinism was a catalyst for higher rates of saving and investment. It has become almost a truism that Jews and Quakers derived commercial advantages in the early modern period because their cultural exclusivity facilitated access to credit.[13] More generally, Abramovitz's emphasis on the importance of 'social capabilities' in economic development concurs with the views of David Landes and Peter Temin as well as McCloskey, that Anglo-American cultural values are in some as yet unspecified way correlated with the emergence of Anglo-American economic hegemony from the early nineteenth century.[14]

The single most controversial episode regarding the relationship between economic behaviour and culture, however, and one which has spawned an enormous literature, concerns the late-Victorian entrepreneur. In the debate about Britain's relative economic decline in the twentieth century, the apparently poor performance of British business looms large. Britain's entrepreneurs allegedly suffered from an anti-entrepreneurial culture. This debate has continued for at least forty years, with remarkably little consensus emerging. It is to this debate that this book aims to make a contribution, in particular, through attempting to test for cultural attitudes towards entrepreneurship in late-Victorian Britain and the United States.

The late-Victorian entrepreneur and British culture: the state of the debate

The economic history of Britain during the period 1880–1914 is a tale of relative decline, a story made more painful by what had preceded it. The United States, by contrast, enjoyed the ascent to unparalleled economic supremacy. One of the most revealing indicators of this surge in American economic power is its relative energy use. Between 1890 and 1913 Britain's energy consumption rose from 145 million tonnes of coal or its equivalent to 195 million tonnes, whereas the United States consumed an almost identical 147 million tonnes in 1890 but by 1913 this had increased to 541 million tonnes.[15] Of course, relative costs played an important role here, but this enormous gap in energy consumption was caused primarily by differences in industrial growth. Britain's industrial potential in 1880 was over 50 per cent higher than the United States', yet by 1913 the United States' industrial potential was more than double that of Britain's. Britain's share of world manufacturing output fell from 22.9 per cent in 1880 to 13.6 per cent by 1913. The United States' share grew from 14.7 per cent to 32.0 per cent.[16]

In the face of the contrast in fortunes that these figures illustrate it is not surprising that both anxious contemporaries and, subsequently, economic historians have pointed an accusing finger at the allegedly poor qualities of the British entrepreneur, who was either not sufficiently flexible in foreign markets or else reluctant to incorporate new technology.[17] The case against the late-Victorian entrepreneur was summed up by Landes in the sixties when he claimed that British enterprise reflected a

> combination of amateurism and complacency. Her merchants who had once seized the markets of the world, took them for granted; the consular reports are full of the incompetence of the British exporters, their refusal to suit their goods to the taste and pockets of the client, their unwillingness to try new products in new areas, their insistence that everyone in the world ought to read in English and count in pounds, shillings, and pence. Similarly, the British manufacturer was notorious for his indifference to style, his conservatism in the face of new techniques, his reluctance to abandon the individuality of tradition for the conformity implicit in mass production.[18]

British businessmen of the late nineteenth century came to be seen as passive, complacent and even arrogant in their alleged blindness to business opportunities, with either, at best, a craft-dominated, production-centred philosophy that neglected both marketing and mass production, or, at worst, a total disregard for all things commercial and industrial. Such apparently self-destructive behaviour has partly been explained with reference to nineteenth-century British culture. This formed the set of attitudes the Victorian proprietorial and managerial classes held towards business, cultural standards which, it is claimed, were anti-industrial. The leading proponent of this view is the American historian Martin Wiener:

> These standards did little to support, and much to discourage, economic dynamism. They threw earlier enthusiasms for technology into disrepute, emphasised the social evils brought by the industrial revolution, directed attention to issues of the 'quality of life' in preference to the quantitative concerns of production and expansion, and disparaged the restlessness and acquisitiveness of industrial capitalism.[19]

The long-run consequences of this alleged culturally rooted entrepreneurial failure have been a persistent ambivalence towards industry, which ultimately, it has been claimed, affected economic development in the most serious of manners.[20] Much of the colour of recent governments' political philosophy, at least since 1979, has been squarely based on these assumptions, and so has impressed upon the nation the need to change from what Keith Joseph called the 'perceptible depressing limpness in individual attitudes' to a dynamic and entrepreneurial economy.[21]

Specialist opinion has, however, questioned this entrepreneurial-failure interpretation of Britain's relative economic decline. Much research since the 1960s has discovered that British entrepreneurs were not as prone to failure as originally believed. Case-study upon case-study was examined and tangible evidence of entrepreneurial failure has proved elusive.[22] Perhaps more importantly, relative industrial decline is explained without reference to diminishing British enterprise. The rapid growth of the United States and Germany relative to the UK was attributed to their relatively late start and, thus, their relative under-utilisation of resources. British entrepreneurs maximised returns in less favourable circumstances. Thus, the argument goes, British relative decline was inevitable.[23]

Indeed, within the late-nineteenth-century liberal trading regime, convergence in the world economy on British aggregate productivity would be expected. British productivity growth would be slow, that of other countries faster. Living standards abroad would catch up with British.[24] Nonetheless, the trends in productivity growth in the British economy in the years preceding the First World War can only be described as disappointing as American productivity leapt ahead of that in the United Kingdom.[25]

This has partly been explained by the emerging patterns of comparative advantage in the global economy. The United States and Germany by 1913 enjoyed comparative advantages in different and faster growing areas of manufacturing, and their higher productivity reflected this. The United Kingdom, by contrast, enjoyed a comparative advantage in older industries, where productivity gains were more muted, as well, perhaps, as in some services such as banking and trading.[26]

Despite its plausibility, however, the explanation that United Kingdom relative decline was inevitable under the constraints of global convergence does not appear to capture the sheer extent of that decline. While much of the dynamic American growth was because of the increasing ability to exploit her much greater natural resources, British economists and historians have claimed that the 'loss of leadership...is ascribable as much to human nature as it is to physical endowments. To an indefinable but considerable extent leadership was not wrested from Britain, but fell from her ineffectual grasp'.[27]

British industry was concentrated in relatively low-growth sectors by 1913, with an obviously slower adoption of mass production technology than elsewhere, facts which have prompted the claim that British firms suffered from technological conservatism. Evidence of this, however, remains muted after rigorous quantitative analysis of the major industries. Conditions for the introduction of new technology in Britain were more limited.[28] American demand and supply conditions were so different from those in Britain – indeed from anywhere in Europe – that mass production was far less of a profitable option in the UK.[29]

Additional partial explanations for the allegedly poor performance of British firms have focused on their marketing, their corporate structures and, latterly, the institutional constraints present in the wider UK economy and society.[30] Institutional constraints in British society such as, in Olson's phrase, 'distributional coalitions' with their rent-seeking behaviour, may have been behind British businessmen making poor decisions. In particular, there is evidence of widespread collusive practices, although whether collusion actually led to slow sectoral productivity growth is so far unclear.[31]

The historical debate on the relative decline of the British economy can therefore be summarised as being between those who hold that British businessmen were largely at fault because of anti-industrial cultural values and those who believe that there was no entrepreneurial failure to be explained, that British businessmen made rational decisions in rather less favourable circumstances than competitors or predecessors faced. The understanding of Britain's industrial experience at the turn of the century is dominated by this 'intellectual stalemate'.[32]

Resolving this stalemate is, in theory, relatively straightforward. As long as all cultural differences between British and American entrepreneurs can be controlled, their sensitivity to straightforward economic signals can be measured and any variations from the expected behaviour can be further investigated for the influence of culture. The trick is, of course, to control for culture. Before explaining how this has been done, a summary of the economics of entrepreneurship is necessary.

The market for entrepreneurship

Entrepreneurship is a factor comparable to any other economic factor, such as land and labour.[33] It is therefore perfectly reasonable, if relatively rare, to think of a market for entrepreneurship, just as there is a market for labour.[34] It may be relatively rare because of a particular conceptual difficulty in the market for entrepreneurship. This relates to the demand for entrepreneurship. A conventional analysis would focus on how changes in the wider economy – an increase in population, for example – would lead to an increase in the demand for a commodity or service. With entrepreneurship, however, it is not immediately clear what is being demanded. One view emphasises that entrepreneurs are intermediators, making business decisions under conditions of uncertainty.[35] Thus, the demand for entrepreneurship is a derived demand emanating from wider economic changes. Schumpeter, however, emphasises the importance of entrepreneurship as innovation, which is partly independent of wider economic change.[36] Regardless of its intellectual roots, the concept of the demand for entrepreneurship is problematical and in consequence often ignored.

The supply of entrepreneurship is conceptually much more straightforward. In the market for entrepreneurship, changes in the supply are responsive to changes in the price paid to the entrepreneurs supplying the service. This price paid is the entrepreneur's profit, usually the rate of return on the sum invested less the investment's next best alternative, although for many forms entrepreneurship, where the capital intensity of production is slight, the next best alternative is income from employment.

It seems reasonable to suppose that culture might be of particular importance when it comes to explaining variations in the supply of entrepreneurship. Entrepreneurship is a risk-taking activity, in contrast to its alternative, wage-earning labour. The supply of entrepreneurship within an economy may well be sensitive not only to profits but also to certain cultural values relating to risk and uncertainty. If the dominant social customs frowned upon risk-taking in one culture, then the rise in real profits required to attract entrepreneurs out of wage-earning occupations would have to be higher than in a society where risk and failure were accepted.

To design an experiment which uses economic theory to test for the relative sensitivity of the supply of entrepreneurship to both profits and culture, two things must be done: first, there needs to be a suitable quantifiable measurement of entrepreneurship, and second, a technique must be devised to measure the differences in the cultural predisposition to entrepreneurship in the societies and periods under investigation.

Measuring the supply of entrepreneurship is in itself conceptually problematical. If, for example, the focus was on Schumpeterian innovation as the most important element of entrepreneurship, then innovations of varying importance would have to be weighted accordingly. Some analyses have attempted to pursue this through patent data (although not without difficulties, it must be admitted).[37] The approach here has been to assume with Schumpeter that the 'entrepreneur will there be found among the heads of firms, mostly among the owners'.[38] This ignores differences in the quality of entrepreneurship among the population, but, by counting the self-employed and taking this group to be the entrepreneurs in a population, it is possible to derive a measurement of entrepreneurship. To be sure this is a conservative and partial definition of entrepreneurship, but it has the pronounced advantage of being both quantifiable and sealed with official approval.[39]

Testing for an entrepreneurial culture: Jewish immigrants as a control population in late-nineteenth-century USA and UK

While measuring late-Victorian entrepreneurship in Britain and America might now be feasible, no meaningful conclusions can be drawn until the underlying cultural differences are estimated and properly controlled for. But because culture is neither defined nor quantified, this is an impossible task. The approach here has been not to measure the cultural differences but rather to factor them out. This can be done through using a control population.

The use of control populations is a relatively common methodology in much scientific research. Medical researchers have tested for environmental determinants in the aetiology of certain diseases, such as coronary artery disease and types of diabetes, for instance. They generally choose members of an ethnic population who have migrated away from their home environment, compare the respective incidences of a given disease and thus infer a measurement of environmental influences.[40]

By contrast, the use of control populations in the social sciences is rare. Social scientists are generally unable to follow the medics' methodology because they can seldom identify an appropriate control population. In the case of comparing migrant with non-migrant cohorts from a single ethnic population, for instance, socio-economic differences between the mobile and immobile groups may be a function not of environment but of selection. In so far as emigration is a voluntary activity, the act of migration implies that those who leave have a different set of preferences and expectations from that of those who stay. Physiologically they may be similar to the wider population; psychologically and culturally they are almost certainly not.

Since these preferences and expectations may themselves be related to the propensity to engage in entrepreneurial activity, those who stay and those who leave may exhibit different entrepreneurial patterns not because of environment – the different signals from the factor markets – but because of culture. What is required therefore is a control population that is homogeneous with regard to entrepreneurial predisposition, and this needs to be a population of migrants that were in Britain – the country with the alleged cultural failings – and in the United States – the nation with a supposedly entrepreneurial culture – at the same time.

Selecting the most appropriate migrant group is not straightforward. Of the great emigrant nations during this period, the Irish have to be discounted because internal migration (Ireland was a member of the United Kingdom until 1922) was different from international migration.[41] The Italian emigration movement is complicated by large regional variations in the choice of destination and the tendency for most to be only temporary migrants, features which international migration statistics largely fail to capture.[42]

Practically this leaves only the East European Jews. The history of the Jewish mass migration to both the United States and the United Kingdom is reasonably well charted (although considerably augmented in the chapters below), and it is beyond doubt that large numbers arrived and settled in both countries, overwhelmingly in the respective commercial centres, New York and London.

The experiment and the book can now be set out and explained quite simply. The first stage is to measure the supply of entrepreneurship among the control population of Jewish immigrants in New York and London. With a long history as 'middlemen minorities' in East Europe, the Jews represent a singularly apposite control population. Any differences in the supply of entrepreneurship in the two immigrant communities ought to be very obvious.[43] Entrepreneurship is measured by counting the Jewish immigrant entrepreneurs as a share of the Jewish immigrant workforce in New York and London.

As Chapters 3 and 4 make plain, Jewish immigrants in New York were much more likely to move into entrepreneurial occupations than those in London. Chapter 5 demonstrates that this was not because of any differences in their backgrounds. The two streams of Jewish migrants were composed of essentially similar people. They are, in other words, a genuine control population.

Chapter 6 considers whether the relative divergence in the supply of entrepreneurship can be explained by changes in its price. The structures of the two local immigrant economies in New York and London are compared and any changes in the underlying demand and real profits paid for entrepreneurship are investigated. The result is that profits fell in New York and rose in London. Given the patterns in the supply of entrepreneurship in the two Jewish communities, this is a curious finding.

Chapter 7 explains how this can be understood by incorporating culture into the model of entrepreneurship. The East European Jews were culturally similar at the outset. They possessed similar tendencies to conform to cultural values whether they ended up in London or New York. On arrival the process of assimilating host country cultural values began. East European Jewish culture emphasised a high degree of conformity, so immigrants in both countries adopted some host cultural values quickly. The observed divergence in the supply of entrepreneurship is therefore best explained as twin responses to the differences in how American and British cultures valued entrepreneurship. Given this conclusion, the final chapter briefly considers how evidence of a relatively anti-entrepreneurial culture can be applied to a more general understanding of Britain's twentieth-century economic performance.

Part II
Jewish Immigrants in New York and London, 1880–1914

2
Jewish History and East European Jewish Mass Migration

Viewed from outside, much of the writing of Jewish history over the last three or four decades seems to be mesmerised by a single event. While the Holocaust is without doubt *the* defining event for world civilisation in the twentieth century, in much Jewish history it is linked to the creation of the state of Israel; redemption after tragedy. With its astonishing fulfilment of Biblical prophecy, it is easy to see why the Zionist interpretation has been so dominant in Jewish circles.[1]

The Holocaust was of course much more than just another demographic shock in the history of the Jewish Diaspora. Nevertheless, from a broad demographic perspective, the decisive episode in the return to Israel was not the Holocaust but the mass migration that preceded it.

In 1870 around two-thirds of the world's Jews lived in Eastern Europe, with another quarter in the rest of continental Europe. Had they remained as immobile for the next seventy years as for the preceding seventy, well over 80 per cent of world Jewry would have come under German control by the end of 1940. If similar mortality rates are assumed for what would then have been a far larger Jewish population, it is unlikely that sufficient Jews would have survived the war for an independent state of Israel to have been a viable entity. The remaining British Palestine would have been ceded to an enlarged kingdom of Jordan, incorporating a small Jewish minority.

In reality, however, today the descendants of the East European Jews dominate world Jewry, and three-quarters of the 13 million Jewish population live in the three principal destinations of the mass migration movement of a century ago – the United Sates, the United Kingdom and Israel. The European Holocaust stands as an eternal reminder of mankind's potential for evil. And while it carries a particular resonance for Jews, its importance is universal. Of more immediate and specific significance for the vast majority of modern-day Jews, however, is the fact that their forebears left Europe in time.[2]

The broad contours of this mass migration are quite easily charted. In 1870 the overwhelming majority of European Jewry had lived for many generations in, and adjacent to, what was the former kingdom of Poland. The successive partitions of Poland left around three-quarters in a region that became known as the Pale of Settlement, running along the western fringe of the expanded Russian empire. Other nineteenth-century border realignments left the rest of these Jews in the Polish provinces of Austria-Hungary and Prussia, with some also in Romania. While the borders moved and the people stayed where they were for the first seventy years of the nineteenth century, the relationship reversed thereafter until 1914. From 1870 onwards, the Jews increasingly left their homes in the small towns and villages in the Pale and moved to Berlin, Lodz, Moscow, Odessa, Warsaw and other fast-growing cities.[3] From the 1880s onwards, the most popular destinations were no longer in Central and Eastern Europe but the United States and Britain.

Approximately 2½ million Jews left East Europe between 1880 and 1914. Some 2 million went to the United States, the vast majority from the Russian empire. About 150,000 East European Jews migrated to Britain during this period, again overwhelmingly from the Russian empire. Around 50,000 settled in Palestine, a similar number in Germany, with a few thousand scattered through the British colonies of South Africa, Canada and Australia, and a yet smaller number settled in Latin America, notably Argentina.[4]

War in 1914 stopped the flow. To be sure, emigration recovered a little for a few short years after 1918, but revolution and civil war in their homelands and restrictionism in America and Britain meant that Jewish mass migration was effectively over in August 1914. By 1938 the immigrants and their descendants in the USA and the British empire accounted for over a third of world Jewry.[5] New York in the United States and London in Britain and the Empire had become two great entrepôts of world Jewry in the space of a single generation. This was the most dramatic demographic event in world Jewry since Moses.

The immigrants arrived in London and New York as paupers. Yet, far from being a drain on metropolitan rates, their self-sufficiency and economic progress were remarkable. These East European Jews in Britain and America represent the most successful immigrant or ethnic group bar none in the history of both nations.

The impact of these immigrants and their descendants on Anglo-American civilisation has been immense. From fields as diverse as science and law, the fine arts and mass entertainment, business and the non-profit sector, their contribution has been overwhelmingly a force for good in Britain and America. After generations of fairly sterile and inward-looking existence in Eastern Europe, their arrival and settlement unleashed a hitherto unsuspected spring of creativity. A detailed comparison of the early years of the Eastern European Jewish settlements in London and New York, with a particular focus on their routes out of poverty, carries a historical significance far beyond the relatively narrow confines of Jewish history.

Before going on to consider the details of immigrant entrepreneurship in the two locations, the remainder of this chapter seeks to illustrate three broad themes of the Jewish immigrant communities' development in both London and New York which are important to the purposes of this book. First, the Jewish immigrants in both host societies were upwardly mobile, considerably more so than the surrounding population. Second, they were upwardly mobile at different rates. Finally, the path of upward mobility was an entrepreneurial one.

As already noted, the condition of the immigrants upon arrival was invariably one of poverty. Indeed, during the initial migratory crisis of 1881–82, the response of the West was to subsidise the passage of thousands of immigrants too poor to afford the journey themselves.[6] In London this initial wave of enthusiasm for aiding the East European Jews quickly gave way to a faint revulsion as their customs offended the chattering classes of the day. This in turn gave way to a grudging respect in recognition of their industriousness and the realisation that the moral fabric of London's East End was changing for the better.[7]

The immigrants enjoyed considerable upward mobility; their propensity to pursue entrepreneurial occupations enabling them to climb into middle-class status very quickly. Henrietta Adler estimated that 23.7 per cent of East End Jews were middle-class by 1929, overwhelmingly through self-employment.[8] Adler was convinced that they had risen from the poverty of the 1880s because of a 'growth in independence and self-help among the descendants of the immigrants'.[9] In 1946 the Jewish Trades Advisory Council claimed that self-employment among the British Jews was twice that of the British Gentiles, a very conservative estimate.[10] By the early 1960s it was recognised that 'the move into the middle class has taken place with remarkable speed and effected the majority of the community'.[11]

It is impossible to know with any accuracy from current knowledge what the actual social mobility of the Jewish immigrants in England was. The only remotely close proxy is the regional mobility of the immigrant population, but the exact mechanism linking suburbanisation to prosperity is unknown and, in any case, few data exist to quantify precisely the move out of the East End.[12]

In New York the advance of the Jew seemed even more rapid. Already in 1890 Max Cohen was pointing to the enormous growth of Jewish business in the United States so that the 2058 Jewish firms with $2000 or more capital invested had a total capital valuation of $207.4m.[13] A few years later, in 1905, the renowned immigrant journalist Abraham Cahan noted that '[h]undreds of Russian and Polish Jews have been more or less successful in business, and the names of several of them are to be found on the signs along Broadway'.[14] Thomas Kessner has shown that within one generation half of New York's Russian Jewish household heads were in white-collar occupations, overwhelmingly through entrepreneurship.[15]

The increasing visibility of the Jewish immigrant success in business led to recognition of their achievements, much of which became unwelcome as tensions in US society over 'American' identity tended to be discriminatory to the disadvantage of the non-Anglo-Saxon Jews.[16] 'The Eastern Jew is the most adroit shoe-string capitalist in the world,' said Burton Hendrik in 1922, but the compliment was double-edged; '[T]he one clear conclusion is that the process of "Americanization" is going to be slow,' he said, before going on to advocate the restriction of any future immigration.[17]

Others were less restrained. Henry Ford republished the notoriously anti-Semitic and fraudulent *Protocols of the Elders of Zion*.[18] The editors of *Fortune* magazine were pushed to consider in 1936 whether there was 'any factual basis for charges of Jewish monopolization of American opportunity'.[19] They concluded that such claims were, of course, exaggerated. But the fact that the question was asked testifies not only to the fairly pervasive anti-Semitism of the time, but also to the impressive upward mobility of Jewish immigrants in the United States.

Jewish immigrants in the United Kingdom and the United States were upwardly mobile. This was exceptional behaviour in both countries. Social mobility in America and Britain was restricted. There was very little upward mobility from working to middle, or from blue- to white-collar classes during this period.[20] An important point to grasp then is that most Jewish immigrants in both cities rose from the direst of poverty to positions of economic security and social respectability within fifty years when most of those around them did not.

The second point is that the Jewish immigrants in New York and London were not only upwardly mobile but were apparently mobile at different rates. Already by the 1920s in New York the immigrants had left the tailoring workshops 'for the counter of the store; the sons of these immigrants...press into professions, commercial employment and clerical jobs'.[21]

In London progress was more muted. According to one Anglo-Jewish historian,

> [a] few had prospered in the immigration period to the extent of being able to send their children to university...Others worked hard to improve the life of themselves and their children. Progress was delayed by the inter-war depression although some movement away from manual work was clearly discernible; but a more rapid rush into the middle class had to await the opportunities available in the years of fuller employment for much of the period after 1945.[22]

Vivien Lipman, the pioneer chronicler of the East European Jewish community in London, thought of the community being middle-class only by 1954, but precision has remained elusive.[23] Unlike in New York, the possibility of quantifying the Jewish experience in London has so far proved impossible. The underlying sources of evidence for such measurement are simply not there. The principal empirical contribution of this volume is the provision of new estimates of the social mobility, immigration and entrepreneurship of the Jewish immigrants in London, all based on previously unpublished sources of data.

In both countries the children of the settlers made extraordinary leaps in the social hierarchies.[24] There were a few professionals among first-generation immigrants, but overwhelmingly the path to material success and economic security was an entrepreneurial one, not littered by educational qualifications or professional examinations or any other source of mobility; 'It was business.'[25]

Successful Jewish immigrant entrepreneurs were not restricted to the famous – retailers like Montague Burton and Michael Marks in Britain, or the Hollywood moguls in America, for example. There were many, many others.[26] Of the first-generation entrepreneurs, the two examples that follow could be multiplied a thousandfold.

Morris Cohen arrived in London in 1877. He had worked as a gentleman's tailor at the Russian court and so was able to secure a position at Hope Brothers, a well established gentleman's tailors in the City. He quickly realised that the burgeoning demand for women's readymade coats and dresses was not being met by conservative London tailors and so established his own workshop. He prospered, built his own factory and then further invested in residential real estate, concentrating on one square of terraced houses in London's East End. He built small workshops in the back yards and let them out to fellow womenswear manufacturers, so stimulating the entire industry. In a very short time the majority of womenswear output in the United Kingdom came from the East End. Morris Cohen was the father of the industry. Even today, some of the leading firms trace their origins back to Morris Cohen.[27]

Harry Fischel was born in Meretz, Lithuania in 1865. His father was a cabinetmaker and Harry went from building furniture in the Pale to becoming a leading Jewish developer in Manhattan. His hopes raised after marvelling at the letters of relatives who had gone on to America, Harry set off to New York in 1885. After initial difficulties, eventually a customer offered him credit to do a building job. With this initial success behind him, he had no difficulty in obtaining credit for his own jobs. After twelve months he had saved enough to invest in an odd-shaped plot of land in the Lower East Side, upon which he built a tenement and made a 200 per cent profit after five months. Harry Fischel went on to become the first successful Jewish builder on the Lower East Side.[28]

Both Morris Cohen and Harry Fischel rose from arriving with very little except youth and initiative and went on to economic and social progress despite many early disappointments. They both experienced the early immigrant pains of transition, the poverty, the discrimination, to say nothing of homesickness and loneliness, but they both established themselves in business by being innovative. They were both entrepreneurs. The first fifty years of Jewish mass settlement in New York and London can be rephrased as being a period of extraordinary entrepreneurial success. The Jewish immigrant populations of New York and London were remarkably entrepreneurial. The next two chapters measure exactly how entrepreneurial they were.

3
Statistics of Anglo-Jewry and the Synagogue Marriage Records, 1880–1914

To measure entrepreneurship, some method needs to be devised that estimates both the total population of Jewish immigrants in New York and London and the share that were entrepreneurs. In principle, this is elementary. In practice, it is entirely dependent upon having reliable sources of occupational and population statistics. The obvious sources would be the different national censuses, and for the United States, reasonable census data do exist and are reported in Chapter 4. For the United Kingdom, by contrast, the successive decennial censuses simply do not provide any kind of reliable basis for the statistical analysis of Jewish immigrant entrepreneurship.

For anyone acquainted with studies of Anglo-Jewry, this comes as no surprise. Historians have long lamented the dearth of meaningful statistics available for the study of the formation and development of the immigrant community in Britain. The demographic data are simply not available. For rates of immigration, for example, the conclusions reached by Lloyd Gartner and Vivien Lipman in the 1950s remain valid today, namely, that despite the problems, we 'must look to the census as our basic source and almost entirely abandon attempts to derive annual immigration figures from other sources'.[1]

The quality of the census evidence is undeniably patchy. For estimating entrepreneurship, the published reports simply contain insufficient detail, with only the most general of occupational classifications used for the vast majority of immigrants. It is impossible to differentiate between the Jewish entrepreneurs and employees in the main immigrant trades, for example, and this for one very good reason: the information is missing from the original census manuscripts.[2] Any attempt to estimate immigrant entrepreneurship has, by default, to depend on additional sources of information. These are not exactly thick on the ground.

Beyond the barely adequate statistics from the decennial census reports, very little is known indeed. Consider, for example, our current estimates about such basic demographic phenomena as the annual changes in late-nineteenth-century immigration and the size of the Jewish population in Britain. These remain little more than guesses, never mind other important features of Anglo-Jewish history, such as social mobility, entrepreneurship and cultural assimilation.

These latter themes have increasingly become the focus of research, as historians of world Jewry have tried to locate the Jewish experience within a broader context. Emancipation, the main focus of earlier generations of historians, was merely the legal outcome of complex social forces rippling through nineteenth-century Europe. The best of the more recent studies of Jewish assimilation and integration tend still, however, to be narrowly focused and based on qualitative evidence. While the quality of scholarship is beyond question and the broad thrust of research is heartily to be welcomed, patterns of Jewish assimilation and integration are simply best captured when both quantified and compared across different nations.[3] Only then do the required generalisations about the Jewish experience in different contexts become valid.

Here, however, especially for Britain, the deficiencies of any genuine statistical base become glaringly obvious. In a word, as one scholar recently concluded in her recent comparison of turn-of-the-century Jews in New York, London and Paris, for 'England, we unfortunately have little data.'[4]

This chapter therefore reviews the scanty statistical sources on Jews in late-nineteenth-century Britain, explaining the deficiencies of both the census and a range of other sources. More importantly, the chapter introduces a new data set: the occupational and other information contained on the synagogue marriage records. If reliable, the information contained in this source would begin to provide very real answers to some of the fundamental questions about the East European Jews in Britain.

This chapter sets out then the advantages and disadvantages of using the collection of synagogue marriage records as a key source of evidence – one which, when used in conjunction with the censuses, provides a far more complete understanding of the Jewish immigrant population of Britain.

Many readers may find the following discussion of different sources a little over-elaborate. Economic historians become sceptical through training, however, and especially so when grand claims are made of newly discovered sources of evidence. We are inclined to judge historical sources cautiously, to sift slowly through various possible alternative interpretations, always alive to potential margins of error. From temperament, we tend naturally to sit firmly on the fence. Those readers quite willing to take the results on trust may skip happily on to the next chapter. For now, however, the existing statistics of Anglo-Jewry need to be reviewed.

The statistics of Anglo-Jewry

The statistical foundation of any existing analyses of the Jews in Britain is the decennial population censuses. These contain information on the number of foreign-born, their geographical location, age and gender distribution, marital condition and occupation. No census is ever perfect, however, and the population censuses of England and Wales have a number of general faults, as well as a number of specific problems concerning any analysis of Britain's Jews.[5]

The most obvious problem is that the censuses remain silent about whether a person was Jewish or not. Census enumerators sought no information about religious affiliation. The published census reports refer to the foreign-born population in Britain: the Austrians and Hungarians, Germans, Russians, Poles, Romanians, Bulgarians, Montenegrins, Serbs and so on resident in Britain. But not all these were Jews.

While Jews were the minority of German, Austrian and Hungarian immigrants in Britain, non-Jewish immigration from the rest of East Europe was thought to be very low. Among contemporaries, the convention arose of counting the enumerated Russians, Poles and Romanians as Jews. While this puts a figure to the East European Jewish immigrants, historians remain ignorant about the population of Jewish immigrants from the eastern provinces of Austria-Hungary and Germany, although, as in America, they were likely to be only a small minority of the total. Furthermore, the assumption that the census even captured total Jewish immigration from its main sources remained highly controversial among contemporaries.[6]

Disproportionate under-enumeration among the Jewish immigrants was widely believed to be prevalent at the end of the nineteenth century. The official investigation into immigration by the Board of Trade, for instance, concluded in 1894 that 'there are reasons for believing that the number of foreigners was somewhat understated at the enumeration of 1871 and of 1881, and overstated in 1891.'[7]

The outcry was sufficient for the established Anglo-Jewish community to take special measures for the next census in 1901. The Chief Rabbi and the London Jewish Board of Guardians issued circulars in

Yiddish and took on volunteers to ensure that the returns were complete and accurate. Subsequently, the Royal Commission charged with investigating immigration in 1903 was satisfied that 'great and unusual care was taken in securing the returns of the Metropolitan Jewish aliens in 1901'.[8] But suspicions remained.

Those lobbying for restrictions to immigration had political capital to make out of the cause of under-enumeration and played it as hard as they could, but even the assimilated Anglo-Jewry believed that it was 'probably true that the number of enumerated [Jewish] inhabitants [in East London]...should also be somewhat larger'; at least, this was the opinion of the leading Jewish statistician of the time, S. Rosenbaum.[9] Unfortunately no one knew by how much.

Almost inevitably no census is ever complete, but the problem for statisticians comes only if the incompleteness is in some way non-random, with one group significantly under-represented relative to the general population. In nineteenth-century America, for example, slaves were undercounted in the US censuses, perhaps because owners feared some sort of capitation tax.[10] In the UK, recent evidence suggests that there was a significant undercount of young men in 1991. In the inner city areas especially, substantial proportions of young black men, almost a third in inner London apparently, were not enumerated, perhaps again for fear of taxation.[11]

In London's East End in 1901 any possible under-enumeration may have been related to other motives for avoiding official recognition. Historians of East European Jewry have assumed that Jewish communities in the Pale of Settlement treated all contact with a hostile Russian state with the utmost suspicion.[12] Transposed into a different setting, so the argument goes, the East European Jews would be more than likely to reduce contact between themselves and the, now, British state, perhaps by avoiding enumeration.

Certainly this was what some contemporaries believed was happening. If so, and if the population censuses undercounted the East European Jewish immigrants by anything like a third, then their value as the foundation of the statistical analysis of the Jewish population is greatly impaired. A report published by Conservative Party Central Office in 1903, for instance, controversially claimed that there were twice as many immigrant Jews in Britain as had been enumerated in the 1901 census, far more than could be accounted for by subsequent immigration alone.[13]

This was more than just low politics. The institutional apparatus for ensuring the accuracy of census statistics was spindly and weak.

The census enumerator simply distributed the schedules to households for completion and returned to collect them at a later date.[14] It was not difficult to imagine that census enumerators might have been the unwitting agents of mass under-enumeration, simply by virtue of being unable to check whether the returned schedules were fully completed.

Despite these concerns, it is nevertheless extremely unlikely that the under-enumeration of the Jewish immigrants was on such a significant scale. They had arrived, after all, from a nation which insisted on far greater amounts of bureaucratic compliance than Britain, and with large penalties if it was not forthcoming. For the Jews in Russia, places of residence had to be registered, many were employed in officially regulated occupations and their principal communal liabilities were vigorously policed capitation taxes. In fact, their Russian background was more likely to have prepared them to be model citizens in terms of complying with the census enumeration.[15] Given the additional efforts made by Anglo-Jewry, the 1901 census, in particular, was likely to have been comprehensive. Censuses invariably undercount – the 1991 British census by 2 per cent apparently – but their overall reliability is rarely questioned.[16] For the Jewish immigrants in London in 1901, it is reasonable to conclude that any undercount was similarly slight and that the census's reliability remained unimpaired.

This is a very useful conclusion. The 1901 census at the very least can be seen as a reliable benchmark. While this is a good start, unfortunately other problems emerge in using the censuses for the analysis of the Jewish population. As noted, all of the censuses refer to nativity, not religion. While the assumption that all East Europeans were Jews gives some idea of the immigrant population, estimating the population of second-generation immigrants becomes parlous indeed. Some of the British-born children of the immigrants may be captured through studying samples of the original census manuscripts, but, once adult and householders in their own right, they are much more difficult to identify.[17] Moreover, the widespread habit of Anglicising surnames means that many of the most rapidly assimilating second-generation Jews would be missed.[18] Studies of the relationship between assimilation and occupation, or age of first marriage, or family formation, or whatever, are simply lost through the British censuses' disinterest in matters religious.[19]

Table 3.1 summarises the basic census statistics concerning the Jewish immigrants in England and Wales from 1871 to 1911. Regardless of any concerns about the overall reliability of the earlier censuses, and putting aside for now the vexed question of how to incorporate the

Table 3.1A   East- and Central-European-born residents in England and Wales, and the County of London, 1871 to 1911

Native of:	1871	1881	1891	1901	1911
England and Wales					
Russia	2513	3789	23626	61789	69580
Poland	7056	10679	21448	21055	36502
Romania	n.a.	n.a.	734	3296	4293
Austria-Hungary	1802	2809	5673	10794	16347
Germany	32823	37301	50599	49133	62992
London					
Russia	1065	1778	12034	38117	42301
Poland	4229	6931	14708	15420	26119
Romania	n.a.	n.a.	286	2106	2532

Sources: see Table 3.1B.

German and Austrian Jews into any study, Table 3.1 confirms an otherwise familiar picture of a rapidly growing East European Jewish immigrant population, biased to young adults resident in London.

Table 3.1 illustrates the strengths and limitations of the census statistics well. As indicators of the overall size and profile of the immigrant population, the censuses, especially for 1901, are reasonably reliable. For estimating the size or characteristics of the wider Jewish population, however, the censuses have more limited use, and statisticians have adopted a number methods in order to compensate.[20]

Joseph Jacobs first derived the population of London Jews in 1882 at around 46,000 from burial returns.[21] Because of their concentration in the capital, estimating the population of metropolitan Jews was the most important task, and the most difficult. From 1897 the Jewish population of Britain was estimated in successive editions of the *Jewish Year Book*. The figure varied wildly according to the methodology chosen, leaving the editors to bemoan the fact that the 'calculation of the Jewish population of Greater London still presents considerable difficulties'.[22] Two attempts to calculate Britain's Jewish population for 1903 differed by more than a quarter.[23] Without reliable sources, estimates of the wider Jewish population were always likely to miss the mark.

There are abundant qualitative and quantitative studies of the occupational structure of the immigrant economy, by contrast. This is because Victorian social investigators viewed with alarm the immigrants' concentration in London's East End, and were dismayed at their apparent link with 'sweating'. The best of these studies is undoubtedly the extraordinary research project coordinated and supervised by Charles Booth.

Table 3.1B   Marital status, gender and age distribution of the Russian, Polish and Romanian immigrants in the County of London, 1901

	Marital status						
	Total	Unmarried	%	Married	%	Widowed	%
Male	29 843	12 885	43.2	16 636	55.7	322	1.1
Female	25 800	9 435	36.6	14 853	57.6	1 512	5.9

	Age structure			
Age (years)	Male	%	Female	%
Under 15	4 108	13.8	4 163	16.1
15–19	2 822	9.5	3 166	12.3
20–24	5 299	17.8	4 635	18.0
25–34	9 005	30.2	6 717	26.0
35–44	5 108	17.1	3 838	14.9
45–54	2 017	6.8	1 822	7.1
55–64	974	3.3	981	3.8
65–74	399	1.3	373	1.4
75 +	121	0.4	105	0.4
All ages	29 853		25 800	

Sources:
1A. Censuses for England and Wales for the years: 1871, P.P. 1873 LXXI, vol. 3, 'Population Abstracts', table 15, 'Number of Foreigners', p. 25; 1881, P.P. 1883 XCV, vol. 3, 'Ages, Conditions as to Marriage, Occupations and Birth-places of the People'; 1891, P.P. 1893-4 CIV-CVI, vol. 3, 'Ages, Conditions as to Marriage, Occupations and Birth-places of the People', table 11, pp. xxxiv-xxxviii; 1901, P.P. 1902 CXX, 'Summary tables: Area, houses and population', p. 260; 1911, P.P. 1912-13 CXI-CXIII, vol. 9, 'Birthplaces', table 3, pp. 114–75. Note that figures for Romania include Bulgaria, Serbia and Montenegro. 1911 returns include foreign-born naturalised British subjects. Romania foreign-born were not ennumerated before 1891.
1B. 1901 Census Report, 'County of London', table 37a, pp. 159, 161.

This gave considerable attention to the Jewish economy of London. In consequence, the Jewish occupational structure of the late 1880s became really quite well known. Jews were credited with being most entrepreneurial, a most dubious compliment at the time.[24] Along with other sources offering additional details, there are frequent insights from one or other of the various relevant official reports, for instance, the pattern of Jewish immigrant entrepreneurship is reasonably clear.[25] But nevertheless, and despite the range of these sources, there is no comprehensive quantitative statement on immigrant entrepreneurship.

Joseph Jacobs's estimate of the occupational structure of London Jews in 1882 was mostly guesswork.[26] The Poor Jews' Temporary Shelter, near Tower Hill and the London docks, kept a register of visitors and their occupations, but its inmates were just off the boat and soon moved on, typically to South Africa.[27]

Once again, attempts to build a statistical base beyond that offered by the census reports have generally been unsuccessful. Apart from the basic information contained in the census reports, historians have no reliable and consistent data. Consequently, any existing estimates about the changing nature of the Jewish community, of immigration, population size and entrepreneurship beyond those captured in the snapshots of the five censuses from 1871 to 1911, are simply unreliable. It is in this context that the possibilities suggested by using the information from the synagogue marriage records need to be judged. The rest of the chapter describes this source in detail.

Synagogue marriage records

There are three kinds of synagogue marriage record in Britain: the *ketubah*, the synagogues' duplicate copies of the civil marriage registers, and the certificates of the Chief Rabbi's authorisation to marry according to Jewish means. Each record relates to a different administrative function.

The *ketubah* (plural *ketubot*) is a document associated with Jewish weddings since antiquity. In late Victorian times, orthodox Jewish religious law required relatively little for a marriage to be contracted. The bride's and groom's consent needed to be given in the presence of two reliable male witnesses. At the ceremony, the bride was presented with a written document signed by the witnesses. This, the *ketubah*, was 'a legal instrument concerned with settlements and money obligations' from the husband to the wife in the event of divorce or the husband's death.[28] For those weddings conducted under the authority of a synagogue, duplicate copies of the *ketubot* were often retained.[29] The historical value of the *ketubot* is limited, however, with information restricted to the names of both parties, their fathers and the witnesses, as well as the date and location of the wedding along with certain financial details.

From 1837 any marriage in Britain was required by the Registration Act 1836 to be recorded in the civil marriage register. In practice, this meant that most weddings took place in one of two locations, either the office of the local superintendent registrar or at the parish church. For Jews, the act allowed a third option. From 1837 Jewish marriages could be registered by officials appointed by the Board of Deputies of British Jews.

This concession was seen as an important victory in the quest for emancipation, in this respect placing the Jews on an equal footing in

British civil society with other dissenting denominations such as the Quakers. The act insisted on strict lines of intra-communal authority, however, with the Board of Deputies having the responsibility of acting as the Registrar General's agents in the Jewish community. In practice, the Board delegated their responsibilities to the Chief Rabbi, giving the incumbent considerable influence over the affairs of Jewish congregations.[30] From that time onwards Jewish marriages in Britain were solemnised at one of the synagogues and by one of the officials authorised by the Chief Rabbi.[31] With the exception of the Sephardic synagogue at Bevis Marks, from 1870 the right to solemnise Jewish weddings was restricted to those synagogues constituting the new umbrella group, the United Synagogue.[32] As the immigrant community grew in size, a new umbrella group, the Federation of Synagogues, emerged, and increasingly its constituent synagogues won the right to register Jewish marriages.[33]

The resultant documentation consisted of an entry for each marriage in the civil marriage register, which would be sent to the Registrar General when the register book was full, and an entry in the duplicate civil marriage register book, which was retained by the synagogue. It is these records which are potentially of great value to the historian because each one contains detailed information about the occupations, ages, marital status and so on of the bride and groom and their fathers. This information gives historians, for the first time, a clear profile of levels of entrepreneurship in the Jewish community.

The third Jewish marriage record, the Chief Rabbi's certificate of authorisation, was an indirect administrative outcome of the Jewish concession in the Registration Act 1836. For the concession to avoid falling into disrepute, it had to be effectively policed. The communal authorities had to ensure that all parties contracting to a Jewish marriage were, in fact, Jews.

From shortly after the act, the Chief Rabbi began to interview all prospective brides and grooms to verify their Jewish status. From 1845 a certificate was issued, called the certificate of the Chief Rabbi's authorisation to marry according to Jewish means. As immigration accelerated, the Chief Rabbi's authorisation certificates changed one vital detail. From 1880 the certificates included information about the brides' and grooms' birthplaces. It is therefore only with the introduction of these amended certificates that it becomes possible to differentiate between immigrant and native-born Jew.

Combining the information from the civil marriage registers with the certificates of authorisation has allowed a statistical profile to be built of a large cohort of the Jewish population, the brides and grooms of all Jewish weddings at the time of their marriage. This profile is potentially of greater historical value than even the successive decennial censuses, because it incorporates more information about each person, it includes information about native-born Jews and it is an annual series. However, it is also important to be aware of the potential limitations of such a body of statistical evidence.

There are two areas where the value of the information from the synagogue marriage records might be questioned. First, there is a possibility that significant numbers of immigrant Jews in London who did marry nonetheless chose not to register their marriage. If such under-registration was either on a significant scale or disproportionately so in some sectors of the Jewish community, then the utility of the information yielded from the marriage records would be much reduced. Second, even if the registered population was fairly complete and any unregistered marriages insignificant, the information contained on the marriage records may not be representative of the general Jewish population for various possible reasons. These two issues, under-registration and the representativeness of the information, need to be explored before the appropriate degree of confidence in the data can be properly attributed.

Registration and the representativeness of the Jewish marriage records

If the under-registration of Jewish marriages was a reasonably common phenomenon in the years after 1880, it must have been because those Jews marrying in London were opting for some sort of alternative arrangements. Immigrants, after all, may not have appreciated or understood the carefully constructed apparatus of the registration of Jewish marriages under English law. Perhaps it was the case that immigrants escaped the official structure simply through ignorance. Conversely, the Jews in London may have been fully aware of the institutional arrangements for registering Jewish marriages but deliberately chose alternatives, perhaps there was a cheaper alternative or perhaps some held strong grievances against the Chief Rabbi.

Under-registration arising from ignorance was, in fact, unlikely to have occurred. As already noted, East European Jews were not unfamiliar with the need for civic compliance. In the Pale of Settlement from 1835, the Russian government appointed official rabbis to the Jewish communities. These 'state' or 'crown' rabbis acted as the official intermediaries between the state and the Jews. The Russian architects of the policy hoped they would be a civilising influence on what they saw as backward Jewish communities. They were therefore deliberately intrusive and backed by the power of an autocratic state. The result was a dual rabbinate, with the state rabbi as the notional leader of the community, and a Talmudic scholar who continued to minister to the religious needs of the community as tradition dictated.

The state rabbi was also the local state registrar and so compiled all the Jewish vital statistics in the 'state registers', the *metricheskie knigi* in Russian (literally, the 'metric' books). It was this information that enabled the Russian government to calculate how much tax to levy on the Jewish communities. Because of its fiscal importance, strict penalties were imposed on any attempts at evasion. The threat of harsh treatment prompted effective self-policing in the Jewish communities, so that any individual failing to inform the state rabbi of their marriage, or a newborn child, 'would not only be fined...but also be treated as a violator of the law of the state' and so handed over to the police.[34] As far as the Jews in the Pale were concerned then, as a Russian lawyer explained to the *Jewish Chronicle* in 1900, it was uniformly accepted that 'besides an ecclesiastical marriage performed by the Rabbi, a marriage certificate issued by the officer in charge of the State register is required'.[35]

For those arriving in London, registering a marriage was normal practice. Aware of the sanctions in Russia, they would surely have discovered how to do so. Moreover, the Chief Rabbi made it known to the immigrants that they needed to register their marriages. It was common knowledge that his authorisation needed to be obtained.[36]

If ignorance was unlikely, an alternative possibility is that Jews in London might have under-registered out of deliberate choice. There are two possibilities. Either Jewish immigrants may have registered their marriages at the local registrar's office, avoiding the religious authority of the Chief Rabbi. Equally, without the equivalent of Russian penalties, registration may have lapsed, simply because for some it was too expensive.

Religious protest was present throughout the immigrant milieu. There was a vigorous, even robust, debate about the nature of Jewish faith in this new land, and about what the ecclesiastical role of the Chief Rabbi was among the immigrants. One immigrant congregation, the *Machzike Hadath*, even went as far as to challenge rabbinical authority of the Chief Rabbi.[37] But such protest is unlikely to have influenced rates of marriage registration. Even the *Machzike Hadath* surrendered to the Chief Rabbi's authority in determining the Jewish status of prospective brides and grooms.[38]

Registering a Jewish marriage was undoubtedly expensive before 1877. It was feared in the 1870s that the poorer Jews were avoiding registration, that they were pursuing 'informal weddings', known in Yiddish as *stille huppahs*. This, it was believed, was entirely an issue of expense, and so, first in 1871 and then again in 1877, marriage fees were reduced so that 'cheap marriages' cost only 10*s*. 6*d*. to be registered.[39]

After the introduction of 'cheap marriages', however, there is far less evidence of under-registration. From 1877 the numbers of registered marriages increased. So much so that in 1890 the Registrar General asserted that Jewish immigration could be determined through examining the increase in the recorded number of Jewish marriages. This brought a vigorous response on what was a very sensitive issue. The *Jewish Chronicle* emphasised that much of the increase in Jewish marriages was because 'cheap marriages' had 'entirely abolished' the practice of non-registration among the Jewish poor. Of course, most of the increase was from immigration, but nevertheless the consensus from all sectors of the Jewish community was that cost no longer represented a hurdle to registration. Indeed, for those arriving from Russia, marriage registration may have been considerably cheaper.[40]

Under-registration of Jewish marriages was seemingly relatively rare. What there was may well have been biased to the very poor, but the numbers of recorded marriages are such that their proportion of the total can only be very low.[41] Genuine cohabitation, and so the deliberate non-registration and non-solemnisation of marriage, was extremely rare. Equally, marrying out of the community was extremely unusual among the immigrants. The number of Jewish marriages registered with the local superintendent registrar was tiny.[42] It is, in sum, reasonable to suppose that essentially all those who married also registered their marriage.

The second area concerning the value of the marriage record data set is whether the information contained on the marriage records was itself representative of the wider Jewish population. One area, for example, where the marriage record information was obviously not representative of the wider community – even if every adult was married and registered – was the distribution of ages. The information contained in the marriage records relates to the population of brides and grooms at the time of marriage. This was mostly in the early to mid-twenties. Some categories of information may be particularly sensitive to age. Whereas one's birthplace is forever fixed, for example, occupation and occupational status do vary with age, although less so then than today.[43] Having occupational details recorded only at the time of marriage may well bias the data set in a particular direction. Fortunately, adjusting for the age bias is relatively straightforward. It is, rather, other potential sources of bias in the data which need to be considered.

The most significant distortion to the data would arise if the proportion of those adults who did not marry in Britain (either because they arrived married or because they chose not to marry) was either very large or varied significantly from year to year. Remaining single was extremely rare in East European Jewish society, where 'well nigh irresistible social habit required every male to marry; an unmarried female was fully unthinkable'.[44] Those who arrived married, however, may in some way have differed from to those who arrived single and subsequently married. These differences would not be picked up in the marriage records data set.

Calculating with any accuracy the proportion of Jewish immigrants who arrived married is impossible. Potentially, it could have been a very large part of the population of adult immigrants, because East European Jewish custom, at least in the earlier part of the nineteenth century, was to marry early, very early. Indeed, it was partly in order to outlaw what were thought to be indecently young marriages that Tsar Nicholas I introduced marriage registration for the Jews. However, by the end of the century the mean age of first marriage among East European Jews was converging with a wider European norm.[45] By the 1890s the mean age of marriage among the Jews in Russia had risen to over 25 years for men and over 23 years for women. This was older than the mean age of migration.[46] The assumption here has been that the East European Jews were following what is a typical pattern of behaviour, where marriage is almost always seen by historians to follow migration.[47] The East European Jews, it is true, were more likely than most migrant populations to opt for permanent settlement and so move as family groups. Nonetheless, on arrival they were still overwhelmingly young and single; marriage for most was delayed until after migration.

This long discussion of the potential weaknesses of the marriage record data set has deliberately tended to over-elaboration. Before acceptance, this new and previously unpublished source of data on Jewish immigrant entrepreneurship must pass several examinations of its reliability and representativeness. Ultimately the only way to test the representativeness of the marriage record data set is to compare it with those sources which are recognised as being reliable. This, in practice, means the decennial censuses of population and, indeed, realistically only the 1901 census. The next section describes how the occupational

information of East-European-born grooms from a sample of the duplicate civil marriage registers and the Chief Rabbi's authorisation certificates – called the CRA database – compares with the occupational
information for East-European-born alien men in London in 1901.
A description of how the CRA database was constructed is contained in
the appendix to this chapter.

Testing the representativeness of the marriage records

As Table 3.2 shows, the occupational structures of the East European
Jewish grooms from the marriage records and the East-European-born
men from the census show a striking degree of similarity. Even where
there are significant differences between the grooms and the men, they

Table 3.2 Occupational structures of Russian, Polish and Romanian male
aliens in the 1901 census and East-European-born Jewish grooms,
1880–1914

Class		Census	%	CRA	%
Total		25091		961	
I	National & Local Govt.	3	–	–	–
II	Defence of the Country	–	–	–	–
III	Professional Occupations	524	2.1	15	1.6
IV	Domestic Services	89	–	–	–
V	Commercial Occupations	670	2.7	17	1.8
VI	Conveyance of Men, etc.	306	1.2	–	–
VII	Agriculture	7	–	5	0.5
VIII	Fishing	1	–	–	–
IX	Mines and Quarries	28	–	2	–
X	Metals, Machines, etc.	311	1.2	7	0.7
XI	Precious Metals, etc.	406	1.6	21	2.2
XII	Building, etc.	643	2.6	15	1.6
XIII	Wood, Furniture, etc.	2797	11.1	115	12.0
XIV	Brick, Cement, etc.	26	–	4	–
XV	Chemicals, etc.	81	–	5	0.5
XVI	Skins, Furs, etc.	614	2.4	30	3.1
XVII	Paper, Prints, etc.	227	0.9	11	1.1
XVIII	Textile Fabrics	280	1.1	11	1.1
XIX	Dress	14976	59.7	626	65.1
XX	Food, Tobacco & Lodging	2033	8.1	65	6.8
XXI	Gas, etc.	73	–	–	–
XXII	Other Undefined & Dealers	994	4.0	12	1.2

Note: percentages not reported when less than 0.5 per cent.

Source: as for Table 3.1B and CRA database.

arise more from the slight underlying differences in the two populations compared than from any fundamental bias in the CRA database.

The grooms are over-represented by some margin in the Dress trades (class XIX), possibly woodworking (XIII), and even perhaps furriering (XVI). Commerce (V), Transport (VI), Building (VII), Food, Tobacco and Lodging (XX) and Dealing (XXII) are over-represented in the census population. Nonetheless, the overall similarity is very impressive, and especially when the unavoidable differences in the two populations being compared is taken into account.

The census of alien occupations includes some East European sailors (class VI) staying close to the London docks, for example, none of whom were in any way connected to the Jewish community of East London. Because the census listed the occupations of the foreign-born in London, rather than the East End, it contains a regional bias. This partly explains the under-representation in the census population of the immigrant staples that dominated the East End, especially the tailoring and furniture trades. In addition there may be some distortion from comparing an occupational profile at a given moment – 1901 – with that for the marrying population over the longer period.

The major reason for the differences, however, is age bias. The young men who were getting married were more likely to be tailors than to be shopkeepers or traders.[48]

Table 3.3 shows the unsurprising fact that the marriage register population was disproportionately composed of young adults. The proportion of grooms who married before their twenty-fifth birthday was much larger than the share of the under-25s in the census population (58.3 per cent to 37.9 per cent). And while the grooms who married in

Table 3.3 Age distribution of Russian, Polish and Romanian male aliens (ten years and older) in 1901 and East European Jewish grooms

Ages (years)	Census	%	CRA	%
Total	28 395		961	
10 to 14	2 650	9.3	–	–
15 to 19	2 822	9.9	6	0.6
20 to 24	5 299	18.7	554	57.7
25 to 34	9 005	31.7	356	37.0
35 to 44	5 108	18.0	28	2.9
45-plus	3 511	12.4	17	1.8

Source: as for Table 3.1B and CRA database.

the 25 to 34 years age group were a similar share of total grooms as the 25 to 34 years cohort in the census population (37.0 per cent to 31.7 per cent), the big difference was that very few immigrants married after the age of 35, but almost a third of the census population was in that age group.

Because the age distributions both of the brides and grooms and of the census population are known, it is quite straightforward to adjust the occupational profile of the marriage record population and so eliminate the age-bias compared with the general population.[49] As Table 3.4 shows, there was a distinct age-bias in the dominant Dress classification. Among the grooms, over 70 per cent of the younger cohort and

Table 3.4 The Occupational structure of Russian, Polish and Romanian male aliens in London in 1901 and East European Jewish grooms in 1880–1914, by age group (percentages)

			CRA		
Classes		Census	up-to-25	over-25	Adjusted
Total			560	401	
I	National & Local Govt.	–			–
II	Defence of the Country	–			–
III	Professional Occupations	2.1	1.6	1.7	1.6
IV	Domestic Services	–			–
V	Commercial Occupations	2.7	1.8	1.3	2.0
VI	Conveyance of Men, etc.	1.2			–
VII	Agriculture	–			–
VIII	Fishing	–			–
IX	Mines and Quarries	–			–
X	Metals, Machines, etc.	1.2	0.7	0.7	0.7
XI	Precious Metals, etc.	1.6	2.2	3.5	2.7
XII	Building, etc.	2.6	1.6	1.0	1.4
XIII	Wood, Furniture, etc.	11.1	12.0	10.9	12.5
XIV	Brick, Cement, etc	–			–
XV	Chemicals, etc.	–	0.5	1.0	0.7
XVI	Skins, Furs, etc.	2.4	3.1	4.5	3.6
XVII	Paper, Prints, etc	0.9	1.4	0.7	1.0
XVIII	Textile Fabrics	1.1	1.1	2.0	1.5
XIX	Dress	59.7	71.3	56.6	62.2
XX	Food, Tobacco & Lodging	8.1	5.9	8.0	7.2
XXI	Gas, etc.	–			–
XXII	Other Undefined & Dealers	4.0	0.4	2.5	1.7

Source: as Table 3.1B and CRA database and note 49. Note that percentages less than 0.5 per cent in the two total columns have not been reported.

only 57 per cent of the older were employed as tailors, glovemakers and so on.[50]

In Table 3.4, the final column shows how the age adjustment results in the near elimination of the main discrepancies in the two populations' occupational structures. As they grew older, Jewish men left tailoring and moved into trading and business (classes V and XXII), or into keeping food stores and tobacconist shops (class XX), furriering, draping, and the jewellery trades (classes XVI, XVIII and XI). The discrepancy in the woodworking trades may arise from a residual regional bias in the two populations, associated with cabinetmaking's close spatial relationship with the East End. However, the most important conclusion is clear. The correlation between the occupational structure contained in the census reports and the age-adjusted sample of marriage registers is very strong, with a coefficient of 0.99.

The very high correlation coefficient suggests that the age-adjusted marriage record population almost completely overlaps with the wider population. As a foundation for the statistical analysis of the Jewish immigrant community, there are therefore more than reasonable grounds for treating it with a considerable degree of confidence.

Conclusion

This chapter has attempted to show that despite the paucity of statistics relating to East European Jewish immigration into Britain, one source of evidence can be utilised in a much more general fashion than previously thought. This is the collection of synagogue marriage records. The results of testing this data set through comparing it with the most reliable other source available builds confidence in its reliability. The next chapter uses this data set to construct estimates of Jewish immigrant entrepreneurship in London, estimates which are then compared with more conventionally derived figures for New York.

Appendix: sampling Jewish marriage records – the CRA database; sources

From 1837 all synagogues in Britain were required to inform the Board of Deputies of British Jews every year of the number of births, deaths and marriages that had come under each individual synagogue's jurisdiction. These figures were published in the statistical appendix in the following year's annual report of the Board of Deputies. The Board of Deputies were acting in their legally appointed role as agents of the Registrar General for the Jewish community. The Registrar General also received this information, as he did with any

Table 3.A1 Registered Jewish marriages in licensed City and East End synagogues, 1880–1914

Synagogue	Marriages	%
*1 East London	14 912	53.2
*2 Great	4 375	15.6
*3 New	1 399	5.0
4 New Road	1 316	4.7
5 Philpot St Gt	1 286	4.6
*6 Hambro	877	3.1
7 German, Spital Sq.	801	2.9
8 Sandys Row	486	1.7
9 Gt Garden St	471	1.7
10 Fieldgate St	461	1.6
11 Bethnal Green Gt	350	1.1
12 Cannon St Rd	295	1.1
13 Gt Alie St	227	0.8
14 Spitalfields Gt	157	0.6
15 Princes St	131	0.5
16 Vine Court	100	0.4
17 Little Alie St	69	0.2
18 Old Castle St	58	0.2
19 Philpot St, Sfardish	57	0.2
20 Old Montague St, Shaas	52	0.2
21 Artillery Lane	46	0.2
22 Greenfield St	33	0.1
23 Dunk St, Spitalfields	22	0.1
24 Peace & Tranquility, Buckle St	16	0.1
25 Whitechapel Rd	7	0
26 Dunk St, Shortkoff	3	0
27 Pelham St	0	0
28 Dunk St, Beth Hamedresh	0	0
29 Stepney Orthodox	0	0
Total	28 007	

Note: Synagogues marked * were United Synagogue members.

Source: Board of Deputies, *Annual Reports* (1881–1915), statistical appendices. The returns for 1884 and 1897 are missing and so not included.

other institution which performed the ceremonies associated with births, deaths and marriages. The Registrar General's information was forwarded by the local superintendent registrars, who annually inspected all registration books and kept the first copy of each register when it became full. Thus, the Board of Deputies figures can be checked and have been verified as accurate.[51]

Table 3.A1 lists the synagogues in the City and East End of London that were licensed to marry, and the distribution of Jewish marriages.[52]

The registers of the duplicate copies of the civil marriage records continued to be held by the synagogues. Most of these synagogues have since closed down, however, so the marriage registers of these now defunct synagogues are found not on their premises but in the archives of the Board of Deputies, in the archives of the umbrella organisation the synagogue was a member of or on the premises of an extant synagogue with which the defunct synagogue previously amalgamated.

The marriage registers of those defunct synagogues belonging to the United Synagogue are housed in the archives of the United Synagogue. These include the Hambro, which merged with the Great in 1936. The Great was then destroyed in 1941 and its marriage records were given to the United Synagogue. The East London synagogue closed in 1988 and its vast collection of marriage records is now in the archives of the United Synagogue.

Of the remainder a number are still extant. The fourth United Synagogue member from the East End, the New Synagogue, relocated to Stamford Hill, in North-East London, in 1913 and still holds its marriage registers on site.[53] The *Machzike Hadath's* Spitalfields Great Synagogue, once housed in the Neuve Église on Brick Lane, moved to Brent Cross, in North-West London, and holds its records there. Sandys Row, Great Garden Street and Fieldgate Street Synagogues are all still in the East End with their records. New Road and Cannon Street Road Synagogues amalgamated with the East London Central Synagogue, now in Nelson Street, and their records are held there (along with one book from the Little Alie Street congregation). Of the rest, most sent their registers to the Board of Deputies on closing. The archives of the Board of Deputies contain the marriage registers of Great Alie Street, Princes Street, Vine Court, Little Alie Street, Philpot Street Sfardish, Old Montague Street Shaas, Artillery Lane, Greenfield Street, Peace and Tranquility, Whitechapel Road and Dunk Street Shortkoff Synagogues.

There are some anomalies. The first book from Princes Street Synagogue is in the local history archive of Bancroft Road Library in Stepney, rather than with the Board of Deputies. The records of the former German Synagogue at Spital Square are housed by the Federation of Synagogues on its premises at Greatorex Street.

Some of the series of marriage records are either missing or were not traced. The Old Castle Street Synagogue's records, for example, are listed as being in the Board of Deputies archives but were not located. The records of Bethnal Green Great, Philpot Street Great and Dunk Street Spitalfields synagogues have not been located either. Both Philpot Street Great's and Bethnal Green Great's registers were presumed to have been destroyed along with the Synagogues in the Blitz.[54]

Some of the series of records are incomplete. The German Synagogue, Spital Square, for example, is missing one book (100 entries) between 1897 and 1900, 72 entries have been lost from the next, 1900–01, and around 80 have been lost from the book covering the period up until 1914. Thus out of a reported 801 weddings only 557 records have been located. The first book from Vine Court is missing, as is the final book in the series up to 1914 from Fieldgate Street Synagogue – meaning that only 17 records out of a reported 100 and 400 out of a reported 461 respectively have been located. Out of the enormous number of books from the East London Synagogue, just one is missing.

It was not possible to assume that choice of synagogue for marriage was random, so every effort was made to complete the total universe of records from which a sample could be selected. Complete, or almost complete, series of marriage registers were obtained from the following synagogues: East London, Great, New, New Road, Hambro, Great Garden Street, Cannon Street Road, Great Alie Street, Spitalfields Great, Princes Street, Little Alie Street, Philpot Street Sfardish, Old Montague Street Shaas, Artillery Lane, Greenfield Street, Peace and Tranquility, Whitechapel Road and Dunk Street Shortkoff. Near complete information was obtained from the German Synagogue, Spital Square, and Fieldgate Street Synagogue, with partial information from Vine Court Synagogue. The records of Philpot Street Great, Bethnal Green Great, Old Castle Street and Dunk Street Spitalfields are missing, presumed destroyed. The records of Pelham Street, Dunk Street Beth Hamedrash and Stepney Orthodox were not included, even though each had been licensed to marry before 1914, because, according to the Board of Deputies' returns, no marriages had taken place before the end of 1914. Sandys Row Synagogue was the only synagogue to deny access to their records and so they are not included in the sample.

Records either destroyed or to which access was denied form less than 9 per cent of the total.[55] Given the uneven distribution of marriages, the absence of some synagogue's marriage records from the sample may matter more than others. The only series of numerical significance without representation come from Philpot Street Great and Bethnal Green Great Synagogues. These were active towards the end of the period, performing over 20 per cent of all City and East End synagogue marriages from 1909 to 1914. For these synagogues only a weighting system (described below) was devised to compensate for their absence from the sample.

The missing records from the German Synagogue, Spital Square, even though concentrated around the turn of the century, constituted only 3 to 4 per cent of the total during these years. This was not considered large enough to damage the overall reliability of the sample and their absence remains without compensation. While having 1.7 per cent of the total records, and between 2 and 3 per cent after 1900, Sandys Row Synagogue is not a significant loss to the sample. The Sandys Row congregation was formed in 1851 by 50 working-class Dutch immigrants. It was the centre of the small Dutch Jewish community in Spitalfields, many of whom were still there after 1880. Even though Sandys Row Synagogue was a part of the Jewish East End, it retained a separate character with little communal commitment. A founder member of the Federation of Synagogues, it suddenly left without any notice in 1899 because the Synagogue committee found they could get better terms with the United Synagogue's Burial Society, a unique case of communal disloyalty.[56] Very few of the East European immigrants would have married there and the brides and grooms at Sandys Row are likely to have been almost entirely from Dutch stock.

The absence of data from synagogues in the regions of secondary settlement, areas like Hackney and Stoke Newington, may at first sight represent a bias in the sample against those successful immigrants who had moved away from the East End. There were, however, relatively few immigrants in these areas before 1914 and, more importantly, very few immigrant marriages solemnised in the synagogues located there. The tendency was rather for those immigrants who had moved out to marry in the synagogues within the main immigrant community in the East End.[57] The synagogues in Hackney, Stoke Newington and other contiguous areas, such as the East Ham and Manor Park Synagogue (established in 1901), Wellington Road Synagogue, Stoke Newington Synagogue (both established in 1902), West Ham Synagogue (1910) and Walthamstow Synagogue (1912) had very few marriages.[58] Older synagogues in these areas, such as the New Dalston and South Hackney Synagogues, were not remotely characterised by immigrant membership.

Synagogue congregations varied. In order to compensate for the absence of the records from Bethnal Green Great and Philpot Street Great synagogues, records from the most closely related synagogue, in terms of the character of their congregations, were weighted to substitute for them.

The New Road Synagogue was the closest in character to both the Philpot Street and Bethnal Green Synagogues (which were themselves quite similar). All three were important immigrant synagogues belonging to the Federation. The New Road synagogue was built as a showcase in 1892 by the Federation.[59] Philpot Street Great replaced it as the leading Federation synagogue after opening in 1907. As the leading community centre, Philpot Street Great quickly became the most popular Federation synagogue for marrying in. The ceremony installing the Federation's chief minister, Rabbi Jung (during its breakdown with the United Synagogue over how to choose the new Chief Rabbi in 1912), also took place there.

While not as important as Philpot Street Great, Bethnal Green Great Synagogue assumed prominence among the Federation synagogues after opening in 1905. The leaders of New Road, Philpot Street Great and Bethnal Green Great Synagogues were all men at the forefront of the immigrant community's resistance to the assimilated Anglo-Jewish families' attempts to dominate the Federation at the end of the period.[60] They were therefore synagogues with similar characteristics. Furthermore, there was a clear statistical relationship between the marriages registered at New Road Synagogue, on the one hand, and at Philpot Street Great and Bethnal Green Great Synagogues, on the other.

While New Road Synagogue had been the most popular place of marriage among the Federation synagogues, from 1909 it lost this position first to Philpot Street Great synagogue and, by the end of the period, Bethnal Green Great. The characteristics of all three synagogues were similar, together attracting a similar proportion of the Federation marriages. Initially, this portion was solemnised solely at New Road, then, as the other two opened, so they became substitute locations for much of that portion of the marrying population that would otherwise have married at New Road. Therefore the absence of Philpot Street Great and Bethnal Green Great can best be compensated for by using the records from New Road Synagogue as a proxy. The New Road records have therefore been reweighted accordingly by the values of 5, 6, 6, 7, 8 and 5 for the years 1909 to 1914 respectively.

Sampling method

From all the records available for inclusion in the sample, the first 5 records in each book of 100 were selected for a 5 per cent sample. Ideally, the records should have been randomly selected, but the original sources were often too fragile to sustain anything other than the most delicate of selection procedures. From this 5 per cent systematic sample of the marriage registers, the related certificates of the Chief Rabbi's authorisation were located from the archives of the Chief Rabbi's Office. Using this record linkage methodology, the birthplaces of the brides and grooms were matched to the occupational and other information in the civil marriage registers.

Table 3.A2   Distribution of marriages in licensed synagogues in the City and East End of London, 1880-1914

	1880	1881	1882	1883	1884	1885	1886	1887	1888
1 Great	126	124	106	116	–	151	155	121	201
2 Hambro	30	46	49	61	–	55	54	103	110
3 New	71	59	70	67	–	69	84	76	105
4 East London	36	52	55	38	–	73	90	61	67
5 German, Spital Sq.									
6 Sandys Row									
7 New Rd									
8 Princes St									
9 Gt Alie St									
10 Little Alie St									
11 Gt Garden St									
12 Old Castle St									
13 Philpot St Gt									
14 Philpot St Sfardish									
15 Vine Court									
16 Peace & Tranquility									
17 Cannon St Rd									
18 Dunk St Spitalfields									
19 Dunk St Shortkoff									
20 Fieldgate St									
21 Old Montague Shaas									
22 Whitechapel Rd									
23 Artillery Lane									
24 Spitalfields Gt									
25 Greenfield St									
26 Bethnal Green Gt									
27 Pelham St									
28 Dunk St Beth Ham									
29 Stepney Orthodox									
Total	263	281	280	282	[315]	348	383	361	483

1889	1890	1891	1892	1893	1894	1895	1896	1897	
218	170	129	117	101	96	102	142	–	1 Great
93	87	9	3	1	2	2	5	–	2 Hambro
98	134	19	18	21	22	11	28	–	3 New
80	135	434	476	497	555	576	601	–	4 East London
1	4	2	1	20	11	22	23	–	5 German, Spital Sq.
		0	0	0	0	2	4	4	–	6 Sandys Row
								2	–	7 New Rd
								0	–	8 Princes St
										9 Gt Alie St
										10 Little Alie St
										11 Gt Garden St
										12 Old Castle St
										13 Philpot St Gt
										14 Philpot St Sfardish
										15 Vine Court
										16 Peace & Tranquility
										17 Cannon St Rd
										18 Dunk St Spitalfields
										19 Dunk St Shortkoff
										20 Fieldgate St
										21 Old Montague Shaas
										22 Whitechapel Rd
										23 Artillery Lane
										24 Spitalfields Gt
										25 Greenfield St
										26 Bethnal Green Gt
										27 Pelham St
										28 Dunk St Beth Ham
										29 Stepney Orthodox
490	530	593	615	640	688	717	805	[874]	

Table 3.A2   Contd.

	1898	1899	1900	1901	1902	1903	1904	1905	1906
1 Great	157	1151	121	141	149	139	146	129	129
2 Hambro	3	2	5	3	2	9	18	14	17
3 New	33	38	57	34	37	24	36	34	41
4 East London	612	700	657	689	765	769	723	837	853
5 German, Spital Sq.	25	37	42	30	20	32	32	45	53
6 Sandys Row	17	21	30	34	30	25	26	29	24
7 New Rd	51	64	70	75	103	85	101	114	118
8 Princes St	15	11	14	10	10	6	7	7	11
9 Gt Alie St	25	19	16	16	11	13	7	10	13
10 Little Alie St									
11 Gt Garden St	4	14	20	30	37	57	49	44	38
12 Old Castle St	0	9	9	4	7	0	5	3	8
13 Philpot St Gt									
14 Philpot St Sfardish									
15 Vine Court	0	7	7	9	10	6	14	11	8
16 Peace & Tranquility		0	0	2	4	4	1	0	2
17 Cannon St Rd			3	25	22	28	19	29	23
18 Dunk St Spitalfields			0	4	2	0	2	1	1
19 Dunk St Shortkoff									
20 Fieldgate St			11	27	35	32	28	27	17
21 Old Montague Shaas				0	9	9	2	4	11
22 Whitechapel Rd					0	0	0	0	0
23 Artillery Lane					0	8	10	7	
24 Spitalfields Gt						0	12	16	
25 Greenfield St							2	3	
26 Bethnal Green Gt							0	18	
27 Pelham St									
28 Dunk St Beth Ham									
29 Stepney Orthodox									
Total	942	1073	1062	1133	1253	1238	1224	1362	1411

Note: Key as in original, nr & * = no return. ? = unknown. 1884 and 1897 values missing, no data, their totals are straight-line interpolations and reported in straight brackets.

Source: As for Table 3.A1.

1907	1908	1909	1910	1911	1912	1913	1914	Total		
107	107	101	120	112	136	117	138	4375	1	Great
15	9	7	10	8	18	14	13	877	2	Hambro
21	33	26	19	14	*	*	*	1399	3	New
746	608	541	519	497	521	495	554	14912	4	East London
59	50	33	44	49	66	48	52	801	5	German, Spital Sq.
28	25	26	16	40	37	38	30	486	6	Sandys Row
123	105	51	53	42	49	41	69	1316	7	New Rd
7	6	7	2	2	10	4	2	131	8	Princes St
26	11	18	4	6	8	15	9	227	9	Gt Alie St
		2	13	12	12	21	9	69	10	Little Alie St
32	22	12	26	16	19	19	32	471	11	Gt Garden St
*	*	0	0	0	4	8	1	58	12	Old Castle St
6	19	188	204	185	227	232	225	1286	13	Philpot St Gt
		0	4	16	15	10	12	57	14	Philpot St Sfardish
7	nr	8	5	0	0	4	4	100	15	Vine Court
1	1	1	*	*	*	*	*	16	16	Peace & Tranquility
29	20	14	20	18	21	24	?	295	17	Cannon St Rd
0	2	7	0	1	1	1	?	22	18	Dunk St Spitalfields
		0	0	0	3	nr	0	3	19	Dunk St Shortkoff
24	22	25	29	98	24	29	33	461	20	Fieldgate St
3	4	4	0	0	3	1	2	52	21	Old Montague Shaas
1	1	1	0	0	1	0	3	7	22	Whitechapel Rd
7	5	0	3	2	3	0	1	46	23	Artillery Lane
13	12	14	15	13	15	25	22	157	24	Spitalfields Gt
9	4	5	3	3	2	2	0	33	25	Greenfield St
38	34	39	36	28	41	50	66	35	26	Bethnal Green Gt
				0	*	*		0	27	Pelham St
					0	0		0	28	Dunk St Beth Ham
					0	0		0	29	Stepney Orthodox
1302	1100	1130	1145	1162	1236	1198	1277	29196		Total

The total number of weddings in the sample was 1362, or 4.7 per cent of the estimated aggregate total in Table 3.A2, slightly less than 5 per cent because of the missing records which were not compensated for, such as from the German Synagogue, Spital Square and Sandys Row, for example. As already stated on p. 38, this sample is called the CRA database, an acronym following the certificates of the Chief Rabbi's authorisation that list the place of nativity.

Of these 1362 brides and grooms, 961 grooms were born in East Europe (Russia, Poland, Romania, the Balkans and Galicia) (73.2 per cent), 277 were born in Britain (21.1 per cent) and 74 were born in other countries (5.7 per cent), overwhelmingly in Holland, Germany and Austria. There were 847 brides born in East Europe (65.2 per cent), 394 in Britain (30.3 per cent) and 58 in other countries (4.5 per cent), similarly dominated by Holland, Germany and Austria.[61] This, incidentally, is the first evidence of the relative importance of Dutch, Germans and Austrians among the Jewish immigrants in Britain.

If the selection procedure had been random, the sample size would be sufficiently large to give statistical validity to all of the major results given below. While not random, the systematic method of selecting the civil marriage records for inclusion did not lead to any obvious sources of bias in the sample. One way of being able to test the sample's structure for any hidden bias is to compare it with the properties of Prais and Schmool's sample of Jewish marriages for 1904.[62]

Prais and Schmool analysed a 10 per cent sample of the Chief Rabbi's certificates for 1904. This is the only other published study ever to use synagogue marriage records, and so is the only benchmark with which to compare this sample. Their geographical coverage was wider, covering authorisations to marry in all mainland Britain. The comparison shows that in Prais and Schmool's database, 74 per cent of the grooms and 60 per cent of the brides were born in East Europe, whereas in the CRA database 85 per cent of the grooms and 71 per cent of the brides marrying in 1904–05 were East-European-born. Given the tendency for immigrants to concentrate in London, this is not surprising.

Two other characteristics can be compared which ought to be less sensitive to any regional bias: the brides and grooms' previous marital status and their ages at first marriage. Here the two samples are very similar. In Prais and Schmool's sample, 97 per cent of the grooms and 98 per cent of the brides, compared with 98 per cent of both brides and grooms in the CRA database were marrying for the first time. The balance in both cases was remarrying widows and widowers; there were no remarrying divorcees. Prais and Schmool's sample showed that the mean age of first marriage in 1904 was 25.1 years for men and 22.9 years for women. The CRA database for 1904 and 1905 gave 24.2 years for the men and 22.2 years for the women, the slightly earlier age of first marriage reflecting, no doubt, the higher proportion of younger marrying immigrants in the CRA database.

The CRA database has therefore been selected from a near-complete universe of Jewish immigrant marriages in London's East End. The sample was appropriately selected and its properties appear very similar to the only other sample of Jewish marriage records previously published. In sum, there are strong grounds for placing considerable confidence in the Jewish marriage record data set and so proceeding with the analysis of Jewish immigrant entrepreneurship resulting from this source.

4
Jewish Immigrant Entrepreneurship in London and New York

Living in the densely packed urban slums, Jews concentrated in just two or three occupations – the so-called immigrant trades. Above all, however, in both New York's Lower East Side and London's East End the immigrant economy was dominated by the clothing industry.[1] While garment production had begun to industrialise in the late nineteenth century, beyond the sewing machine mechanisation was slight.[2] With the simple sewing machine as the main organisational locus, clothing firms were typically small and easy to establish.[3] The road to entrepreneurship in the garment industry was therefore broader than in almost any other sector. Once established, however, Jewish firms competed through cutting labour costs. Ruthless competition forced many immigrants to endure a volatile existence, in and out of business.[4]

Contemporaries in both countries were astonished at the speed with which impoverished Jewish immigrants became entrepreneurs. At a time when social commentators were pressing for labour's right to combine, the urgency of the new arrivals' scramble out of wage-earning work and into self-employment seemed somehow indecent.[5] The British writer Walter Besant dolefully commented that 'the transformation of the poor, starving immigrant, willing to do anything at any wage, to the prosperous master workman is unlovely'.[6]

Beatrice Potter, one of the contributors to Charles Booth's *Life and Labour of the People in London*, concluded that the 'strongest impelling motive of the Jewish race' was 'the love of *profit* as distinct from any other form of money-earning'.[7] This explained their compulsion for self-employment. She went on to describe what she thought of as an immigrant's 'typical' path from the near-slavery in a sweatshop after arrival to learning a trade. And then, after a few more months, the by-now settled immigrant

> employs the enforced leisure of the slack season in some form of petty dealing. He is soon in a fair way to become a tiny capitalist – a maker of profit as well as an earner of wage. He has moved out of the back court in which his fellow countrymen are herded together like animals, and is comfortably installed in a model dwelling; ... his wife wears jewellery and furs on the Sabbath; for their Sunday dinner they eat poultry. He treats his wife with courtesy and tenderness, and they discuss constantly the future of the children ... He remembers the starvation fare and the long hours of his first place: he remembers too the name and address of the wholesale house served by his first master; and presently he appears at the counter and offers to take the work at a lower figure, or secures it through a tip to the foreman. But he no longer kisses the hand of Singer's agent and begs with fawning words for another sewing machine; nor does he flit to other lodgings in the dead of night at the first threat of the broker. In short, he has become a law-abiding and self-respecting citizen of our great metropolis, and feels himself the equal of a Montefiore or a Rothschild.[8]

The rise into entrepreneurship for the newly arrived immigrants was, according to the stereotype, swift and inevitable. 'The ease with which a man may become a master is proverbial in the East End,' claimed Potter.[9]

Similar observations were made in New York. There the Jewish immigrants also propelled themselves into positions of entrepreneurship, especially in the garment trades. The pattern was similar, first enduring heroic sacrifices (or 'ruthless underconsumption', as one scholar aptly described it), before branching out into business.[10] Successful entrepreneurs then diversified out of clothing into retailing, wholesaling, property and other ventures.[11]

While the observations of Potter, Besant and others were certainly memorable, it remains to be seen whether they were accurate. No doubt the stereotype was true for some, but for how many is simply unknown. As the last chapter has shown, the only evidence available to answer this question for the London Jews has hitherto been too uneven and unreliable for any credible conclusion. Moreover, historians have exhibited unease with some of Potter's and others' generalisations in the Booth survey.[12] Now, however, through using the marriage records for

London and census records for New York, these stereotypes can be put to the test. It is possible to measure the share of entrepreneurs among the Jewish immigrant labour force in both cities for the first time, and this chapter presents those measurements.

Our preferred indicator of entrepreneurship is to count the share of entrepreneurs in the working population. Bearing in mind the definition of an entrepreneur as the head of a firm, in practice this means summing the immigrant merchants, masters and manufacturers in the Jewish workforce. First, one significant limitation of the study needs to be mentioned: the absence of women.

Evidence of the occupational status of women in the late nineteenth century points to their marginalization in the workforce. When they did work, their wages supplemented the male contribution to the so-called family wage. Hence the long-standing pay differential for similar work. Unsurprisingly, female participation rates were low, inversely related to the earnings of the male household head.[13]

Among the Jews, the near-universal practice was for women to stop work after marriage.[14] Perhaps in consequence, female Jewish occupations were largely left unrecorded by census enumerators and synagogue secretaries alike.[15] Evidence of the occupational structure of Jewish immigrant women is patchy and incomplete. Because there can be little confidence in the representativeness of the underlying data, the occupational information for Jewish women is therefore devalued. In common with practically all similar studies of occupational distribution, the focus here must, alas, be restricted to men.[16]

While earlier work has rarely focused exclusively on entrepreneurship, considerable scholarship has focused on immigrant occupational structures as the principal measurement of patterns of social mobility. These studies are not unrelated to the current one. Furthermore, a number of studies published previously have focused on the changing social structure of the Jewish immigrant communities in the United States. Pioneered by Stefan Thernstrom in the 1960s, comparisons of ethnic mobility in late-nineteenth-century United States flourished through the 1970s and early 1980s.[17] The common approach was to derive the social stratification – the shares of blue- and white-collar workers – of different ethnic communities from the original census manuscripts.[18] Partly in deference to this renowned classification system, and partly for the ease of comparison with these existing studies, the tables here show entrepreneurs as a share of the white-collar workforce as well as of the total.[19]

London

For the Jewish immigrants in London over the period, Table 4.1 shows that one groom in eight was an entrepreneur. As a proportion of the general population this presents a strikingly high percentage and fore-shadowed Noah Barou's later comment suggesting that Jewish workers were at the very least twice as likely to be self-employed than were non-Jews.[20] While the Jews moved disproportionately into business, relatively few were in the non-entrepreneurial white collar professional and clerical sectors.

The previous chapter has shown that Jewish immigrants did not concentrate in these classes. Only 2.1 per cent of the East European aliens in London in 1901 were in census class III, the Professionals. Even then, they were typically very low-order professional occupations. Most of the non-entrepreneurial white-collar grooms were religious func-tionaries, 6 were clerical workers, and 2 were musicians. There were only 2 engineers and 1 solitary teacher.

The entrepreneurs concentrated in the clothing industry, furniture-making, and retailing – especially the retailing of food and clothing. For both white- and blue-collar classes, tailoring and the related branches of the clothing industry were the leading trades. Of the 118 entrepreneur grooms, for instance, 46 were in the clothing trades, mostly in manu-facturing but some in dealing. Entrepreneurs in the food and grocery trades totalled another 23, with jewellers and dealers in precious metals providing another 11, and 3 furniture manufacturers. There were 35 in various forms of commerce, from cotton seed importers to estate agents, including some general dealers and job buyers, many of whom would also have been active primarily in the distribution of clothing, so that, in sum, half at least were in the clothing trades.

Table 4.1 Entrepreneurship and occupational status of the Jewish immigrant grooms marrying in London's City and East End synagogues, 1880–1914 (percentages)

	1880–89	*1890–99*	*1900–06*	*1907–14*	*1880–1914*
Total number	91	264	315	291	961
White collar	13.2	12.2	13.3	17.9	14.4
of which:					
entrepreneurs	9.9	9.5	11.4	16.5	12.3
Blue collar	86.8	87.9	86.7	82.1	85.6

Source: CRA database.

While the occupational distribution of the blue-collar workers does not affect the measurement of entrepreneurship, it does underline the immigrant trades' sheer dominance of the Jewish East End. From the 823 blue-collar grooms, 588 were in the clothing and footwear industries (overwhelmingly in tailoring) and another 111 in furniture-making. Along with a number of related trades in the residual category, such as employees of sewing machine agents, lumber suppliers and so on, around 90 per cent of the blue-collar East European grooms were occupied in the principal industries of the immigrant economy.[21]

While Table 4.1 highlights the division in the Jewish labour force between entrepreneurs and workers, it also suggests that there was a switch from blue- to white-collar work over the period, although the age-bias in the marriage register population highlighted in the previous chapter needs to be eliminated before this can be confirmed. Table 4.2 shows the trend once the adjustment is made.

This confirms the growth in entrepreneurship among the Jewish immigrants. Entrepreneurs as a share of the Jewish immigrant workforce first fell from 14.2 per cent in the 1880s, to 10.9 per cent in the 1890s, before increasing to 13.3 per cent during 1900–6 and then to 18.0 per cent in 1907–14. This is broadly consistent with the little that is known of levels of Jewish entrepreneurship in this period. David Feldman, for example, estimated that 11 per cent of Jewish men in East London occupied in manufacturing were entrepreneurs in the late 1880s.[22] What is surprising, however, is how the level of entrepreneurship increased after the 1890s. Over the whole period there was a net increase in the share of entrepreneurs in the male immigrant workforce of 3.8 per cent, and from the 1890s to 1907–14 of 7.1 per cent. With the blue-collar and the non-entrepreneurial white-collar classes declining in relative importance and the entrepreneurs growing, the Jewish

Table 4.2 Entrepreneurship and Occupational status of Jewish immigrant men in London's East End, 1880–1914 (percentage of age-adjusted grooms)

	1880–89	*1890–99*	*1900–06*	*1907–14*
Total no.	91	264	315	291
White collar	17.6	13.9	15.1	19.4
of which:				
entrepreneurs	14.2	10.9	13.3	18.0
Blue collar	82.4	86.1	84.9	80.5

Source: Age-adjusted CRA database.

immigrant labour market was behaving rather differently from the wider one.

There was little structural change in the London labour market. Despite London's increasing role as a commercial centre, which caused occupations in the clerical and transport sectors to grow in importance, the overall impact on the relative shares of white- and blue-collar occupations was trivial. When contrasted to the structural mobility in London generally therefore this increase in the white-collar workers among the Jewish immigrants appears impressive indeed.[23] This represented a genuine shift in the balance of white- and blue-collar workers in the Jewish immigrant community, and one not seen in the wider society around them.

In the later nineteenth century the condition of working class became one of society's dominant issues.[24] J.E. Cairnes developed the concept of 'non-competing groups' within the UK labour market to describe the caste-like conditions in British society.[25] Halsey has famously commented that an 'integrated inequality was the central principle of social life in Britain before the First World War. A status hierarchy lent legitimacy to class inequality'.[26] Recent research has modified this picture only a little. Late-Victorian Britons did move from one sub-group of blue- (or white-) collar class to another, but hardly ever did they rise (or slip) across the principal divide.[27] The Jewish immigrants behaved very differently compared with the general population, as the commentators of the day perceived.

New York

To measure entrepreneurship among the New York Jewish immigrants, the best sources of evidence are the American censuses. The federal censuses for 1880, 1890, 1900 and 1910 and the New York State censuses of 1892, 1905 and 1925 give an enormous amount of information concerning the size of the rapidly growing immigrant community in New York and its occupational profile. As with the censuses for England and Wales, however, the published census reports are insufficiently detailed to allow one to distinguish between employees and entrepreneurs in the immigrant trades. For this it has been necessary for historians to go back to the original census enumerators' books and reclassify the Jewish immigrants according to the more detailed information contained in the original manuscripts.

Thomas Kessner, in his 1977 volume *The Golden Door: Italian and Jewish Immigrant Mobility in New York City, 1880–1915*, took a large sample of the original census records from the main Jewish immigrant wards in New York City for the 1880 and 1905 censuses. He then repeated the process in a later study for the 1925 state census. This revealed the changing occupational structure of the East European Jews in New York from 1880 to 1925.[28]

Kessner's Russian- (and Russian-Polish-) born household heads in the Jewish Lower East Side bear great similarities to the East European grooms in the CRA database (pp. 41–50). Both populations lived in the main immigrant neighbourhoods in the principal settlements, and both were composed of male household heads. The only difference reflects Kessner's decision to focus exclusively on Russian natives. Just over 10 per cent of the East European grooms were from Galicia and Romania, although these are very unlikely to have been more entrepreneurial or less, sharing a near-identical ethnic and occupational background with the Russian and Polish Jews. Like is therefore being compared with like. Kessner's results are summarised in Table 4.3.

The increase of the white-collar occupations among the East European Jews in New York City during the years of mass immigration was quite remarkable. Immigrants in white-collar occupations grew from 21 per cent to 40 per cent of the workforce from 1880 to 1905, further increasing to 50 per cent by 1925. The increase was particularly marked in the higher white-collar class (I), consisting of the more senior professionals and established businessmen. While the Jewish immigrants in London displayed an aptitude for moving into white collar occupations, by comparison Jewish immigrant upward mobility in New York was astonishing.

Such a remarkable rate of mobility needs to be related to any relevant changes in the New York labour market as well as to the prevalence of

Table 4.3 Occupational status of Russian Jewish household heads in New York City, 1880–1925 (percentages)

	1880	*1905*	*1925*
Total no.	524	963	1535
White-collar I	5.2	15.1	13.2
White-collar II	15.8	25.1	36.8
White-collar total	21.0	40.2	50.0
Blue-collar total	79.0	59.8	50.0

Note: Peddlers are here included as blue-collar workers (see note 19).

Source: Kessner, 'Selective Filter', tables I and II, pp. 172 and 178.

social mobility in the United States generally. During this period the New York economy experienced rapid growth and some change in the balance of the city's occupational profile. Kessner concluded, however, that the 'changes in New York's occupational structure were neither sufficiently rapid nor dramatic enough to account for the kinds of progress exhibited by the…Jews between 1880 and 1905'.[29] For New York's Russian Jews 'previous experience, attitudes toward education, ambition for status and security played far more important roles than the structural "pull-effect" of the New York economy'.[30]

Social mobility in late-nineteenth-century United States was actually relatively muted, despite the Horatio Alger ideal.[31] Levels of inter- and intra-generational mobility had declined and levels of inequality had risen, in particular between the so-called old and new immigrants, the Anglos, Irish and Germans on the one hand, and the Italians, Poles and Jews on the other.[32]

The divergence in Jewish immigrant mobility between New York and London was therefore not especially influenced by any underlying changes in the social structure of one location compared with another. It was not the case that the Jews arriving in New York were in a much more mobile society. In both countries in this period mobility was marginal. Not only then were the Jewish immigrants in London and New York both exceptional when compared with the wider populations, but the Jews in New York were much more upwardly mobile than the Jews in London. This was entirely the result of higher levels of entrepreneurship. For the Russian Jewish immigrants in New York City, Kessner concluded that 'it was not medicine, law or even their vaunted thirst for education that carried them forward. It was business.'[33]

Kessner's results were presented in terms of broad social groups, whereas the interest here is in one sub-group of the white-collar workers, the entrepreneurs. While Kessner did not explicitly list the occupations in each socio-economic class, a careful reading of his writings enables the entrepreneurs to be separated from the non-entrepreneurs.[34] The reclassification of Kessner's figures gives estimates for the levels in entrepreneurship among adult male East European Jews in New York from 1880 to 1914 which are directly comparable to those of the East European Jewish immigrants in London. These are reported in Table 4.4.[35]

Table 4.4 shows that East European Jewish immigrant entrepreneurship in New York and London differed hugely. While levels of entrepreneurship among London's Jewish immigrant workforce increased from around 1 in 7 to nearly 1 in 5, probably more than 1 in 3 Jewish

Table 4.4 Levels of Entrepreneurship in the male workforce for the East European Jewish immigrants in London and New York, 1880–1914 (percentages of age-adjusted grooms and Russian household heads)

London	1880–89	1890–99	1900–06	1907–14	Increase 1880s–1907–14
	14.2	10.9	13.3	18.0	3.8
New York	1880		1905	1914	Increase 1880–1914
	18.0		34.3	35.0	17.0

Source: see Tables 4.2 and 4.3 and text.

immigrant men were entrepreneurs in New York by 1914.[36] Moreover, this remarkable rise in the levels of entrepreneurship in New York was earlier than the more modest rise in London. By 1905 over a third of Jewish immigrants were entrepreneurs in New York, a level which stabilised thereafter. True, this rise appears to come from a higher base, with 18 per cent of the New York Jews being entrepreneurs in 1880 compared with only 14 per cent in London in the 1880s, although levels of entrepreneurship fell among those in London from the early to the late 1880s.

Recent research has confirmed this high level of self-employment among the Jewish immigrants. Chiswick, for example, calculates that self-employment among Yiddish-speaking male immigrants in America was 38.4 per cent in 1910 and 45.5 per cent in 1920. Given that most studies suggest that rates of self-employment were higher among Jews outside New York, the 1914 estimate given in Table 4.4 is likely to be reasonably close to the actual figure.[37]

Entrepreneurship among the Jewish immigrants in New York therefore rose from 18 per cent in 1880 to nearly 35 per cent in 1905, from when it stabilised. Unfortunately, without a continuous series of data for entrepreneurship in New York, it is impossible to know exactly when after 1880 this rise in self-employment occurred, or whether it was continuous, or whether, as in London, it was preceded by a fall.

Conclusion

The levels of entrepreneurship among the East European Jewish immigrants in London show an extraordinary difference from those in New York. Starting from broadly similar levels, the Jewish immigrants in New York increased their share of entrepreneurs in the workforce by 17 per cent from 1880 to 1914, from 18 per cent to 35 per cent. With London Jewish entrepreneurship increasing by only 4 per cent (from 14.2 per cent in the 1880s to 18.0 per cent before 1914), the rate of growth was four times greater in New York than in London. While the impressions of observers in both New York and London are confirmed (the Jews were exceptionally entrepreneurial in both cities), the social advance by the Jews in New York was much more rapid than in London.

This divergence in Jewish entrepreneurship may have arisen from fairly straightforward differences in the immigrant trades in New York and London. It may have arisen from the assimilation of different cultural values. But first, it needs to be established whether or not the East European Jews in New York were simply more likely to become entrepreneurs before arrival.

5
Jewish Mass Migration and the Choice of Destination

The weight of quantitative evidence suggests that New York was the preferred destination. After all, around ten times more Jews settled there than in London. It is tempting to think that those who failed to move to the more popular city were therefore demonstrating some sort of inferiority, a disposition which may have spilled over into those strikingly different levels of entrepreneurship. Perhaps they were too poor to go further, perhaps there was some sort of psychological association with Europe which prompted the less adventurous to stay, perhaps there were other even less specific reasons which prompted the more entrepreneurial to go to New York and the less to settle in London. Perhaps, though, the temptation must be resisted because in truth we do not know.

There is certainly evidence that some contemporaries viewed the London bound Jews in a less favourable light. The *Jewish Chronicle* lamented the difference between them; those going on to America during the crisis migration of 1881 and 1882 were 'a far superior class to the usual poor Jews that reach London from Poland'.[1] Chaim Bermant summarised the view of the two destinations, or at least how it appeared to their descendants:

> The ultimate destination was America, *die goldene medine*, the golden land. Britain, at best, was thought of as the silver land, a poor man's America, but those who did come brought others over and many who had thought of England as a staging-point remained for good.[2]

If this view is correct, then the implication for entrepreneurship in the two streams is that those immigrants moving to New York were surely more likely to become entrepreneurs, a likelihood determined by differences in their backgrounds and make-ups. It is a big 'if', however. The testimonial evidence is by no means conclusive.

A Jewish immigrant in London countered the suggestion of New York's greater economic attraction, saying 'if New York's streets were paved with gold, London's were paved with platinum and diamonds'.[3] In contrast to the focus of the *Jewish Chronicle's* complaint, the typical immigrants to London were a people 'of a more capable and self-reliant nature than those who seek refuge here in times of persecution'. Differences in the two streams of immigrants were not so obvious.[4] While the recorded opinions of contemporaries are both conflicting and selective, some obvious influences on the levels of entrepreneurship among the London and New York Jews ought to be considered first – namely, any differences in the wealth and structure of the two groups of emigrants.

Entrepreneurship and capital

It is difficult to judge whether crossing the Atlantic was likely to have led to the more entrepreneurial migrants moving to New York. For one thing a psychological profile of a typical entrepreneur remains elusive. There is no consensus among social scientists about whether entrepreneurs have more or less adventurous personalities. Furthermore, as a matter of historical fact it is probably unwise to assume that moving to America was especially adventurous – it was simply the obvious choice. So regardless of the subsequent outcomes, New York might rather have been the choice of the conservative majority of emigrants, London the choice of the entrepreneurial few.

Economists avoid psychological stereotyping and assume that entrepreneurs essentially select themselves, primarily on the basis of their access to capital, both financial and human.[5] Either entrepreneurs have preferential access to the necessary funds for entering business, or they are more talented, or both. Some evidence exists of the amounts of financial and human resources brought by the two streams of Jews.

Immigrants had to declare the funds they were carrying on arrival both in New York and London, so a comparison of how much financial capital each immigrant brought with them ought to be relatively straightforward. For instance, between 1895 and 1902 each East European native that arrived in steerage at the Port of London from Rotterdam, Hamburg or Bremen and on board a German or Dutch steamer expressing an intention to stay brought, on average, 26.3 shillings, or $6.40.[6] East European Jewish immigrants to the United States during the same period declared similar amounts upon entering, an average of around $8 up to 1905.[7]

There are some legitimate concerns about the underlying statistics here. We don't know whether the amounts brought by Jews coming to Britain from other continental ports differed, for example, or for those on British ships rather than German and Dutch, or those arriving in first and second classes rather than steerage. Around two-thirds of those who declared their intention to stay did not in fact do so, and we have no way of knowing whether those that actually did stay were relatively rich or not. Putting these (and other difficulties) to one side, however, there were apparently differences in the amounts brought. 1902 is the only year when a direct comparison is possible. On average each Jewish immigrant arriving in the USA brought $7.29 but only $5.37 to London, a quarter less.[8] For easing the route into entrepreneurship, this $2 difference might have been important. Its importance is best assessed, however, by comparing the Jews with other immigrant groups.

The Jews took the lowest amounts of any immigrants to the USA. English immigrants, for example, brought on average $58.50 in the early 1900s, eight times more than the typical Jew.[9] This kind of sum would indeed have enabled an immigrant to establish a small business soon after arrival. The $6 to $8 brought by the Jews to London and New York was frankly trivial by comparison. The Jews were not bringing seed capital for business ventures but just enough to cover the bare necessities for the first few days in their new homes. In all probability these sums would have been remitted to them by friends and family members already settled in New York and London, so that the $2 difference was no reflection on any inherently superior preparation for self-employment among the New York arrivals; it may simply have reflected the higher costs of living there.[10]

If the amounts of savings on arrival were essentially very similar among the two Jewish immigrant streams, they could not account for the big differences in the New York and London levels of entrepreneurship. An alternative explanation might lie in any significant variations in talent. Perhaps the talented Jews went to the USA and the less talented to the UK. Talent, or human capital, is very difficult to capture in any statistical sense. Economists have often tried to measure literacy rates across countries to get some idea. Measurement difficulties mean that the average number of years of schooling among a given population is a more common though less preferred proxy. Despite their crudeness, literacy and schooling are surprisingly good indicators of human capital in historical studies.[11]

For the Jews there is some evidence of literacy rates among the two streams, although it is not exactly comparable. The proportion of Jewish immigrants to the USA able to read in any language was 75 per cent. This compares with 58 per cent for the Jews in Russia, so immigrants were somewhat more literate than the base population.[12] Unlike in America, aliens were not asked about their literacy on arrival in the UK. However, 60 per cent of East-European-born Jewish brides and grooms signed their names in English on their marriage records. Furthermore, a substantial number of those unable to sign in English nevertheless signed their names in Yiddish, using the Hebrew script. While these were not counted, they were a memorable feature of the records. Easily over 70 per cent of the immigrant brides and grooms were therefore able to sign their names in either English or Yiddish. The ability to sign one's name is not strictly speaking an indicator of literacy comparable to the ability to read in any language, although traditional Jewish education in the Pale did emphasise the learning of reading to quite an advanced level before writing. So while it is impossible to quantify their literacy in exactly the same way, it was surely the case that considerably more than 70 per cent of immigrant brides and grooms in London ought to have been able to read in any language.[13] With a 75 per cent literacy rate among those arriving in America, the two measures suggest a broad similarity in basic literacy among the Jews arriving in Britain and America.

Any further analysis of the human capital endowments of the two immigrant streams is severely hampered by a lack of evidence. It would be particularly illustrative to compare the two streams' occupational backgrounds, for example. Differences here are very likely to have been closely related to any differences in human capital and so to any differences in the levels of entrepreneurship subsequently attained. It is, however, practically impossible to make any comparison because of the almost complete absence of evidence on UK Jewish immigrants' previous occupations.[14] Indeed, even when the occupational backgrounds of the Jews arriving in the USA are considered, it is clear that these data must be interpreted with extreme caution.[15] It is, in sum, a forlorn hope that it would be possible to evaluate the level of talent in the two groups. For one reason or another, the evidence is simply inadequate to the task.

It is also apparent that the difference in the level of entrepreneurship was not attributable to any underlying difference in the demographic structure of the two streams. For the Jews arriving in the United States from 1899, 56 per cent were male, compared with 59 per cent of those arriving in Britain from 1906. Equally, the share of children was almost identical – 24 per cent of arrivals in America were under 14, compared with the 19 per cent of arrivals in Britain who were under 12. Assuming a roughly equal distribution of children across the ages up to 14, then 20 per cent of American arrivals were under 12.[16] Compared with non-Jews, children were twice as likely to migrate both to America and Britain.[17] The different levels in entrepreneurship were no simple consequence of demography.

Differences in entrepreneurship might plausibly have been related to regional backgrounds, however, for the Jewish Pale experienced sharp regional variations in economic activity over the period. Kuznets suggested that of the four regions in the Pale of Settlement – the Northwest and Congress Poland regions in the north and the Southwest and South regions in the south – emigrants from the Northwest region would be significantly over-represented because of the slower economic growth there. This contrasted with the two southern regions, which were less crowded and benefited more from Russian industrialization.[18]

One contemporary commentator, Rubinov, also suggested that the 'vast majority' of Jewish immigrants to the USA came from the Northwest region, a region dominated by Lithuanian Jews. Certainly population growth in the north of the Pale was apparently much slower than in the south, suggesting emigration came disproportionately from there.[19] However, the evidence is not conclusive. Another contemporary, Obolensky-Ossinsky, cited evidence of increasing Jewish emigration from the two southern regions over the period, so that the overall 'distribution of emigrants from different parts of the Hebrew Pale corresponds roughly with the distribution of population.'[20]

The only existing estimate of regional migration is one recently published by Stampfer based on the members of Jewish communal societies in New York. These communal societies, or *landsmanshaftn*, drew their members, as the generic name suggests, from fellow 'landsmen', thus they may be a reasonable proxy of regional migration.[21] Table 5.1 shows that 50 per cent of society members belonged to *landsmanshaftn* named after a town or area in the Northwest region, 20 per cent from the Southwest, 6 per cent from the South and 24 per cent from Poland. The only evidence of regional background for UK Jewish immigrants is the evidence of birthplace from the certificates of the Chief Rabbi's authorisation to marry which is also given in Table 5.1 along with the distribution of Jewish population in the four regions of the Pale.

While there were seemingly some differences in the regional backgrounds of the two migration streams (the Southwest had a far higher

Table 5.1   The regional distribution of Jewish Immigration to Britain and America, 1880–1914 (percentages)

Regions	London [N = 1496]	New York [N = 26368]	Pale of Settlement
Northwest	45.3	50.0	29.0
Poland	38.5	24.0	26.9
Southwest	2.7	20.0	14.9
South	13.5	6.0	29.1

Sources: London is the brides and grooms from the CRA database. New York City is the members of *Landsmanshaftn*, from S. Stampfer, 'The Geographic Background of East European Jewish Migration to the United States before World War I', in Glazier and de Rosa, *Migration*, p. 227. The Jewish population in the Pale is from the 1897 census, listed in Kahan, *Essays*, table A4.

share of *landsmanshaftn* members in New York than brides and grooms in London, for example), the principal result is that both were indeed disproportionately composed of the Lithuanian Jews from the Northwest region. Indeed, if the comparison is of the northern and southern shares, then the two northern regions accounted for 83.8 per cent of the London brides and grooms, and 74.0 per cent of the *landsmanshaftn* members in New York, compared with only 55.9 per cent of the Jewish population in the Pale.

The deficiencies of the underlying sources warn against any further inferences. In the absence of any consistent testimonial evidence, it would be difficult to place too much weight on the apparent difference in the regional migration from the Southwest and South regions to London and New York. The best interpretation is that both migrant streams were composed predominantly of Lithuanian and Polish Jews, a suggestion that fits in well with what most contemporaries believed.[22] On balance therefore the evidence suggests that there were few differences of any significance in the regional background of the two migration streams. The differences in the subsequent levels of entrepreneurship cannot be accounted for here.

Any analysis of how the differences in the levels of entrepreneurship might be linked either to differences in the wealth, talent and structure of the Jewish migrations is therefore thwarted. The sums brought were trivial, and, apart from basically similar levels of literacy, it is impossible to gauge any differences in human capital. Furthermore, both the demographic structure and the regional background of the two streams were essentially the same.

What is possible, however, is to compare the overall patterns in the arrival of the East European Jews in Britain and America. Differences in immigration patterns may well have been related to economic factors, which in turn might have influenced subsequent levels of entrepreneurship. In this bigger picture, however, any differences between the two streams at first appear slight. One of the most learned commentators on the Jewish mass migration, Lloyd Gartner, has underlined the similarity between the two streams, a similarity 'which we would call astounding were we not so accustomed to it'.[23]

Economic historians now have a fairly good understanding of why some people left their European homes and others remained, so it is possible to apply their basic insights in order to understand why the Jews left Eastern Europe for Britain and the United States. Such a comparison ought to highlight any differences in the make-up of the two immigrant streams, differences that may have influenced their subsequent levels of entrepreneurship.

Nevertheless while this is possible it is hardly straightforward. The deficiencies of existing sources of evidence preclude any simple comparison and so once again some discussion of the drawbacks and revisions to these sources is necessary. If some readers may begin here to feel that so far there has been rather more gristle than meat, I can only reiterate the importance of grasping the nature of the underlying evidence, with all its strengths and weaknesses. Almost all quantitative economic history is an exercise literally by proxy – the economic historian's alchemy being to conjure the pure gold of historical insight from the base metal of partial and limited statistical sources. Nevertheless, some readers may prefer to skim over the section entitled, *Jewish Mass Migration: the numbers*. Before that, however, the bare outlines of the mass migration of East European Jewry need to be sketched.

1850–1914: the era of mass migration

Jewish migration did not take place in a vacuum. During the long nineteenth century, when transport costs were falling, over 50 million people left Europe.[24] Typical characteristics of an emigrant population were that it was coming from a background of rapid population growth, industrialisation and agrarian reform, features which conspired to increase labour market competition and squeeze out the unskilled or those with newly redundant skills.[25] The Russian economy was, in a general sense, no different, with both demographic and economic pressures, as well as the well-known political ones, combining to push the Jews out.

First was the rapid rise in population. The Jewish population in Russia increased at least fivefold between 1800 and 1900; it was the fastest-growing population in nineteenth-century Europe.[26] Second, the Jews had their rights of residence restricted by Russian law to the most densely populated part of the Empire, the Pale of Settlement. Moreover, even within the Pale the Jews were forced to leave rural areas from 1882 and their urbanization increased dramatically thereafter. Restrictions on internal migration therefore increased the population pressures.[27] Third, the traditional occupations of the Jews in the Pale were as middlemen. Many Jewish breadwinners were market-makers, providing an essential service among the overwhelmingly agricultural local population.[28] While the population growth led to an oversupply of traders and merchants generally, the residence restrictions exacerbated its effect; market-makers were most needed in rural not urban areas.[29] Fourth, the industrialisation of the 1880s and 1890s perversely increased this oversupply. This because while the Jews were excluded by official policy from those areas of the economy benefiting most from industrialisation (notably railroad development), they nonetheless had to suffer increased competition from travelling merchants coming into the Pale on the new railway branchlines.[30] The net result of such unparalleled population growth unmitigated by economic growth was that the average income of Jewish families in the Pale fell over the period. It was an anti-Semitic twist to the Malthusian trap, and perhaps as much as a fifth of the Jewish population had fallen into genuine poverty by 1900.[31]

The tradition of movement and communication between the centres of Jewry ensured that enough information about conditions elsewhere was generally available. Moreover, once the railway connections and steamship technologies were in place from the 1860s, the price of movement was no longer prohibitive.[32] In this fertile environment all that was required was a slight shift in momentum for emigration to begin. For the Russian Jews the mass migration movement was triggered by the political turmoil and civil disturbances that followed the assassination of Tsar Alexander II in 1881.

Deep rooted anti-Semitism spilled over into a series of pogroms as elements in Russian society ridiculously blamed the Jews for the Tsar's death. Riots against the Jews in Elisavetgrad and Kiev were followed by pogroms in the provinces of Chernigov, Poltava, Kherson and Ekaterinoslav. The anti-Jewish violence was encouraged by the permissive attitude of the Russian state. In 1882 the notorious May Laws were brought into force restricting Jewish economic activity still further.[33]

Such was the combination of violence and injustice during these few months that the Jews of Russia contracted 'emigration fever'.[34] Many of these first migrants were refugees from this violence. They simply fled to the border and were met by representatives of the western Jewish agencies, who shipped them on to London and New York.[35] Alive to economic opportunities, these immigrants once they had settled sent for their families and friends, causing further migration to take place. So began one of the largest mass migrations of modern times.

Between them the British Isles and Italy accounted for well over half of all European emigrants during the long nineteenth century from 1815 to 1914. A comparison of the emigration rates of these leading sending nations with the Russian Jews ought then to be particularly illustrative.

Table 5.2 shows that even if Great Britain contributed the largest aggregate number of migrants, when compared with its total population, emigration was less significant than in either Ireland or Italy. Irish emigration was particularly influenced by the Famine of course, its shock reverberating through the high Irish emigration rates for decades after.[36]

Along with the Germans and Scandinavians, the British and Irish were considered as traditional groups of immigrants by turn-of-the-century Americans. The Irish excepted, among these 'old' immigrants emigration rates were typically low, and certainly lower than the Italian emigration rate after 1900. The Italians, Greeks and Iberians along with

Table 5.2   Gross (G) and net (N) emigration rates, 1870–1913 (emigrants per 1000 population: decade averages)

		1870–9	1880–9	1890–9	1900–13
Great Britain	G	3.9	5.7	3.9	7.1
	N	1.5	3.2	0.9	3.3
Ireland	G	11.3	16.0	9.7	7.9
	N	–	–	–	–
Italy	G	4.3	6.1	8.7	18.0
	N	–	–	6.8	13.0
Russian Jews	G	–	4.8	8.1	19.7
	N	–	4.5	7.5	18.3

Sources: Rows 1–3, Hatton and Williamson, *Migration*, table 3.2, p. 58. Row 4, gross, Kuznets, 'Russian Jewish', table v, pp. 50–1 (1900–13 actually 1901–14). Row 4, net, is the gross multiplied by 92.89 per cent (or 100 per cent minus the repatriation ratio of 7.11 per cent). Repatriation ratios from Gould, 'Return Migration', table 3, p. 60.

the East Europeans, called the 'new' immigrants, dominated arrivals after the 1880s. While their gross migration rates were very high, much was temporary.[37] The Italians, Slavs and so on were mostly sojourners.

The Russian Jews were also lumped together in Yankee eyes with the other new immigrants but, unlike them, they stayed. Table 5.2 shows that Russian Jewish gross emigration rates were the highest of all, higher even than the Italian. Given the inevitable difficulties over accurately measuring emigration rates, however, this is probably not the most significant result. The most important finding is that, regardless of any measurement errors, the net emigration rate of Russian Jews was so much higher for than any other population.

The Jewish rate of return between 1908 and 1914 was only just over 7 per cent, the lowest return rate of any ethnic or national group.[38] At the peak, over 2 per cent of the Jewish population of the Pale of Settlement were leaving each year never to return. And as already noted, this was disproportionately from the north. Occasionally similar rates of emigration have been witnessed, but only as very localised phenomena: sometimes entire villages moved, for instance. But the sheer extent of the emigration of the Jews from the northern Pale is really only comparable to that of the Irish after the Famine.

This is an important result. The attention scholars have devoted to Irish and Italian migration movements has been understandable given their impact on both home and host economies. However, as Table 5.2 makes clear, the emigration of Jews was actually more intense. And, while the previous chapter has begun to show that their impact was quite profound, by contrast, the migration of the Jews is nevertheless an enormously under-researched topic.

The Jews went overwhelmingly to the United States, over 80 per cent of the total. Britain was the second most important destination with around 7 per cent of the total emigration.[39] Evidently, given such a difference in the magnitude of immigration to these two principal destinations, they were not competing alternatives of anything like equal attraction.

Migration specialists have long tried to explain a destination's attraction to emigrants. The traditional view is that emigrants opted for the location where labour market conditions were most attractive. Certainly, contemporaries assumed that there was a 'close connection' between US immigration and economic growth.[40] The relative unattractiveness of immigration to North America during the depressed 1890s, as well as the 'disastrous effects upon European emigration of the [depressed] industrial conditions in America during 1908' appeared to confirm it, although subsequent attempts to specify the exact relationship have met with limited success.[41]

While it is apparent that for immigration to take place more needs to be on offer in the destination than higher incomes, it is not wholly clear what else is required. Obviously the cost of migration must not be prohibitive, but equally there is a recognition that the cost of emigration is not simply the price of the fare plus the income forgone during travelling. Rather, a more important cost is the risk premium associated with the move to a foreign land.

Immigrant calculations will no doubt have owed more to intuition than actuarial science, but the premium must have seemed very high when detailed information was absent. If accurate and trustworthy information was available, the premium fell. Thus the most attractive destinations were not necessarily those with the highest real income (actually, initially Australia and then Canada during this period) but those with a sufficiently high income and about which potential migrants had sufficient information.[42] Information came primarily from the letters sent home by friends and relatives and then spread from family to family, as if they were links in a chain.

In recent years, migration specialists have increasingly relied on this 'friends and relatives' effect to explain both the variations in emigration rates from nation to nation and the choice of destination.[43] If such chain migration was important, then a destination's attraction was based not only on conventional labour market factors, such as the differences in wages and in rates of unemployment, but also on the size of the existing immigrant community and its network of relations with the sending region. With this kind of understanding of migration, the selection of destination for most emigrants may have been dependent on factors which, while important to the pioneers, may have been totally unimportant to the majority. What mattered most to them was where those pioneers had settled.[44]

There is clear historical evidence about both the flow of information and how the Jews responded. An agent of a steamship company in London said that the Jewish immigrants 'have a great many friends, and it is astonishing to find how reports go from one friend to another'.[45] If the response was positive, both prepaid tickets and cash were sent home. An American Report of 1890 discovered that 'at least 90 per cent' of the Russian Jews benefited from assisted passages.[46] Between 1908 and 1914 official statistics showed that 62 per cent of the Jewish immigrants to the USA had their passage paid by a relative and 94 per cent were on their way to join a relative.[47]

As already noted, the vast majority of Jewish immigrants arriving in London had their passages assisted by relatives already in Britain. The UK Government's Inspector under the Aliens Act claimed that Jewish immigration 'consists very largely of persons who come here to join either relatives or friends who may have been settled some years in the country'.[48] The unanimous testimony of officials from the Poor Jews' Temporary Shelter was that 90 per cent of the Jewish immigrants arriving in London had addresses to go to.[49]

The evidence of extensive chain migration among the East European Jews is overwhelming. They migrated to particular destinations because friends and relatives sent back tickets, money and addresses. Because the costs of moving and settling were reduced by the existence of the informal networks of kith and kin, chain migrants generally arrived with less in their pockets.[50] The Jews arrived with least because of all the immigrants they could count most on a welcome reception. The density of social relations among the East European Jews subsidised both passage and settlement. Such extensive chain migration allowed even the poorest to leave.

There has emerged something of a consensus among economic historians in recent years about how to capture some of the effects of chain migration. This work is particularly associated with Tim Hatton and Jeff Williamson. Their explanation of a number of different streams of migration to different destinations has generally been very successful. The real benefit of the Hatton–Williamson approach is its relative simplicity, in that it assumes that most of the effect of chain migration is going to be proportionate to both the size of the existing immigrant population and previous migration.[51] Adopting the Hatton–Williamson (H–W) model for the Jewish mass migration ought to tell us more about the relative similarity or difference of the two streams of migration. Before proceeding, however, it is essential to have proper estimates of the annual immigration of East European Jews into the USA and UK.

Jewish mass migration: the numbers

While the problems of establishing reliable estimates for immigration are notorious, for the Jews the difficulties are even more pronounced.[52] Official records of immigration were kept for the USA throughout and, despite some difficulties, they form the statistical basis of any study of international migration during this period. The same cannot be said of Britain, where the doctrine of *laissez-faire* was so entrenched that the free movement of persons was not even impeded by any systematic counting before 1906. It is possible, however, to proceed by the way of informed approximations and by building on the work of others. First, the series of figures for Jewish immigration to the USA are considered, and then those for the UK. For both countries new estimates have been derived and are presented here.

Jewish immigration to the United States

Annualised immigration records were published by the US Commissioner General for Immigration and these official records provide the most reliable series of immigration statistics for the period. However, they still need to be treated with some caution. The basis of enumeration changed over time, for example, leading to potentially significant differences in classification. Enumeration was initially of 'immigrants arriving', then from 1904 to 1906 of 'aliens admitted', and from 1907 onwards of 'immigrant aliens admitted'.[53] Moreover, until 1899 the immigrants were reported by nation of origin rather than religious, racial or ethnic group.

Before then the East European Jews were only one among a larger group of immigrants from Russia, Austria-Hungary and Romania.[54] So American official figures for Jewish immigration only begin in 1899. Even then the official definition was not based on whether an immigrant was a Jew, but whether Yiddish was the immigrant's first language, a caveat that introduces some minor complications into the official series, as will be seen below.[55]

For the years preceding 1899 other sources have to be used to construct estimates, and the best of these is the work done by Samuel Joseph. Joseph used the reports of Jewish immigrant welfare societies based at the three main ports of arrival, New York, Philadelphia and Baltimore, to construct estimates for 1886 to 1898.[56] For the earlier years from 1881 to 1885, Joseph assumed that Jews were a fixed proportion of all the immigrants enumerated under the official series from Russia, Austria-Hungary and Romania.[57] Table 5.3 lists the official figures and Joseph's estimates for the years prior to 1899 and these can be taken as the basis for the following discussion.[58]

Table 5.3 shows that Jewish immigration was dominated by the three main East European sources of Russia (72 per cent), Austria-Hungary (17 per cent) and Romania (4 per cent). The existence of the UK (3 per cent) and Canada (1 per cent) as notional sources of indigenous Yiddish-speaking Jewish migrants was a curious feature of the official

Table 5.3 Jewish immigration to the USA, 1881–1914

Year	Russia	Austria-Hungary	Romania	UK	Germany	Canada	Other	Total
1881	3 125	2 537	30					5 692
1882	10 489	2 648	65					13 202
1883	6 144	2 510	77					8 731
1884	7 867	3 340	238					11 445
1885	10 648	3 938	803		1 473			16 862
1886	14 092	5 326	518		983		254	21 173
1887	23 103	6 898	2 063		780		200	33 044
1888	20 216	5 985	1 653		727		300	28 881
1889	18 338	4 998	1 058		758		200	25 352
1890	20 981	6 439	462		633		124	28 639
1891	43 457	5 890	854		636		561	51 398
1892	64 253	8 643	740		1 787		950	76 373
1893	25 161	6 363	555		1 814		1 429	35 322
1894	20 747	5 916	616		1 109		791	29 179
1895	16 727	6 047	518		1 028		1 871	26 191
1896	20 168	9 831	744		829		1 276	32 848
1897	13 063	5 672	516		586		535	20 372
1898	14 929	7 367	720		296		322	23 634
1899	24 275	11 071	1 343	174	405	5	52	37 325
1900	37 011	16 920	6 183	133	337	0	49	60 633
1901	37 660	13 006	6 827	110	272	0	49	57 924
1902	37 846	12 848	6 589	55	182	0	21	57 541
1903	47 689	18 759	8 562	420	477	0	74	75 981
1904	77 544	20 211	6 446	817	669	8	196	105 891
1905	92 388	17 352	6 854	14 299	734	11	772	132 410
1906	125 234	14 884	3 872	6 113	979	429	1 297	152 808
1907	114 937	18 885	3 605	7 032	734	1 818	952	147 963
1908	71 978	15 293	4 455	6 260	869	2 393	1 079	102 327
1909	39 150	8 431	1 390	3 385	652	2 780	748	56 536
1910	59 824	13 142	1 701	4 098	705	2 262	801	82 533
1911	65 472	12 785	2 188	4 895	799	2 420	2 664	91 223
1912	58 389	10 757	1 512	4 308	629	1 896	3 104	80 595
1913	74 033	15 202	1 640	4 001	806	1 467	4 181	101 330
1914	102 638	20 454	2 646	3 614	1 127	2 559	5 013	138 051
Total	1 419 576	340 438	78 043	59 714	23 815	18 048	29 865	1 969 499

Sources: Joseph, *Jewish Immigration*, p. 93, up to 1898. From 1899–1914 these are the official statistics; see Ferenczi and Willcox, *International Migration*, vol. I, pp. 374–500, esp. table XIII, pp. 460–70.

series, no doubt an incorrect one. Simon Kuznets assumed that they were transmigrants from the three main East European sources, arriving via the UK and Canada but having been incorrectly allocated to these nations of transit. Certainly any Jewish British and Canadian national immigrants were so rare that they had never figured in Joseph's lists for the earlier years.

Kuznets's revisions to the data in Table 5.3 are worth dwelling on for three reasons. First, his study is the only systematic analysis of Jewish immigration to date. Second, his stature as a Nobel laureate demands respect, in particular given that his citation was in part for the careful study and construction of statistical series. Third, in many points of detail his revisions are nonetheless inaccurate. The impact of Kuznets's revisions on the total Jewish immigration was only to increase the figures in Table 5.3 by 7.7 per cent, but his revisions were particularly significant for the earlier and later periods. Each needs to be dealt with in turn.[59]

Kuznets's first revision was to reallocate all the Yiddish-speaking Jewish immigrants in the official series from Britain, Canada, Germany and so on to the three main East European countries. Yiddish speaking Jewish immigrants from the UK, for instance, jumped from an annual average of 285 between 1899 and 1904 to 14 299 in 1905, a fiftyfold increase and representing an 11 per cent share of total Jewish immigration to the United States. But these were not emigrating British nationals. Ruppin concluded that they were 'almost without exception East European Jews'.[60]

Mistakes by immigration officials were not unknown. There were hundreds of thousands of transmigrants that went to the USA via the northern English corridor, from Hull and Grimsby to Liverpool, many of them Jews.[61] At the other end some were mistakenly recorded as being UK nationals.[62] The sudden change in 1905 may well have been an unintended consequence of the change in the basis of enumeration from 'immigrants arriving' to 'aliens admitted'. It may also have been a consequence of the simmering Atlantic 'rate war' between the German and British shipping companies.[63] It may simply have been a combination of hard-pressed immigration officials and confused immigrants.[64] Whatever the reason, these notionally British Yiddish-speaking Jewish immigrants to the USA were not British but East European.

Kuznets went beyond a simple reallocation of the notional British Jewish immigrants to the USA, however, and included the Yiddish-speaking immigrants from all other non-East-European sources as well.[65] This appears a little excessive. Joseph's estimates from the three ports listed in Table 5.3 show that the share of the 'other' countries out of total Jewish immigration was just under 5 per cent from 1886 to 1898. There is no reason to suspect that this was not the case in later years and so there is no real need to reallocate the German and other non-East-European Jewish immigrants to the main three sources. The most

appropriate way of adjusting the official US immigration series therefore
is simply to reallocate those Yiddish-speaking immigrants notionally
from the UK from 1905 onwards to their true East European origins and
to ignore the rest.

The one exception is the rising stream of Yiddish-speaking Jews arriving from Canada. This reached 4.8 per cent of total East European
Jewish immigration to the USA in 1910.[66] These were definitely Jews of
East European origins who arrived via Canada and ordinarily they
would simply be included in the aggregation of American East
European Jewish immigration. Unlike the notionally British Jewish
immigrants to America, however, they appear to have spent some years
in Canada before moving south. There was an obvious time-lag between
the notional Canadian Jewish immigration to the United States and the
two East European Jewish streams to the United States and to Canada –
the peaks in the two East European streams occurring in 1905 and 1906
and the trough in 1909. By contrast, the notionally Canadian Jews
arriving in the USA peaked in 1909 and troughed in 1913, a time-lag of
about four years. Because we want to compare the sensitivity of the two
streams to conditions in the Russian, American and British economies,
these Canadian stage-migrants need to be ignored. They were presumably responding to Canadian factors as well as anything else and so present an unnecessary complication to our analysis.[67]

Kuznets also revised Joseph's series of estimates for fiscal years 1886
to 1898. Kuznets divided these years into two periods: 1886 to 1893,
for which he had data for the port of New York only; and 1894 to
1898, for which he, like Joseph, had data for all three ports. For this
latter period, from 1894 to 1898, he assumed that Jewish immigration
at all other US ports would have accounted for an extra 10 per cent,
'a figure suggested by the comparison of similar entries in the subsequent years with the official totals'.[68] This seems a judicious increase
and has been retained here.

For the earlier period, 1886 to 1893, Kuznets's revision to Joseph's
original data is more questionable simply because he apparently misunderstood Joseph's sources, which were quite comprehensive.[69] Thus
for the years 1894 to 1898 Kuznets's upward revision of 10 per cent, in
order to account for arrivals in the lesser ports, seems justified and has
been retained, but his multiplier for the years 1886 to 1893 is certainly
too high and has been discarded. However, in order to take account of
the buildup in arrivals at the lesser ports, this revision of Joseph's port
data has used a multiplier, following Kuznets and for the same reasons,
but with a lower value. Joseph's original estimates for 1886 to 1889
have been kept.[70]

Kuznets's final revision was for the period 1881 to 1885. Joseph calculated the proportion of Russian Jews to total Russian immigrants for the period 1886 to 1898. This ratio was then taken to be the share of Russian immigration for 1881–85 that was Jewish. A similar calculation for the Jews from Austria-Hungary and Romania was undertaken. Kuznets justified his revision to Joseph's estimates because Joseph's ratios were thought to be too low.[71] It had the effect of increasing Joseph's estimates by about 12 200, and even though this was a relatively small number of people, it still constituted an increase of 30 per cent on Joseph's estimate for these first five years.[72]

Joseph's estimate was clearly too low, as he himself admitted.[73] He made an error in calculating the ratio of Jews to total Austro-Hungarian immigrants and his choice of 0.62 as the ratio of Jews to total Russian immigrants during the years of political crisis and pogroms in the early 1880s was surely an underestimate. Using Joseph's revised calculations for the Austro-Hungarian Jews and the 1886 ratio of Jews to Russian immigrants a more realistic estimate can be reached.[74] These two revisions to Joseph's data give a total for the years 1881 to 1885, which ends up quite close to Kuznets's. The revised figures for East European Jewish immigration to the USA are given in Table 5.4. The magnitude of the adjustments can be measured by comparing Tables 5.4 and 5.3.

Jewish immigration to the United Kingdom

While official figures of Jewish immigration to the USA begin in 1899, reliable figures for any immigration into the UK do not start until the executive machinery of the Aliens Act 1905 first ground into gear. From January 1906 the Inspector under the Aliens Act collected figures on the movement of alien people into and through the UK, recording the numbers of those who were genuine immigrants. Before then what figures existed were unreliable, unrepresentative and never really considered by official bodies to even approximate the real numbers of immigrants.[75] Even then the official figures for 1906 are something like a 20 per cent overestimate because of the failure by officials to distinguish between immigrants and returning foreign national UK residents.[76] The returns for 1914 were not reported because of the passing of the Aliens Restriction Act on the outbreak of war.[77] UK official figures of Russian immigration are therefore restricted to 1907–13, a mere 7 years out of the 35 from 1880 to 1914.[78]

Because immigrants from Russia were almost entirely Jews, the figures are assumed to be valid for Russian Jewish immigration.[79] Alas, the same assumption does not hold for Austria-Hungary and Romania,

Table 5.4 Revised estimates of East European Jewish migration to the USA, 1881–1914

Year	Russia	Austria-Hungary	Romania	UK	Multiplier (%)	Total
1881	**3 993**	**3 882**	30			7 905
1882	**13 399**	**4 051**	65			17 515
1883	**7 848**	**3 840**	77			11 765
1884	**10 050**	**5 083**	238			15 371
1885	**13 589**	**3 938**	803			18 330
1886	14 092	5 326	518			19 936
1887	23 103	6 898	2 063			32 064
1888	20 216	5 985	1 653			27 854
1889	18 338	4 998	1 058			24 394
1890	20 981	6 439	462		02	28 440
1891	43 457	5 890	854		04	52 209
1892	64 253	8 643	740		06	78 054
1893	25 161	6 363	555		08	34 645
1894	20 747	5 916	616		10	30 007
1895	16 727	6 047	518		10	25 621
1896	20 168	9 831	744		10	33 817
1897	13 063	5 672	516		10	21 176
1898	14 929	7 367	720		10	25 340
1899	24 275	11 071	1 343	174		36 689
1900	37 011	16 920	6 183	133		60 114
1901	37 660	13 006	6 827	110		57 493
1902	37 846	12 848	6 589	55		57 283
1903	47 689	18 759	8 562	420		75 010
1904	77 544	20 211	6 446	817		104 201
1905	92 388	17 352	6 854	14 299		127 893
1906	125 234	14 884	3 872	6 113		150 103
1907	114 937	18 885	3 605	7 032		144 459
1908	71 978	15 293	4 455	6 260		97 986
1909	39 150	8 431	1 390	3 385		52 356
1910	59 824	13 142	1 701	4 098		78 765
1911	65 472	12 785	2 188	4 895		85 343
1912	58 389	10 757	1 512	4 308		74 966
1913	74 033	15 202	1 640	4 001		94 876
1914	102 638	20 454	2 646	3 614		127 352
Total	**1 430 202**	**346 129**	73 683	59 714		1 929 332

Sources: Table 5.3 and as per text. UK is listed as a country of transmigration, not origin. All figures in boldface are revisions.

although the decennial censuses show that immigrants, many of whom were Jews, did come from these nations. In sum, the official statistics are simply inadequate, covering only a short span out of the period and with no indication of the non-Russian Jewish arrivals. It is therefore essential to have some sort of reliable estimate of East European Jewish immigration to the UK before proceeding.

The best indicator of Jewish immigration to the UK between 1880 and 1914 is the information contained on the certificates of the Chief Rabbi's authorisation to marry, the marriage records described earlier in Chapter 3. Of course, these data are obviously less than a perfect proxy for immigration, but they are the only data available that remotely approximate annual immigration for the years not covered by the official series and, moreover, they include immigrants from all East European countries not just Russia. While marriage was clearly not contemporaneous for most with migration, the only satisfactory test of whether the CRA data are a reasonable proxy for UK Jewish immigration would be to compare them with the few years when official figures exist. Happily the correlation between the two series is extremely strong, with a coefficient of 0.90 between 1906 and 1913.[80] While immigrants may not have married immediately after arrival, marriage within a few months was apparently sufficiently common to allow the trends in marriages to be a very close substitute for immigration.

The official figures for UK Russian Jewish immigration from 1907 to 1913 (along with the estimate for 1906) are listed in Table 5.5, column 1. The Russian Jews comprised 82 per cent of all East European immigrants to the USA during these years. Column 2 adjusts the Russian immigrants by a similar margin to estimate total East European Jewish immigration into Britain.

For the years before 1906 the ratio of East European brides and grooms to immigrants from 1906 to 1913 has been used to extrapolate backwards to 1881 and forwards to 1914 to derive annual estimates of immigration. This series has then been spliced onto the official figures in column 3. Finally, the revised estimates of East European Jewish immigration to the USA from Table 5.4 are listed.[81] This table then presents both of these new series of estimates of East European immigration to the USA and UK from 1881 to 1914.

Jewish mass migration: the trends

With these new estimates of East European Jewish immigration to the USA and UK, a systematic analysis of its determinants can take place.

Table 5.5   Estimates of East European Jewish immigration to the United Kingdom and United States, 1881–1914

Year	Russia	East Europe	East Europe + CRA	Index (1906 = 100)	USA	Index (1906 = 100)
1881			853	7.0	7 905	5.3
1882			1 231	10.2	17 515	11.7
1883			568	4.7	11 765	7.8
1884			1 042	8.6	15 371	10.2
1885			1 610	13.3	18 330	12.2
1886			1 516	12.5	19 936	13.3
1887			2 936	24.3	32 064	21.4
1888			2 747	22.7	27 854	18.6
1889			2 747	22.7	24 394	16.3
1890			3 315	27.4	28 440	19.0
1891			2 179	18.0	52 209	34.8
1892			5 494	45.4	78 054	52.0
1893			4 073	33.7	34 645	23.1
1894			4 925	40.7	30 007	20.0
1895			5 020	41.5	25 621	17.1
1896			3 884	32.1	33 817	22.5
1897			4 073	33.7	21 176	14.1
1898			6 536	54.0	25 340	16.9
1899			7 388	61.0	36 689	24.4
1900			5 778	47.7	60 114	40.1
1901			6 536	54.0	57 493	38.3
1902			8 904	73.6	57 283	38.2
1903			8 146	67.3	75 010	50.0
1904			8 051	66.5	104 201	69.4
1905			9 567	79.0	127 893	85.2
1906	9 897	12 103	12 103	100.0	150 103	100.0
1907	7 661	9 369	9 369	77.4	144 459	96.2
1908	4 388	5 366	5 366	44.3	97 986	65.3
1909	3 998	4 889	4 889	40.4	52 356	34.9
1910	4 235	5 179	5 179	42.8	78 765	52.5
1911	3 641	4 453	4 453	36.8	85 343	56.9
1912	4 267	5 218	5 218	43.1	74 966	49.9
1913	5 907	7 224	7 224	59.7	94 876	63.2
1914			7 672	63.4	127 352	84.8
Total	43 994	53 782	143 450		1 929 332	

Sources: see text.

Figure 5.1 shows how similar the two streams were. This is interesting both for the periods when the two series appear to have been behaving with great similarity and for the periods when they were not. In the 1880s and early 1890s the two series follow nearly identical paths. The

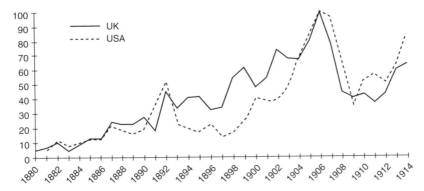

Figure 5.1 East European Jewish migration to the USA and UK, 1880–1914 (1906 = 100)

Source: Table 5.5.

divergence in trends from 1893 to around 1900 saw Jewish immigration to the USA fall relative to the UK. Thereafter the two series appear once again to have been very closely matched.

Some of the variations, however, are simply down to the differences in the underlying sources. For example, while Jewish immigration to Britain fell quickly after 1906, it apparently continued at a high level in the USA into 1907. This, however, is nothing more than the peak in immigration in calendar year 1906 being reported differently; the American fiscal year 1907 included the second half of calendar year 1906.

The apparent divergence between the two streams in 1914 is another consequence of the different reporting periods. European emigration slowed dramatically on the outbreak of war, but this fell into the second half of 1914 and so was reported in US fiscal year 1915. Jewish immigrant marriages in London fell sharply after August 1914, which is reflected in the lower rate of inferred immigration seen in the figure for Britain compared with America. The correlation coefficient of the two series for the entire period is 0.768. This confirms what the figure suggests, namely that the overall degree of similarity was very high. If differences in reporting periods could be accurately factored out, the coefficient would rise. The true picture therefore reveals a pronounced similarity in immigrant trends outside the mid to late 1890s, during which the United States experienced an unusually severe economic contraction.

It is worth emphasising that the rather dramatic fall in British immigration from 1906 to 1909 is not some sleight of hand arising from using the brides and grooms as a proxy for immigrants. From 1906 to 1913 both the American and the British series are based on official records. The six-month lag in the reporting periods notwithstanding, the degree of similarity for these few years is particularly obvious in the chart (with a correlation coefficient of 0.903). The trends in East European Jewish immigration to Britain and America in this short period were essentially identical, if at different levels.

Three conclusions follow. The first is that the total number of East European Jews settling in Britain over the period can be estimated as just shy of 145 000, as the total in Table 5.5 reports.[82] This is certainly not inconsistent with earlier estimates. Moreover, because this total is mostly dependent on counting marriages rather than arrivals, it is likely to be much closer to the total of permanent rather than gross immigration; temporary migrants were far less likely to marry during their sojourn in a foreign land.[83] Given that there is some evidence of British Jewish charities subsidising and therefore presumably inflating rates of return migration, this is an important distinction in the British case.[84]

The second conclusion follows. Focusing on the shorter period from 1905 to 1914 makes it impossible to avoid the conclusion that the Aliens Act 1905 had a negligible impact on the restriction of Jewish immigration to Britain. Jewish immigration to Britain and America was almost identical over these years, but only Britain had legislation designed to restrict Jewish arrivals. If the Aliens Act had any bite, then Jewish immigration to Britain would have fallen relative to America in the years after its introduction in 1906; the sharper the bite, the greater the fall.

In the past the picture has been confused by the fact that immigration to both countries fell, but that is irrelevant when considering the impact of the Aliens Act. Falling immigration across the board simply indicates that fewer people were leaving Eastern Europe. If the Aliens Act had carried any force, then those migrants who left would have gone increasingly to the United States and not to Britain. Figure 5.1 shows, however, that this switch never took place. Given the emphasis on the impact of the Aliens Act in the historical literature, this is a somewhat surprising result, although perhaps one more in line with what is known about how the act was policed.[85]

The third conclusion follows on from the very marked degree of overall similarity in immigration trends to the two destinations. The traditional understanding of what prompts migrants to leave at any specific moment emphasises the importance of earning power in the destination. Because the British and American economies followed different cycles, there were significant variations in immigrant earnings at different moments in this period. Had the Jews been responding to these short-term variations, the timing of emigration to each destination would have been different. This may have been the case in the 1890s, for example, when the American economy was in the doldrums. Jewish immigration to the USA fell, in common with all immigration, whereas Jewish immigration to British fell by less.

The overall similarity between the two streams, however, implies that the relative attractions of neither the British nor the American economy were uppermost in emigrants' minds. The implication of such similarity in immigration rates when economic conditions varied in the two destinations is that the Jews were more pushed out of Russia than pulled into either Britain or America. Bearing the pogroms, persecution and violence in mind, this is perhaps not so surprising. It does, however, suggest that the Jews were a little different from most migrant groups at this time.

Table 5.6 gives a good idea of how the Jewish mass migration to Britain and America compared with the emigration movements from Britain, Ireland and Italy by applying the Hatton–Williamson (H–W) model to all five different streams. The H–W model incorporates the influences of unemployment levels and changes, and the levels and changes in wages in home and destination in both home and destination economies, as well as two measures of chain migration, namely the total stock of an immigrant group in the destination and the previous year's emigration rate.

As explained earlier, the justification for this model is unimpeachable. Survey upon survey has concluded that people migrate because of economic conditions, so both relative wages and unemployment rates are likely to determine much of the decision to move. Furthermore, the accumulated evidence of chain migration requires some account of this to be taken.

Irish, British and Italian emigration rates are largely explained by this simple model, with the R^2-values of 0.88, 0.59 and 0.83 respectively. Furthermore, the explanation of each individual nation's emigration rate is entirely consistent with what would be expected. Wages and rates of unemployment were important determinants of emigration from Ireland, Britain and Italy. Moreover, it was the economic conditions in the destination that were the most important determinants, the likelihood of finding employment emerging as statistically both the most significant and the most important determinant of emigration in all three of the principal sending nations.[86] To be sure, home employment

Table 5.6 Ordinary least-squares estimation of the determinants of international migration: the H–W model compared

Dependent variable	1 East European Jews to USA, 1882–1913	2 East European Jews to UK, 1881–1913 #1	3 East European Jews to UK, 1881–1913 #2	4 Ireland, 1877–1913	5 Britain, 1870–1913	6 Italy, 1877–1913
Constant	−517.38 (1.10)	−30.28 (0.94)	−11.14 (0.30)	−17.46 (2.94)	−3.65 (0.79)	−23.57 (2.02)
a. Changes in foreign employment rate	42.12 (0.74)	2.42 (0.81)	0.26 (0.09)	119.49 (4.84)	38.50 (2.53)	16.06 (2.45)
b. Foreign employment $(t-1)$	108.68 (1.92)	0.96 (0.37)	−0.29 (0.12)	74.68 (2.90)	34.76 (3.01)	8.36 (2.00)
c. Change in home employment rate	−3.32 (0.04)	0.77 (0.13)	−0.15 (0.03)	–	6.97 (0.94)	–
d. Home employment $(t-1)$	114.88 (1.10)	6.66 (0.94)	2.43 (0.30)	−14.57 (2.20)	−18.59 (3.27)	−5.17 (1.58)
e. Change in relative wage	3.82 (0.44)	−0.05 (0.06)	−0.18 (0.23)	–	9.75 (1.90)	–
f. Relative wage $(t-1)$	−0.54 (0.05)	0.02 (0.03)	0.29 (0.34)	17.94 (4.44)	6.69 (1.92)	−5.75 (2.18)
g. Migrant stock	0.02 (1.15)	0.01 (0.33)	0.01 (0.51)	26.54 (2.57)	24.77 (0.64)	–

h. Lagged dependent variable	0.54 (2.38)	0.78 (4.34)	0.77 (3.67)	0.37 (2.75)	−0.56 (3.82)	0.36 (2.05)
x. Change in US employment rate	—	—	10.25 (2.20)	—	—	—
y. US employment rate $(t-1)$	—	—	2.64 (0.58)	—	—	—
Diagnostics						
R^2	0.84	0.74	0.79	0.88	0.59	0.83
RSS	254.00	2.28	1.84	83.45	22.35	103.66
LM(1)	2.32	0.07	0.98	0.31	1.16	0.14

Notes and sources:

Columns 1–3. Dependent Variables from Table 5.5 (columns 3 and 5) divided by estimate for Russian Jewish population from Kuznets, 'Russian Jews', table v, pp. 50–1, with straight-line interpolations for missing figures. US Employment from R. Vernon, 'Unemployment Rates in Post-Bellum America, 1869–1899', University of Florida, mimeo., 1991. UK employment rates from C. Feinstein, *National Income, Expenditure and Output of the United Kingdom, 1855–1965* (Cambridge, 1972). Russian employment rates estimated from the deviation of the fitted log of Russian NNP on Russian NNP. Russian NNP from 1885–1913, Gregory, *Russian National Income*, Table 3.1; and for 1880–84, a composite of Goldsmith's 'All Crops' (weight = 0.9) and 'Industrial Output' (weight = 0.1) indices for 1880–85; R. Goldsmith, 'The Economic Growth of Tsarist Russia, 1860–1913', *Economic Development and Cultural Change*, 9 (1961), table 1, col. 5, and table 7, col. 5, pp. 446–7 and 462–3. US and UK real wages from Williamson, 'Global Labor Markets', table A2.1 (inc. erratum p. 553). Russian real wages are Russian NNP per capita in 1913 £s from Gregory, ibid. Migrant stock for USA based on estimate of New York East European Jewish population in 1880 from Rischin, *Promised City*, table 2, p. 271, with US Jewish immigration (from Table 5.5) aggregated. UK Jewish stock based on 1901 census figure for East European aliens and then with UK Jewish immigration estimates simply deducted to 1880, and aggregated (but allowing for a return rate of 0.071 and a stage-emigration rate of 0.055: see note 81) to 1914.

Columns 4–6. From Hatton and Williamson, 'After the Famine', table 2, p. 584 (col. 2); Hatton, 'Model', Table 1, p. 20 (col. 2); and Hatton and Williamson, *Migration*, table 3.5, p. 67 (eq. 4). These equations and columns 1–3 all use common sources where applicable.

t-statistics in parentheses. The reported diagnostics for the Jews here replicate those reported by Hatton and Williamson in the three sources cited.

conditions also appear to have played a role, and the differences between home and destination wages were of some importance (although only really for the Irish). Chain migration was important for the Irish (on both measures) and the Italians, but acted as a deterrent for the British emigrants, who were increasingly choosing pastures new in Canada, Australia and South Africa at this time.

When we turn to the East European Jews, the first issue of importance is to see how similar Jewish emigration was to that of the Irish, British and Italian. Overall, the H–W model explains just as much of the Jewish mass migration, with R^2-values of 0.84 for Jewish immigration to USA and 0.74 to Britain. Furthermore, the importance of employment conditions in the destination appears also to have been the single most important determinant of emigration, or at least of the Jewish emigration to the USA.

Jewish emigration seems to have been less sensitive to economic conditions in the home country of Russia, although measurement difficulties are particularly acute here; it may well have been the case that the Jewish economy in the Pale was unrepresentative of the wider Russian economy over this period, the global data for which are analysed in Table 5.6.

Table 5.6 gives six different equations, each purporting to capture the determinants of each migration flow. When the second equation is considered, of Russian Jewish emigration to the UK, the results can only be described as somewhat disappointing. Jewish emigration to the UK appears to have been driven by chain migration alone. Of course, this can only be far from a complete explanation. The third equation introduces an alternative view, including the employment conditions in America as a determinant of Jewish emigration to Britain.

This shows that Jewish immigration to the UK was more sensitive to US than UK economic cycles. It is not obvious how to interpret this unusual result. The insignificance of the UK employment rate might be interpreted as evidence of the local Jewish labour market in London following a path different from that of the rest of the UK, for which there is certainly some support (see the next chapter). The London Jewish economy hardly followed American business cycles, however.

On the other hand, given that emigration to the UK was less than a tenth of that to the USA, it is reasonable to suppose that emigrant expectations in Russia were primarily determined by the performance of the American and not the British economy. If the decision to leave was fostered primarily by American conditions, but the choice of destination by the existence of chains, then American employment conditions could well have influenced British immigration.

Furthermore, a more direct mechanism may have been for remittances from the US to have both stimulated consumption and fuelled the liquidity of the Jewish economy within the Pale, thus facilitating emigration to all destinations. Nevertheless it does seem strange that the emigration to the UK should have been so insensitive to either UK or Russian economic variables. Here, however, it must be remembered that the underlying data for the UK Jewish immigration is mostly the marriages of East-European-born brides and grooms. The decision about how soon to marry after arrival for immigrants was inevitably one with some variation. Immigrants who arrived as children, for example, married some years after immigration. Their presence in the CRA database leads to some degree of smoothing in the UK immigration series relative to the more volatile US series, and therefore perhaps to a dampening of the true relationships with British economic indicators.

The overall interpretation of Table 5.6 must be that Russian Jews were broadly behaving like those from other principal emigrant nations, with the caveat about the difference in the intensity of emigration. Conditions in the Pale of Settlement may have been particularly harsh, with political persecution giving an additional but general incentive to leave. Nonetheless, the Russian Jews were principally economic migrants, not political refugees. In considering the determinants of the two emigration streams perhaps the best interpretation of the results is that both streams appear to have been responsive to economic conditions in the USA, even though for the UK Jewish immigrants the USA was not their destination. Both streams were also sensitive to one or other of the proxies for chain migration.

To summarise: while the timing of emigration shows that they were economic migrants, it would appear that the East European Jews were desperate to leave, more so than any other emigrant group. They left Russia at the merest encouragement, which directly or indirectly came from the USA, and they chose destinations where they already knew previous emigrants.

Jewish mass migration and the determinants of destination

The purpose of this chapter was to clarify the differences between the two immigrant streams, in particular with regard to the predisposition to entrepreneurship. There must have been some differences, or the immigrants would not have chosen different destinations. There were apparently some differences in perceptions of the two destinations and these may have influenced the entrepreneurial make-up of the two streams. After all, if London really was only the silver to New York's golden land, then it might be expected that only those who were willing to settle for second best would have stayed in London – a psychological characteristic that would surely have altered the relative predisposition to entrepreneurship. However, no evidence for differences in the two streams has been found, rather the opposite. The amounts of capital brought by immigrants to both destinations were similar, and similarly low. The evidence on human capital endowments is limited, but whether the time-pattern of settlement is considered, or the age and gender structure or regional backgrounds of the migration flows, the two streams appear to have been composed of fundamentally similar people.

This can best be understood by considering the importance of the existing immigrant community in subsidising the cost of further migration and settlement, perhaps by providing employment, a place to live, or familiar surroundings and a common language. Chain migration may have been a more important factor in the East European Jewish migration than for any other migration.

In terms of statistical analysis, chain migration implies a model of path determination, where the probabilities of choosing a location are dependent upon previous choices.[87] This type of statistical model predicts that from a certain point fairly early on outcomes stabilise. In other words, history matters, and the initial choices made by the pioneering few, a tiny proportion of the total population, influence the vast majority. From very early on, then, migration to either of the specific destinations acquired its own momentum.

The principal conclusions of this chapter are therefore that the two Jewish immigrant streams were essentially homogeneous, and that the choice of destination was overwhelmingly dependent on where the prospective migrant's closest friend or relative had moved to. The claims of some contemporaries and subsequent commentators that London was an inferior destination were true in numbers only. There is no evidence to suggest that the actual immigrants saw the choice of destination in these terms. Rather, it was the case that the pressure to leave was so intense that choosing between New York or London became relatively unimportant. This decision simply rested on who the migrants knew and where they were.

For the purposes of this book, this is an important conclusion, for it is impossible to attribute any qualitative difference to the two streams. They were to all intents and purposes the same group of people travelling to two separate destinations. The Jews going to London were, in other words, just as likely to move into entrepreneurship as those going to New York. The large differences in entrepreneurship observed in Chapter 4 cannot therefore be explained by any differences in the characteristics and abilities of the arrivals. The answer must lie in how they responded to differences in New York and London.

6
Entrepreneurship and Profits in the Jewish Immigrant Economies of London and New York

The Jewish immigrants in New York were much more likely to move into entrepreneurial occupations than those in London. But this cannot be explained by any differences in their entrepreneurial abilities on arrival, so it must have been because of differences between the two local environments. Given that entrepreneurship is an economic activity, our first attempt to explain the differences in Jewish immigrant entrepreneurship must focus on the economics of entrepreneurship in the two cities during this period.

The simplest way to analyse entrepreneurship is to focus on the demand and supply for entrepreneurship in the two cities. Entrepreneurship can be thought of as a service and therefore subject to market forces. The demand for entrepreneurship will generally be proportionate to the value of these services to the wider community. This value, or marginal revenue product, is what gives the entrepreneurs their profits. The relationship between the demand for entrepreneurship and other economic conditions is, however, anything but straightforward. Current knowledge does not allow us to predict that entrepreneurship will increase in line with economic growth, for example. Rather, it is more likely to be related to new developments in technology, knowledge and design, and their diffusion through society. The demand for entrepreneurship is, in other words, a slippery concept, something which no doubt accounts for its near absence in the economics literature. Nevertheless, because entrepreneurs specialise, in Kirzner's phrase, in 'alertness' to profit-making opportunities, so focusing on profits enables us to minimise the analytical difficulties.[1] When the demand for entrepreneurship is high, profits will rise accordingly; as demand falls, so profits will also.[2]

As long as there are minimal restrictions on leaving wage-earning employment and entering profit-earning entrepreneurship, focusing on trends in profits at least allows us indirectly to track trends in the demand for entrepreneurship. As will be seen below, barriers for the Jewish immigrants entering entrepreneurship were minimal indeed.

For profits to give a reasonable indication of demand, however, the supply of entrepreneurship needs to be known. This measure is, of course, simply the share of entrepreneurs among the immigrant work-forces in the two cities reported in Chapter 4. Because, as Chapter 5 has shown, the two streams of immigrants were composed of essentially the same group of people, so the willingness to supply entrepreneur-ship for any given profit level ought to have been identical in both groups. With the same backgrounds, they would have shared similar attitudes to risk aversion, industriousness, thriftiness, alertness to opportunities and so on.[3]

Entrepreneurship increased in New York from 18 per cent to 35 per cent of the East European Jewish male immigrant workforce over the period (and to 34 per cent by 1905), compared with a rise from only 14 per cent to 18 per cent in London. This represents a substantial shift out of the employed sector of the Jewish labour market in New York, and, by comparison, one that barely happened in London. Because more entrepreneurship not only increases the demand for labour but also diminishes the pool of non-entrepreneurs left behind, other things equal it bids up wages. So the large shift out of wage-earn-ing and into profit-earning ought to have had the effect of raising the wages of the Jewish non-entrepreneurs in New York also.

Despite the oft-cited conceptual difficulties associated with the eco-nomic analysis of entrepreneurship, this simple model suggests that the most obvious explanation in the divergence in entrepreneurial out-comes in the two Jewish streams lies in a much greater increase in the demand for entrepreneurship in New York than London. We don't need to know exactly how this occurred; we simply recognise that this would have led to higher profits there, thus attracting more and more immigrants out of wage-earning occupations and into entrepreneur-ship. While the higher profits may then have been bid down a little, the seemingly permanent increase in the share of immigrant entrepre-neurs in New York compared with London from 1905 (at the very lat-est) onwards implies that profits remained relatively high. Moreover, given that the increase in entrepreneurs represented a fall in the pool of Jewish immigrant workers, so wages in the Jewish sector ought also to have been higher in 1905 compared with 1880.

In London, by contrast, the shifts into and out of the entrepreneurial sector were far less dramatic. Nevertheless, as entrepreneurship diminished we would expect profits to have fallen in the 1890s compared with the 1880s. Because the pool of wage-earners was then relatively large compared with the 1880s, we would also expect wages to have fallen. With the share of entrepreneurs increasing in the early and, especially, the late 1900s, so we would expect to see both higher profits and higher wages in the years before the First World War compared with the 1890s, although it is unlikely that these rises were on the same scale as in New York.

In other words, if this simple model of economic behaviour is to explain the observed differences in the supply of entrepreneurship among the two cities' immigrant Jews, then profits must have increased in New York by much more than in London. Figure 6.1 illustrates how changes in the demand for East European Jewish immigrant entrepreneurship in New York and London would have caused profits to rise and fall, so leading to the observed divergence in the supply of entrepreneurship. Tracking Jewish profits then becomes the litmus test.

Contemporaries in both cities were fascinated by the Jewish immigrant economies of the time conducting numerous surveys. These have generated considerable data on the Jewish economies of New York and London, so that following trends in wages and profits is relatively straightforward.

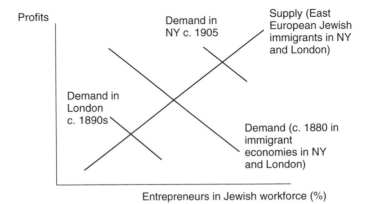

Figure 6.1   The profits and demand for Jewish immigrant entrepreneurship in London and New York, 1880–1914

Two caveats need to be raised. First is the cost of entry and whether there were significant differences between the two cities; it might have cost less to become an entrepreneur in New York, for instance. Second is structure and whether the two immigrant economies were so different that there were simply more opportunities for self-employment in New York than London. Both need to be investigated before considering trends in profits.

Cost of entry

To become an entrepreneur requires capital, and access to capital may have varied between the two cities. As noted in Chapter 5, the Jews arrived with trivial sums too small for seed-capital. Once settled, however, capital may simply have been more costly in London, restrictions on credit more burdensome.

In fact, while both countries had long-established banking systems, neither had yet evolved a personal or business bank account with an overdraft facility. Clothing manufacturers typically used banks to discount bills, but the minimum size of business needed to be much larger than the typical Jewish immigrant small workshop. Business loans were never very risky or very small. Established manufacturers could get credit from banks, but the Jewish immigrant entrepreneurs typically only needed small amounts for working capital. For them, bank doors were closed.[4]

The only exceptions came not from banks but charities. By the end of the nineteenth century, small loans became a popular form of philanthropy among the pioneer Jewish charities, the London Jewish Board of Guardians and the New York Hebrew Free Loan Society.[5] 'Loans do not rob a man of his self-respect; he does not feel degraded in receiving this form of help,' claimed the manager of the Hebrew Free Loan Society in justification.[6]

The loans department of the Jewish Board of Guardians started in 1866 and became easily the most significant part of the charity by the 1890s. Between 1890 and the 1904 peak the amount lent increased more than eightfold.[7] It was so successful that Jewish master tailors in London complained of how it was undermining their businesses through artificially stimulating competition.[8]

The New York Hebrew Free Loan Society started later in 1892.[9] It grew quickly, however. Already by 1903 it claimed that

> there are in the City of New York about 600 people who started business by a brotherly loan from our society who are today rated at

between $3,000 and $20,000 – and there are a few thousand people who began in the same manner and today have a good solid business existence.[10]

The two soft-loan societies clearly had an impact on facilitating entry into the immigrant trades. But their activities cannot account for the difference in entrepreneurship in the two immigrant communities. The average sums lent were similar, as were the amounts injected into the two immigrant communities when compared on a per capita basis. Indeed, if anything, the mean size of loan and per capita financing was greater in London than in New York.[11]

The Jewish economies of London and New York

If capital availability was not important, the structures of the two immigrant economies might have influenced the levels of entrepreneurship. New York Jews may have concentrated in a sector with smaller firms than those in London and therefore had more numerical scope for self employment.

The specialisation of both Jewish immigrant economies was extreme. The 1901 census for England and Wales showed that 60 per cent of East European born men living in London were occupied in the Dress trades (census class XIX).[12] The clothing industry completely dominated the Jewish East End. Indeed, once those occupied in the ancillary trades are included, such as furriers, sewing machine agents and the various merchants and dealers involved in its distribution, but enumerated under different census classes, the share of the East European immigrant male workforce involved in the East End clothing industry rose to around 70 per cent.

In New York's Lower East Side there was a similar bias to the garment industry. Unfortunately the presence of significant numbers of non-Jewish East European immigrants in New York renders the occupational information based on national origins in the federal and state censuses less helpful than for the United Kingdom. However, in 1890 a privately commissioned census of the immigrant Jewish labour market showed that over 60 per cent of the population questioned were employed in the clothing industry and ancillary trades.[13]

Outside the clothing industry and its web of supporting services, most of Jewish immigrant entrepreneurs simply provided goods and services to the immigrant community. Meat and milk, for example, needed specialist suppliers in accordance with religious custom. Bread consumption also followed customary preference and so there was a demand for specialist retailers, as well as a whole host of sundry communal services from rent collecting to undertaking.[14] While collectively the provision of communal services gave rise to large numbers of self-employed immigrants, the demand for these services was proportionate to the size of the immigrant population and so cannot account for the differences in the relative share of entrepreneurs in the two immigrant communities.

Kessner noted that real estate businessmen were second in numerical importance to garment manufacturers in his high white-collar class of New York Jewish immigrants.[15] The Jewish involvement in the speculative manias of the New York property market was legendary, and it has been suggested that a 'major route for social advancement was real estate'.[16] However, the Jewish immigrants in New York were not unique in their penchant for investing in real estate, as the East End saw an immigration-inspired property boom in the early 1900s.[17] Overall, however, the numbers of property entrepreneurs were simply not that large in either city.

Other sectors where Jewish immigrants supplied entrepreneurial services were also simply numerically subordinate to the dominance of the garment industry. In both London and New York technology was changing the furniture industry, for example, making it increasingly less attractive for immigrants to pursue entrepreneurship. By the end of the period, furniture industry employment was concentrated in just a few large firms in both cities.[18] Jewish bootmakers also suffered from new technology and both employment and entrepreneurship declined through factory competition.[19]

It is difficult to avoid the conclusion that the clothing industry was of paramount importance in both cities' immigrant Jewish communities. They were both essentially one-sector economies. Given both the dominance of the clothing industry in both immigrant economies and the extent of the divergence in entrepreneurship, if there was one sector where the demand for entrepreneurship must have changed, it was the clothing industry. Other sectors were simply not important enough to have accounted for the degree of change seen in the levels of entrepreneurship in New York and London.

The clothing industry was attractive to the immigrants for two reasons. First, many Jews had experience of tailoring work in Eastern Europe. Even allowing for any recording errors, the largest single occupational category cited by the Jewish immigrants on arrival was tailoring.[20] The clothing industry in the Pale was far less mechanised than in

New York and London, but it provided a large proportion of the Jewish immigrants with some sort of familiarity with the construction and selling of garments.[21]

The second reason for its attraction was its ease of entry. To start, all that was needed was a sewing machine, a pressing table and an iron, all of which could be bought on the instalment system. The cloth was provided pre-cut by the wholesalers either to master tailors or to middlemen. Middlemen would break up the packages into smaller and smaller bundles, giving these out to homeworkers. For these tailors, start-up capital was minimal. Abraham Rosenthal, a master tailor in London's East End, thought that 'a man could start off if he had a £1 in his pocket'.[22] But at that end it was a perilous trade, confined to only the busiest weeks of the year, with minimal work for the rest, and conducted under awful conditions. The bulk of the industry was workshop-based.

To set up a workshop typically required at least two sewing machines and one pressing table, eight or nine workers and good relations with the foremen of the wholesalers' warehouses. With a weekly cycle the working capital requirements were not large but demanded regular payment and included bribes for warehouse foremen.[23] So, while it was true that only petty sums of cash were required to enter, the capital required to dip in more than a toe during the busy season was somewhat higher.

In 1901 it was estimated that about $50 was required to open a clothing workshop in New York.[24] In Leeds, where larger workshops of just over twenty workers were the norm, £25, or around $120, was reckoned to be the minimum start-up requirement.[25] The equivalent figure for London is unknown, but it can hardly have been as much as half the Leeds figure, given that the typical size of workshop in the East End was eight or nine workers.

These were still relatively small sums for start-ups, so the clothing industry was undoubtedly attractive to the potential entrepreneurs among the Jewish immigrants, but their role has often been misunderstood. Sidney Webb, for example, thought that the East End clothing industry was pre-industrial and of no 'profit to the community...not even self-supporting'.[26] While the ease of entry certainly had a deleterious effect on conditions, the truth is that the Jewish immigrants created new industry sectors. Contemporaries universally failed to understand how these worked, preferring to tar Jewish workshops with the brush of racial inferiority. In fact, it was their willingness to apply and modify techniques from readymade production to the working-class coat and suit trades that enabled the Jewish clothing industries in New York and

London to prosper.[27] In the broader context of the industry's overall development in the two countries the true impact of the Jews is clear.

The development of the American and British clothing industries

The British and American clothing industries in the nineteenth century were overshadowed by developments in the readymade sector. Before 1850 readymade clothing was rare. In the USA the early readymades came from a few New York and Boston factories, supplying very cheap, coarse garments for sailors and slaves. Even with the beginnings of a market for cheap readymade work clothes in the 1840s (especially among migrants to California during the Gold Rush), the industry's total output remained dominated by the custom or bespoke trade.[28]

By 1860 there were around 60,000 clothing workers in the United States. New York was the leading centre with two-fifths of the workforce and another 15,000 worked in Philadelphia. These were still mostly custom tailors. However, a combination of the Civil War and new technology changed the way in which entrepreneurs viewed the manufacturing process in the clothing industry. Military demand for uniforms from the Union and Confederate armies accelerated the process of standardisation, because the New York manufacturers (who provided most of the uniforms) were given thousands and thousands of measurements, and hence the opportunity to set standard sizes for military and civilian garments alike.[29]

With standard sizes the true potential of the sewing machine was unlocked. The first practical sewing machines were patented in the late 1840s and early 1850s. But the early 'machine-stitching would rip, and the hand-made garments were much firmer'.[30] It was only with successive refinements and improvements in the stitch-forming mechanisms and tension devices through the 1860s that clothing manufacturers began to purchase the machines in any numbers.[31] Sales in the American market jumped from around 65,000 machines in 1865 to 770,000 in 1872.[32]

New cutting machines were also introduced from the 1870s. Together the new cutting and sewing machine technology dramatically increased the speed of stitching. In the late 1890s the US Commissioner of Labor demonstrated that cutting machinery reduced the time to fulfil a set series of tasks to less than fifteen per cent of that required when they were done by hand. The sewing machine similarly reduced the time needed to stitch vests (waistcoats) and pants (trousers) to fifteen per cent of that required in handstitching. To sew up the seams of coats by machine required only 6.7 per cent of the time taken by hand, a fifteenfold increase in productivity.[33] If batch sizes were large enough, the efficiency gains were huge. Standardisation therefore became increasingly significant.

By 1880 the number of clothing workers had increased from the 60,000 of 1860 to 160,000. The majority, however, were still custom tailors. Despite the technological improvements, readymade clothes had yet to move out of their downmarket niche in the United States. After 1880, however, the readymade industry came into its own. With the emergence of the readymade sector, the industry's centre of gravity moved more firmly into New York. By 1900 the total workforce in the United States had more than doubled to over 360,000 with New York dominant. By contrast, custom work was practically extinct.[34] Philadelphia, for instance, saw employment drop from over 20,000 clothing industry workers in 1880 to less than 7,000 in 1890.[35]

The catalyst for this dramatic change in the industry was not technology but fashion.[36] The lessons learned by manufacturers during the Civil War regarding standard sizes were applied to an ever greater variety of garments and to increasingly upmarket niches. After the 1873 economic downturn consumers began to purchase cheaper readymade goods instead of the more expensive custom coats and suits. By the 1890s the demonstration effect had led to an enormous change in consumption patterns. One of the leading New York manufacturers estimated that 'perhaps nine tenths of the men and boys of the country were wearing clothing made ready to put on'.[37] By 1910 the substitution of readymade for custom garments was complete and the industry workforce had further grown to over half a million.

By comparison, the United Kingdom's readymade clothing industry has a much longer history. As early as the seventeenth century the demand for soldiers' uniforms prompted some standardisation. This in turn allowed the manufacturing process to become concentrated in ever larger firms and regional specialisation followed. In 1851 the cheap labour to perform the handstitching was supplied in the port towns of the South-West and the market towns of East Anglia, and by the vast army of London's underemployed. From the 1880s onwards, however, the industry became increasingly concentrated into the two core centres, London and Leeds. A quarter of the tailoring workers of England and Wales worked in the Leeds and London industries by 1911, half by 1935.[38]

In contrast to the USA, consumer demand for readymade garments in Britain was well advanced already by the 1850s, stimulated by innovative retailing practices.[39] The leading retailers of readymades in Britain came from the mid-nineteenth-century secondhand clothes trade. The key entrepreneurial skills for developing the readymade sector were the organisation of marketing and manufacturing. With so much alteration and repair of used garments required before their resale, both qualities were necessary in the secondhand trade.

The retailing of readymades was centred in London and their manufacturing was put out to local women workers. One leading retailer, Nichols, employed 1200 outworkers in the East End in 1850.[40] By the early 1850s the London retailers had created a mass market based on saturation advertising and sold vast quantities of readymade garments. E. Moses & Son, the largest readymade retailer, spent the prodigious amount of £10,000 annually on advertising. Nichols spent £5000.[41] It must have worked. In 1860 Moses claimed that 80 per cent of the English population bought readymades.[42] Even allowing for some exaggeration, this is still impressive. Unfortunately no statistics survive, and indeed it is unlikely any were ever compiled, but it was surely the case that by 1860 perhaps the majority of the population bought at least some items of clothing readymade.

In comparison with the United States therefore the readymade industry in Britain attained organisational maturity before the introduction of the new sewing machine technology. This was why wages were so low and conditions so deplorable in the famous 'sweating' controversy of the 1840s and 1850s.[43]

The early maturity of the British clothing industry may explain why it never attained the labour productivity of the American industry.[44] Organised through homework, the British industry was slow to concentrate into large factories. One British commentator in the early 1890s observed that in New York the 'ready-made clothing trade especially, is carried on upon a gigantic scale, of which we have but little experience in this country, large as our trade is'.[45] These big factories concentrated on low-quality, mass-produced factory garments, and employed hundreds of workers.

With capital requirements representing a substantial barrier, Jewish immigrant entrepreneurs did not compete in the factory sector. Rather they concentrated on producing medium-grade goods in their small workshops. The competition here was mostly with the upmarket custom trade and so the garments needed a better fit and more styling than the factory goods. Because more skill was needed to produce these higher-grade garments, factories held no advantages over smaller workshops. The great and good fortune of the Jewish immigrants in both the United

States and Britain is that it was precisely this segment of the clothing market which grew most rapidly in the late nineteenth century. The growth of British demand is indicated by the rise in the number of clothing retail outlets, from 544 to 5681 between 1880 and 1915.[46]

Despite the growing market and increasing technological gains, non-Jewish English tailors were remarkably reluctant to leave the custom trade. They shunned the machine, leaving the newly emerging field open to the more flexible and innovative Jewish tailors. English tailors 'were mired down by the traditions of their trade and the fear of economic and status decline which might accompany innovation'. A factory inspector commented that it 'is really the conservatism of the English clothing manufacturer that prevents him entering the field that has been marked out by the Alien'.[47] By 1888, Beatrice Potter noted, the 'art of the English tailor has been exchanged for the perfect mechanism of Jewish organizations'.[48]

The Jewish workshops in both New York and London were therefore both able to exploit the new technology and subdivisional techniques developed in the factory sector and apply them to ever higher grades of garments. These garments had previously only been made by custom tailors, and so carried a bespoke price tag. Because the Jewish workshops were so much more efficient, the price of work fell, creating a vast new market of the ordinary working families in both Britain and America. There were slight differences in the principal product – the Jewish workshops in New York focused more on readymades, those in London on a semi-custom, semi-readymade output. But the most striking feature of both industries was how quickly they grew.[49]

The Jewish clothing industries of New York and London

As the industry developed, the newly arrived immigrants found themselves at the very bottom, as under-machinists and under-pressers in the small workshops. The people at the head of this industrial structure were the wholesalers. The wholesalers received the orders from the retailers, bought the cloth, cut it to order and gave it out to subcontractors. The subcontractors were responsible for returning the stitched garments, or the daily 'task', by a certain time, for which they received a fixed price per piece. It was this daily task that defined the Jewish clothing firm's structure.

In order to complete the daily task, Jewish workshops were organised for speed. There needed to be a baister or general tailor to hand stitch with big temporary stitches along the seams to prepare for the machinist.

There also needed to be a finisher to take the machined item and fell the sleeves and linings, remove the baister's thread and trim any edges. After this a buttonhole worker was needed to cut and stitch the buttonholes, and the finisher would normally sew on the buttons. The final procedure before the item of clothing could be returned to the wholesaler's warehouse was its pressing. The master would supervise his team, making sure that the machinist was kept working, helping out with the baisting, or perhaps finishing the coat before its pressing, as well as going to and from the wholesalers.

The determining factor in any workshop therefore was the sewing machine. Work was organised around the machine. Moreover, because pressing was a special skill and 1 presser needed the product of 2 machines in most grades of work to be kept fully occupied, workshops tended to be organised around 2 machines and 1 presser, with 8 or 9 workers in total.[50]

In the early 1880s the typical New York workshop followed the same structure but consisted of 3 teams feeding 2 pressers, or 12 to 13 workers. As these workshops grew in number they came to dominate the New York industry and the factory trade diminished in importance. In consequence the average number of employees per tailoring establishment halved from 31 in 1889 to 15.6 by the mid 1900s.[51]

In both New York and London the Jewish workshops concentrated only in certain sectors. Mark Moses, a well-known Jewish master tailor in the London's East End, insisted that 'Jews cannot compete in trousers & common suit trade as prices would not allow them to live and pay the high rates of wages which their men earn.' It was only through 'improved machinery and perfecting the system of division of labour' that the Jews managed to compete at all, he concluded.[52] In those sectors of the garment industry which were wholly given over to readymade techniques, like trousers, Jewish employment and entrepreneurship were less evident.[53]

In those sectors where fit and fashion were important, the Jewish workshops predominated, overwhelmingly so in womenswear. In both cities after the 1890s womenswear was the fastest-growing subsector as demand for readymade and semi-readymade fashion goods took off. With bigger profit margins, this sector was a vital route to prosperity in both communities during the period.[54]

Compared with any other immigrant group of the period, the Jews in both cities were therefore presented with a substantial opportunity for progress in their rapidly growing niches of the clothing industry. Wages and profits were, however, continually under threat in an industry with minimal entry barriers and with a pool of labour continually refilled with new immigrants. Competitive forces led to large price cuts. In London the prices were said to have been cut by half in the fifteen years before 1888.[55] In New York the fall in prices occurred just a little later: average wholesale prices fell from their 1882 peak by around one-third to 1897.[56] Indeed it was not until the late 1900s that prices began to rise in both London and New York. In the overcoats and suits trades in Britain (Jewish niches), prices only really made significant increases after 1909 and 1910 respectively.[57]

The trends in the prices in New York and London were strongly influenced by the arrival of the immigrants. As each successive wave of immigrant entrepreneurs pushed their way in, so the competition for work led to continual underbidding. The fall in the price paid to contracting master tailors for their stitching up of work meant a continual pressure on profits and working conditions, giving rise to both long hours and a relentless search for increasing the speed of production through applying more and more readymade techniques to higher grades of clothing.

This in turn led to an increase in the size of the typical Jewish workshop by the turn of the century, as work was subdivided and mechanised with ever greater precision and for ever greater speed. By 1908 workshops were more likely to employ 20 or more than 10 or less. The work was organised around teams, with a principal machinist helped by 3 or 4 under-machinists, a principal presser helped by an under-presser, and so on. The pace was unrelenting.[58]

Profits in the New York and London Jewish clothing industries

The Jewish sectors of the clothing industries in both New York and London were therefore remarkably similar in the early 1900s. The New York workshops had more readymade output than in London, but the differences were less obvious then than they had been in the early 1880s, when the New York workshops had more traditional custom work than in London's East End. Already in 1880, the factory end of the market was already closed to them (in London) or else was soon to become so (in New York). Nevertheless in both cities, the Jewish immigrants located their niche between the high-quality handmade clothes for the well-dressed elite and coarse factory readymades. While the structures of the two cities' Jewish industries were therefore similar, what is of particular importance here is the trends in profits.

First, in New York the early Jewish immigrants employed the task system to great benefit, replacing journeymen tailors in both the custom and readymade branches in the late 1870s. According to the United States Industrial Commission on Immigration, in its detailed review of the New York clothing industry, profits in the Jewish workshops in the early 1880s were high:

> The coat for which the tailor received $5 or $6 as custom work, and for which he received $2.50 to $3 in the dull season as ready-made work, was made in the Jewish task shops for $1.50 to $2. At this price the Jews earned as much and even more money than the merchant tailor.[59]

The good times did not last, though. The readymade trade gravitated to the factories and so passed largely out of immigrant hands. Moreover, the increasing numbers of Jewish immigrants bid the price of all work down, and with it profits and wages. The average weekly wage in the Jewish workshops in 1881 would have been just a little lower than a presser's average weekly wage of $14.31.[60] An 1890 privately commissioned census of the Jewish population of New York found that average weekly wages for male Jewish immigrants in the Lower East Side had fallen to $10.13.[61]

Matters did not improve much. In 1893 John Burnett reported on the impact of Jewish immigration in New York to the British Board of Trade. He had earlier reported on the East London clothing industry and so was a particularly well-qualified investigator. He concluded that 'the sweating system in the United States is worse that it is in England':

> [The] doubting Londoner, who thinks there is nothing on earth to equal the sweating shops of East London, is quickly undeceived... Rates of pay are higher, and, possibly, the standard of living a little better than in the worst shops of this kind in the east end of London; but in a considerable number of cases the sanitary conditions of the places used as workshops are much worse.

He cited evidence of typical wages and profits in a New York Jewish workshop using the task system. Wages had fallen by at least a quarter since the mid 1880s, with daily wages normally about $2, or, with a four-and-a-half-day week, only around $9 a week. According to Burnett in 1893, the entrepreneur's daily profit was around $5 to $8, giving a weekly profit of between $22.50 and $36.[62]

The Industrial Commission estimated that wages had fallen from an overall average of $7.55 (including female wages) in 1893 to $6.96 in 1895. In 1899 male wages varied from between $3 and $6 for those learning the trade, to between $10 and $12 for the majority. While some earned more, on average wages had barely changed from the early 1890s. A typical workshop would generate $5.68 profit per day, or $25.56 per week in 1901, perhaps 10 per cent less than in 1893, considerably less than in 1880.[63]

The Dillingham Commission on Immigration to the USA reported in 1911. It did not publish any information on profits but it did survey the typical wages earned by Russian Jewish immigrants in the New York clothing industry. It concluded that '[p]oor wages, however, prevail in the clothing industry', finding that the mean weekly earnings in 1909 were $13.88 for men and $8.74 for women.[64] Wages had perhaps therefore risen a little from the late 1890s and were higher than anytime since the early 1880s. The cost, however, was in the much larger daily task. A typical daily task of 8 to 10 coats in the late 1880s and early 1890s had risen to between 20 to 22 by 1901.[65] Profits must also have improved by 1909 after falling from the early 1880s, since they ran after all in tandem with wages. But the cost for entrepreneurs as much as workers was longer hours and an increased intensity of work.

London's tailoring industry also experienced a fall in profits. The testimony of various master tailors recorded by Booth's investigators gives a clear indication of the average profit levels among sweaters in the late 1880s. Moreover, such was the level of complaints from these tailors about falling profits that it was common to hear them state that they could work for no less, that there was no margin left.[66] Some were turning to innovative work practices, however, deskilling the individual tasks, subdividing and intensifying the work processes and reducing wage costs. One wholesaler's foreman 'knew for instance that two middlemen whom they employed on the same work & who for the same wages, earned very different profits, the one clearing about £3 & the other about £5 a week', or from $15 to $25.[67]

In 1888 the typical male Jewish immigrant in London's East End would earn 6s. to 7s. a day as a machinist or presser. The average week's work in the larger shops was four to four and a half days but in the smaller shops only about three days. Most immigrants worked in the smaller shops, so the mean weekly wage over the year would have been a paltry 20s., or less than $5.[68]

By 1893 there had been no improvement. Clara Collet's investigation into wages in the UK clothing industry revealed that male Jewish tailors in the East End coat industry earned only 6s. to 7s. per day. With an average working week still less than four days, the mean weekly wage was only just over 20s. According to Collet, industry conditions in 1893 had clearly not improved from the late 1880s; East End tailors blamed the competition from the Leeds-based factories.[69]

Conditions did improve from the later 1890s onwards, though. A Board of Trade report showed that clothing industry wages had risen by 60 per cent more than the average for all industries from 1899 to 1908.[70] A report on clothing industry conditions in 1906 confirmed that weekly wages in the East End tailoring trade sector had risen along with the general trend in the clothing industry. Jewish immigrant tailors in 1906 enjoyed increases of perhaps 50 per cent compared with the late 1880s and early 1890s rates of pay. Baisters' average weekly pay was 26.75s., machiners' 29.75s. and pressers earned 34.75s., or anything from $6.50 to $8.40. More readymade techniques were used and in more profitable sectors. When demand faltered, lower-grade readymades filled in, so that the industry had a longer, more regular working week and was much less seasonal. Indeed, outside the peak month of May and the trough of November, employment levels in the East End barely changed.[71]

In March 1908 the president of the Jewish Master Tailors Improvement Association (the leading employers' organisation in the East End), Abraham Levi, confirmed that Jewish master tailors were also benefiting from improved conditions in his evidence before the Parliamentary Select Committee on Homework. The Jewish tailoring industry, he claimed, enjoyed far better conditions than in the late 1880s. Indeed, Jewish tailors were earning 20 to 30 per cent higher wages than the English Gentile tailors, benefiting from the subdivision of work under the task system.[72]

The force of new immigrant-inspired competition, so apparent in the testimonies of master tailors to the Booth investigators in the late 1880s, was not mentioned. Profits were seemingly stable. Levi stated that 'we middlemen, as a rule, demand a certain price for our work, which will give us an adequate wage to our workpeople and leave us a fair share of profit for our work and responsibility'.[73] Wholesalers still attempted to force prices down, but the situation in London before 1910 was clearly not as bad as in New York. The average working day for male tailors in the Jewish East End had increased to thirteen hours, including around one and a half hours off for meals, but this compared with fourteen hours with few breaks in New York.[74]

Tawney's investigation of the tailoring industry immediately prior to the outbreak of war found that 'the Jewish workshops show no signs of depression', and that the 'wages earned in Jewish workshops are relatively high'.[75] Tawney was particularly impressed by the intensity of work under the task system – the 'Jewish workshop holds its own, in fact, by its minute attention to detail, and by an extreme degree of application which may be compared with the intensive cultivation of a small holder.'[76]

The purpose of Tawney's investigation was to measure the impact of the minimum wage on employers' profits in the clothing industry, and while he discovered that the less efficient tailoring workshops had suffered from declining profits since 1909, the Jewish small master was more than 'holding his own'.[77] This was especially helped in London's East End by the growing trend for Jewish tailors to move into the most profitable sectors of the clothing industry such as womenswear.[78] After the depressed conditions of the 1880s and 1890s, by the end of the period both profits and wages improved in the Jewish workshops in London.[79]

By contrast, in the New York Jewish workshops profits and wages never recovered their 1880 level, at least not until after the early 1900s. Given that wages did increase from 1901 to 1909, the likelihood must be that profits also increased. But it is most unlikely that they recovered their 1880 level before the 1910 'Protocol for Peace'.[80]

Trends in profits in the two Jewish communities would thus appear to have diverged. In London profits increased from the 1880s and 1890s to 1907–14. In New York they fell from 1880 to 1905, although they were beginning to recover. The partial reason for this divergence is not too hard to discover. In both cities the profits were bid down by successive waves of immigration and bid up by the domestic demand for clothing. The difference was that in New York the number of Jewish immigrants was so much larger and their impact on clothing industry so much greater that profits and wages were bid down relative to London.

In 1910, 39.1 per cent of the workforce in the New York garment industry were East European Jews.[81] With New York dominant in the American industry, East European Jews comprised around a quarter of the American industry's workforce. In Britain, with less regional concentration and a much smaller immigration rate, East European Jews accounted for only around 5 per cent of the industry's workforce by 1911. In the USA the growth of domestic demand for Jewish-made clothing from New York was insufficient to maintain profit and wage levels in the face of a much larger growth in the supply of Jewish immigrant labour. Furthermore, already by 1905 Italian immigrants were entering the New York labour market and competing with East European Jews for clothing profits and wages. By 1910 Russian and other East European non-Jewish immigrants had further bid down industry wage levels.[82]

For incumbents the costs of exiting this overpopulated sector were unfortunately high. Constrained by language and cultural ties and with little knowledge of opportunities in other sectors, only a few were able to diversify into real estate, retailing and other sectors where capital costs were sufficiently high to deter immigrant entry.[83]

While the evidence for the divergence in profit trends seems quite clear, the divergence is not in the direction expected. Given the trends in the supply of entrepreneurship in the two immigrant economies, profits were expected to have grown by much more in New York than in London, not the other way round.

In London the supply of entrepreneurship fell from the 1880s to the 1890s from 14.2 per cent to 10.9 per cent, in line with falling profits. As profits increased in the 1900s and 1910s so the supply of immigrant entrepreneurship in the Jewish East End increased to 13.1 per cent in 1900–06 and to 18.0 per cent in 1907–14. By comparison, however, the trends in New York seem perplexing. Entrepreneurship rose there from 18.0 per cent in 1880, when profits were high, to 34.3 per cent in 1905, when profits were lower.

It may have been the case that the overwhelming majority of Jewish immigrants there were restricted to very few economic options, that they were essentially either entrepreneurs or employees in the clothing industry. If so, the relative attractiveness of entrepreneurship in 1905 compared with 1880 may have been more a function of wages having fallen by more than profits. The evidence to support this is hardly overwhelming, however. Most observers thought wages less flexible than profits.[84] Our simple economic model is struggling to explain the divergence in Jewish immigrant entrepreneurship.

The Jews in the Pale were forced into petty entrepreneurship by persecution. The *Jewish Chronicle* described how persecution had led to a 'pogrom mentality', a strong cultural belief in the necessity of independence and security which could best be achieved in the economic sphere by self-employment.[85] Contemporaries often concurred, one noting 'that the tendency of the Jew to become an employer is strong'.[86]

This cultural belief was shared by both Jewish immigrant communities and, given their similar backgrounds, it was shared to a similar degree. It is therefore remarkable that while those in New York moved into entrepreneurship with little or no pecuniary encouragement, the response from those in London was so extraordinarily muted. The higher profits there should have attracted many more immigrants out of wage-earning occupations and into profit-earning ones.

This strong cultural predisposition to self-employment may suggest, however, that motives other than immediate financial gain may have been uppermost in the minds of Jewish immigrants. Certainly they were not responding to financial signals alone. It is therefore to these cultural motives for self-employment, and to how they may have been influenced in the two cultural environments of New York and London, that this enquiry now turns.

7
Cultural Assimilation among Jewish Immigrants in London and New York

The assimilation of British and American cultural values by the East European Jews was rapid. There is abundant testimonial and biographical evidence that many immigrants were enthralled by their new homes. Assimilation was also strongly encouraged by the established Jewish communities in both cities. They initiated a series of programmes to 'Americanise' and 'Anglicise' the new arrivals, for instance; to turn the immigrants, in the words of the Chief Rabbi, into 'loyal citizens'.[1] These were often crude and condescending, resented by the older immigrants, but not wholly unwelcome among the younger ones.[2]

The younger immigrants – and most arrived in their teens and twenties – rather looked at the world around them and, not surprisingly given that Tsarist Russia was predominantly their only earlier experience of Gentile culture, they liked what they saw. 'To be an American, dress like an American, look like an American, and even, if only in fantasy, talk like an American, became a collective goal, at least of the younger immigrants,' wrote the renowned Jewish historian Irving Howe.[3] By the 1900s the typical Jewish immigrant in New York wore American clothes, read English newspapers and used one hundred English words in the increasingly mangled Yiddish of the Lower East Side.[4]

The Jews in London were similarly captivated. In 1900 a detailed study of the Jewish East End concluded that 'most immigrants are moved with the ambition to become Englishmen; and seven or eight years' residence in this country is often enough to fill them with contempt for "foreigners"'.[5] Those who had arrived as children quickly followed English habits, acquiring 'something of the English stolidity and inertia'.[6]

The Jewish immigrants therefore assimilated American and British cultural values. This was a partial and highly selective process; they were not simply the passive recipients of some kind of forced socialisation. But assimilation was an important influence on immigrant behaviour. It should not be surprising therefore if it influenced their economic behaviour.

Cultural explanations of economic behaviour are clearly secondary to economic ones. Most economic activity is typically well explained by relatively few variables; using just the concepts of demand, supply and equilibrium price alone enables a surprisingly large amount of human activity to be understood. These, however, have not satisfactorily explained the divergence in the supply of entrepreneurship in the two Jewish immigrant labour markets of New York and London.

Our simple economic analysis has failed to identify any differences in the demand for Jewish immigrant entrepreneurship in New York and London after 1880. In both cities the immigrant economies were dominated by just the one sector, which experienced a similar technological and institutional development in both locations. There was no obvious source for any divergence in the demand for entrepreneurship. Unsurprisingly, there was little difference in the scope for generating profitable opportunities in the two immigrant economies. The divergence in the supply of entrepreneurship therefore remains unexplained. Whereas New York Jews followed the cultural stereotype and moved into self-employment with great gusto, the London Jews' response was much more sluggish. A cultural explanation is therefore worth exploring.

What is apparent is that the immigrants were eager to adopt the language, customs and mores of their new homes. How they selected specific values and how they adapted them in their own environments is not known – the exact process is probably not knowable. But cultural assimilation did happen. And, moreover, the force of assimilation actually makes the perplexing relationship between profits and the willingness to supply entrepreneurship in London and New York much easier to understand.

Figure 7.1 illustrates how a cultural change after arrival in immigrant preferences for supplying entrepreneurship may have influenced profits in our simple economic model of entrepreneurship. The divergent immigrant experience is now no longer explained through differences in the demand for entrepreneurship, but rather through changes in the willingness to supply entrepreneurship – changes that arose from assimilating the values of the two host cultures: the entrepreneurial, dynamic American culture and the anti-entrepreneurial, conservative British culture.

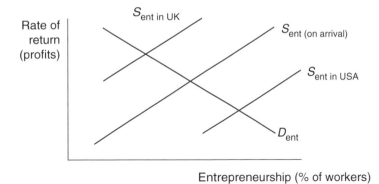

Figure 7.1 Cultural assimilation and changes in the supply of entrepreneurship in London and New York

The figure shows how the assimilation of British and American values could have changed the supply of Jewish immigrant entrepreneurship. In America Jewish immigrants assimilating the cultural preference for entrepreneurship above wage-earning could therefore have moved into entrepreneurship for lower profits. Their supply curve moves down to the right, indicating that, with more entrepreneurs, profits were bid down. In Britain, by contrast, the Jewish immigrants may have become increasingly reluctant to leave paid employment and so required higher profits for any given level of entrepreneurship. Their supply curve moves up and to the left, indicating that many who would ordinarily have been entrepreneurs chose to stay in wage-earning work, leaving higher profits for the remaining entrepreneurs. This hypothesis explains the facts very well. But it remains purely hypothetical until a clear link can be established between cultural assimilation and entrepreneurship among the immigrants.

Indeed, more pertinently, what is required is evidence of whether the more assimilated Jewish immigrants in London became more reluctant to move into entrepreneurship, preferring to remain in the employed sector. After all, the cultural stereotype of the Jewish entrepreneur was well grounded in their East European background. That the American immigrants followed this stereotype is not so remarkable. What seems so strange from the perspective of the Pale is why there were so few immigrant entrepreneurs among the Jews in London. This chapter considers this in detail, focusing on one group of immigrant grooms in particular, the Jewish immigrant journeymen.

Jewish immigrant journeymen in London

English culture has been widely criticised as having been relatively anti-entrepreneurial. If this was in fact the case, then some Jewish immigrants in London, assimilating English culture, may have chosen non-entrepreneurial occupations, whereas an equivalent group in New York, assimilating entrepreneurial American values there, may have chosen entrepreneurship.

Obviously talent, fortune and so on played a role. But if the most talented and determined became entrepreneurs in both cities then there may have been a lesser talented, or fortunate, or whatever, cohort in both cities, who, being susceptible to American values, moved into entrepreneurship in New York, and, being equally susceptible to English values, remained in some form of blue-collar work in London.

Recall that the share of entrepreneurs in the Jewish immigrant workforce in New York rose from 18 per cent in 1880 to 34.3 per cent in 1905 and remained around 35 per cent in 1914. Table 7.1 repeats the earlier reported findings (from Chapter 4) that immigrant entrepreneurship rose in London only from 14 to 18 per cent. The table also elaborates on this developing occupational structure, reporting how the important status demarcation among the London Jewish immigrants by the end of the period was not between blue- and white-collar occupations but between skilled craft workers and the other blue-collars – for one of the most notable features of the occupational data is how many immigrant grooms described themselves as journeymen on their marriage records.

These journeymen were distinct from all other blue-collar workers because, apart from a handful of tailors' cutters, there were no other

Table 7.1   Occupational status of East European Jewish immigrant men in London's East End, 1880–1914 (percentages)

Class	1880–89	1890–99	1900–06	1907–14
i. Entrepreneurs	14.2	10.9	13.3	18.0
ii. Non-Entrepreneurs	3.4	3.0	1.8	1.4
Total, i + ii	17.6	13.9	15.1	19.4
iii. Journeymen	–	0.8	4.2	26.3
Total, i + ii + iii	17.6	14.7	19.3	45.7
iv. Other blue-collar	82.4	85.3	80.7	54.2

Source: Age-adjusted CRA database.

blue-collar grooms with occupations in the highest-skill category. Almost all the rest, from the machinists and pressers to the clickers and mechanics, were in some form of semi-skilled class. The journeymen were therefore different from the typical blue-collar worker. Compared with the typical Jewish immigrant in New York, moreover, these journeymen may have been much more like some of those who moved into entrepreneurship than those who remained in blue-collar work there. They may, in other words, have been a cohort of the Jewish population who, but for the assimilation of English cultural values, would have moved into entrepreneurship in London.

The emergence of the term journeyman was extremely rapid. Before 1905 it was barely used among the immigrants, but by 1910 over a third of the immigrant grooms were journeymen. If this is considered as a relatively high-status occupation, then almost 46 per cent of the Jewish immigrants in London were in a high social class between 1907 and 1914, a dramatic gain on the 1 in 6 or so from the 1880s through to the early 1900s.[7]

The existence of so many Jewish immigrant journeymen is also clear evidence of cultural assimilation. This is for two reasons. First, it was a term which was mostly borrowed from the host English culture. Journeymen hardly existed in the Pale. Compared to England, there were no such craft distinctions in the Jewish artisan trades there. Moreover, there was no Yiddish word for journeyman.[8] Second, not only did it come from the English rather than the Russian environment, but, in borrowing it, the Jewish immigrants had given it a new meaning, because the one thing clear about these Jewish immigrant journeymen is that they were not journeymen.[9]

Overwhelmingly they were in the garment and furniture industries, with 58 per cent and 27 per cent respectively and with only 15 per cent for all other occupations. They were tailors and cabinetmakers in Jewish workshops. This is why they cannot have been journeymen. Well before 1900 the journeyman function had become redundant in the Jewish workshops. There were some Jewish journeymen in late-nineteenth-century London of course. There were one or two Jewish unions which used the term in their title, for example, but these organisations were for English working-class Jews and not the immigrants.[10]

The term journeyman had a very specific meaning. In the tailoring trade the journeyman tailor was a craftsman, and the two terms became synonymous in the high-class West-End trade. A journeyman was someone sufficiently skilled to cut, sew and finish an entire garment to a high standard.[11] This was how tailoring had been traditionally organised, was still organised in London's West End trade in 1914 and remained so there long after.[12] The Board of Trade's study into conditions in the clothing trades in 1906 confirmed that while journeymen were a key part of the West End bespoke, or custom, trade, they were absent from the East End trade.[13] Moreover, hardly any East European Jews worked in the West End. The custom industry there employed a number of immigrants, but, as Collet reported in 1894, '[v]ery few of the foreigners, even including the Russians and Poles, seemed to be Jewish'.[14] Jewish East End workshops were unable to meet the quality thresholds required for the West End custom trade. As noted in Chapter 6, they were successful in supplying the rapidly growing niche for middling quality readymade and custom mens- and womenswear. They were successful because they pursued specialisation and speed, combining extensive subdivision of tasks with mechanisation. Over the period the degree of subdivision and specialisation became ever more elaborate. In the workshops of the Jewish East End there was therefore simply no room for journeymen. In a 1908 description of a typical Jewish workshop, the president of the Jewish Master Tailors' Improvement Association made no mention of any role for a journeyman, despite a detailed listing of all the different specialities and functions of all the workers.[15] By then the expanded task system was entrenched in the East End. The typical workshop contained 20 to 30 workers, each specialising on one minute function in the construction of garments.[16] The inescapable conclusion is that Jewish immigrants were describing themselves as journeymen on their wedding certificates when strictly speaking they were not.

The question remains as to what they actually were. Here, alas, the historical record is silent. Despite the apparent consensus on its meaning (the journeyman made the garment all the way through), Feldman makes the point that by the end of the period even English journeymen tailors were beginning to exploit subdivisional principles by using anything from 2 to 6 female assistants.[17] The meaning of the term may therefore have been more plastic in London's clothing industry than is generally assumed. In the years before 1914 its meaning in the Jewish workshops may simply have become a corrupted term for a skilled worker, or one with more responsibility in the larger workshops, a team leader perhaps.

Nevertheless, as Tawney and other reporters testified, by the period's end the modest degree of specialisation practised by English journeymen was far removed from the sheer degree of subdivision in the East End workshops. Whatever their function may have been in the Jewish workshops in the years around 1910, no English journeyman would have recognised them as his peers.[18]

By contrast, in New York there were no Jewish immigrant journeymen, or journeymen of any description. There were cities in the United States where a craft system of work still predominated, where therefore there were still journeymen in 1914 and where a craft culture still existed. But New York was not one of them.[19]

New York's manufacturing sector in the 1900s was populated almost entirely by ethnic East Europeans (Jews and Gentiles), southern Italians and Irish.[20] None of these ethnic groups had a strong artisan or craft tradition. The Irish, Italians and non-Jewish East Europeans came mostly from rural and agricultural backgrounds. Without a craft-dominated manufacturing sector and with no craft culture, there was no equivalent in New York of the high status accorded to high-skilled blue-collar workers in English culture – especially in London's working class culture. The only practical route to higher-status occupations open to the Jewish immigrants in New York was entrepreneurship.[21]

The Jewish immigrant journeymen grooms in London therefore may well have assimilated English cultural values. These values might have given higher status to the journeyman function in a way that made it relatively attractive to many of those who might otherwise (as in New York) have gone into entrepreneurship. This could explain the divergence in entrepreneurial outcomes. The exact mechanism will no doubt remain opaque. But, if it could be demonstrated that the immigrant journeymen were relatively assimilated, this would then provide strong supporting evidence for a cultural explanation of the different paths in immigrant entrepreneurship. It would tell us that, all else equal, the relatively assimilated became journeymen while the relatively unassimilated did not.

Unfortunately cultural assimilation is not directly observable. There is no accepted definition of what it involves, never mind any particular technique of measuring it. Researchers have, however, tried to use various proxies, such as naming patterns, trends in fertility and marriage.[22] A similarly tangential approach is followed here.

Cultural assimilation among Jewish immigrant journeymen

Assimilation is likely to have been associated with the amount of time spent in the host culture since arrival. After all, it seems unreasonable to expect a new arrival in London to have been acquainted with English customs, whereas a longer-settled immigrant might well have acquired a glimmer of appreciation of the attractions of Queen and Country, Yorkshire pudding and the Epsom Derby. A reasonable proxy for assimilation therefore ought to be the number of years since settlement. If the journeymen were more assimilated than the average immigrant, they surely had spent more time in Britain before marriage. Unfortunately the marriage records give no indication of how soon before the marriage the immigrants had arrived in Britain, so the length of time since settlement is not directly measurable.

A crude proxy can be constructed, however, which builds on the observation that immigrant marriage rates were less volatile than immigration rates.[23] Those marrying in any one year consisted of two groups of brides and grooms, the recently arrived and those who had arrived earlier, during childhood perhaps. If immigration followed a straight-line trend over this period, then the share of these two cohorts would be constant during the years when immigration was close to its trend.[24] In years of above-trend immigration, the share of the newly arrived brides and grooms would be higher. Conversely, during years of below-trend immigration, the share of the longer-settled and so more assimilated would be higher. One way of estimating when the cohort of brides and grooms consisted disproportionately of the more assimilated is therefore simply to identify the years of below-trend immigration and weight them accordingly in what then becomes a modified time trend running for the thirty-five years from 1880 to 1914.[25]

Time, however, is not the only variable with some relationship to cultural assimilation. Additional characteristics from the marriage records may well have been sensitive to cultural assimilation. Those characteristics which were most likely to be related to assimilation ought to be isolated by comparing the East European grooms with the English grooms included in the same sample. Once a range of indicators of assimilation have been identified, their prominence among the Jewish immigrant journeymen can be measured.

Because time since arrival was likely to have been correlated with cultural assimilation, the acquisition of certain skills specific to the host country would also have been related to both assimilation and time. One skill never required in the Pale was literacy in English. The ability to be able to sign the marriage register in English signified the acquisition of a basic English literacy because it required a different alphabet from the Yiddish language's Hebrew alphabet. The acquisition of English literacy must therefore have taken place after arrival.[26] The presence of this characteristic was therefore, like cultural assimilation, a function of time spent in Britain since arrival.

Table 7.2 compares the English literacy of the English- and East-European-born grooms to see if there is any reasonable basis for using it as an indicator of cultural assimilation. Unsurprisingly, almost all of the English grooms and their brides signed the register, whereas only around half of the immigrant grooms and their brides did. If the relatively assimilated immigrant grooms were increasingly likely to share characteristics of the English, then they would be more likely to have signed the register than the average immigrant. Moreover, the more assimilated may have married the more assimilated brides – in which case they married brides

Table 7.2 Indicators of cultural assimilation, English and immigrant grooms

Assimilation indicators	English [N = 277]	A %	Immigrant [N = 961]	B %	Assimilation index [A/B]
1 Grooms signed in English	268	96.8	578	60.2	161
2 Brides signed in English	249	89.9	438	45.6	197
3 Brides born in UK*a*	212	77.9	150	15.8	495
4 Married in the East London Synagogue	106	38.3	550	57.2	67
5 Married in United Synagogue	133	48.0	162	16.9	285
6 Married in Federation Synagogues	38	13.7	249	25.9	53
Status: 7 White-collar	79	28.5	138	14.4	202
8 Journeymen	34	12.3	97	10.1	124
9 Blue-collar*b*	157	56.7	787	81.9	77

Notes:
a Bridal birthplaces on some records not listed. Therefore N = 272 and 952 for English and East European-born respectively.
b Seven English and seven immigrant high blue-collar (but not journeymen) cutters were excluded from the blue-collar class, who were otherwise all semi-skilled workers. Therefore N = 270 and 954 respectively.

Source: CRA database.

who signed the register more than average, meaning that bridal literacy would also be an indicator of immigrant assimilation.[27]

Researchers of ethnic assimilation today use interracial marriage as one of their key indicators. According to this measure, even by the 1990s assimilation had still not progressed very far, especially in the United States.[28] Interracial marriage is therefore an indicator of only very pronounced assimilation.

While not the same as interracial marriage, the differences between the English and immigrant grooms were at their starkest when comparing bridal nativity. Overwhelmingly immigrants married immigrants, and English married English. Then, as now, marriage tended to remain within rather than across the social divide, and in the East End there was a strong division between the native working-class Jews and the immigrant Jews. As one commentator described it, there 'appears to be a stronger line of severance between the English and foreign Jew than between the English Jew and Gentile'.[29] The small number of immigrants marrying English brides might very well therefore have been the among most assimilated grooms.

The next group of characteristics (rows 4 to 6) compare the location of marriage. All the marriages were solemnised under the authority of a synagogue, but not all the synagogues were the same. Religious tensions between immigrant and native Jews in both New York and London were the source of conflict during the period. The orthodox immigrants were shocked at the laxity of religious observance among the British and American Jews, who, in turn, thought the Judaism of the Pale offensive superstition. In consequence, immigrants belonged to immigrant synagogues, and native Jews to longer-established institutions.[30] In London the established synagogues were all members of the United Synagogue and it is not unreasonable to assume that an immigrant marrying in one of these might have been relatively assimilated.

The first synagogue listed in the table is the East London Synagogue. This was a member of the United Synagogue but was exceptional for being the location where almost all the 'cheap marriages' (with reduced fees) took place. Consequently, almost all those who were relatively poor would have married there. Contemporary opinion was universal in believing that there was a strong inverse relationship between poverty and time since arrival, so we would expect this group of grooms to be dominated by the impoverished newly arrived immigrants.[31] Nevertheless, a substantial number of English Jews also married at the East London Synagogue. Some of these may have been from families of regular synagogue members but the vast majority were also 'cheap marriages' between the relatively poor English working-class Jews. Overall, however, immigrants were more likely to marry there than English grooms, so that marrying at the East London Synagogue was probably inversely associated with cultural assimilation.

The second group of synagogues is composed of the other three United Synagogue constituent members in the City and East End of London. These synagogues – the Great, the Hambro and the New – were almost exclusively patronised by English Jews. By contrast, the third group of synagogues, belonging to the Federation of Synagogues, were immigrant synagogues. Not surprisingly, most of the marriages in this group were with immigrant grooms. Only 14 per cent of English grooms married in a Federation synagogue compared with 26 per cent of immigrant grooms. Marrying in a Federation synagogue was therefore a characteristic of immigrant and not English behaviour. This suggests, on the one hand, that marrying in a Federation synagogue may have been inversely related to cultural assimilation, and, on the other, that immigrants marrying in the United Synagogue (other than the East London) were following the behaviour of the English Jews, and so were presumably relatively assimilated.

The final rows in Table 7.2 present the differences in occupational status of the two populations of grooms. Unsurprisingly, English grooms were twice as likely to be in white-collar occupations. They were also around a quarter more likely to be journeymen, whereas immigrant grooms were more likely to have low status blue-collar occupations.

Occupational status is of course a function of many different factors: parental background, education, talent and fortune, to name only the most obvious. But immigrants may have preferred employment as journeymen to entrepreneurship for cultural reasons. What is undeniable is that both the entrepreneurs and journeymen were pursuing unusual paths for the immigrant but not for the English Jews.

Table 7.3 separates the immigrant grooms into the three principal occupational groups listed in Table 7.2 and considers whether there was any relationship between immigrant occupational attainment and assimilation. The four indicators of assimilation derived from Table 7.2 (English literacy in brides and grooms, bridal English nativity, and marrying in an assimilated synagogue) along with the modified time trend (to accentuate those years when it was likely that a higher share of grooms than normal were the longer-settled young arrivals) are used to test for assimilation in each group.[32]

In addition to testing for the sensitivity to cultural assimilation, the table also includes a test of the sensitivity of occupational attainment to

Table 7.3. Occupation and assimilation among immigrant grooms (ordinary least squares estimation)

Independent variables	Dependent variables		
	Entrepreneurs $N=138$	Blue-collars $N=719$	Journeymen $N=97$
Constant	−0.060**	1.161***	−0.111***
	(2.02)	(31.16)	(4.10)
Longer settled = high	0.101**	−0.493***	0.437***
	(2.01)	(7.74)	(9.50)
Grooms signing	0.051**	−0.100***	0.013
	(2.22)	(3.42)	(0.64)
Brides signing	0.059**	−0.146***	0.077***
	(2.49)	(4.87)	(3.55)
Brides born in UK	0.057*	0.029	−0.095***
	(1.80)	(0.77)	(3.30)
Assimilated synagogue	0.074**	−0.141***	0.052*
	(2.38)	(3.61)	(1.85)
Father's status	0.055***	−0.005	−0.052***
	(2.57)	(0.18)	(2.68)
Father-in-law's status	0.088***	−0.084***	−0.013
	(4.05)	(3.05)	(0.66)
R^2	0.075	0.155	0.139
D–W test	1.97	1.99	2.03

Notes: *t*-statistics in parentheses. * = significant at 10 per cent; ** = significant at 5 per cent; *** = significant at 1 per cent.

Source: CRA database.

parental status. Occupational status may have been derived partly from cultural assimilation, but it was also surely at least as likely to have been influenced by the groom's father's occupational status. A childhood exposure to white-collar work, especially entrepreneurship, may have given considerable advantages to the subsequent adult career path.

It is, of course, self-evident that the occupational status of these grooms was determined primarily through various demographic and economic factors not included here, which is why the R^2-figures are so low. However, the purpose of the analysis is not to explain why grooms ended up in these different occupational classes at the time of marriage, but only to examine if cultural assimilation had any significant influence at all. It is therefore the indicators of statistical significance, the *t*-statistics, which give the most important information here. Moreover, the very real constraints of the available evidence need to be remembered. We simply do not have the kind of biographical information required to understand why each groom chose his specific occupation.

Occupation and assimilation

Entrepreneurs

Consider the immigrant entrepreneurs first. The most significant results (with the highest *t*-statistics) are that the immigrant entrepreneurs were from, or married into, relatively advantaged parental backgrounds. The indicators of assimilation were also positively correlated with immigrant entrepreneurship. English literacy in both brides and grooms was strongly associated with entrepreneurial status, as was marrying in one of the more assimilated synagogues. Moreover, entrepreneurs were more likely to marry in those years when immigration was below trend, when the cohort of immigrant grooms had more longer-settled and relatively assimilated men in than normal. Finally, they were more likely to marry English brides.

Given the difficulties of isolating and measuring culture, there is simply no possibility of generating some pure indicator of assimilation. All of the chosen indicators of assimilation here are partial; they are at best only indirect indicators of assimilation. If the analysis only focused on one or two, then any interpretation using English literacy, say, as an indicator of cultural assimilation would have to remain cautious in the extreme. However, because all five indicators are mutually consistent here, it is reasonable to see the results in the table as strong prima facie evidence that the immigrant entrepreneurs were relatively assimilated.

The entrepreneurs were no doubt different from the average immigrant in many other ways not recorded here, but the results from the table show that, for at least the characteristics listed here, they were more like the English Jews than the other immigrants. Furthermore, inspection of the coefficients suggests that their status benefited from assimilation at least as much as from parental advantage.

There is no strong theoretical preference for emphasising either of the indicators of advantage or any of the indicators of assimilation. Arguments can be made in support of all of them. Given, however, that the coefficients for the two indicators of advantage were 0.055 and 0.088, and ranged from 0.051 to 0.101 for the five indicators of assimilation, the suggestion is that, on balance, assimilation was as important as parental advantage in attaining entrepreneurship.

Blue-collars

This interpretation is reinforced when we turn to the blue collar workers in the second column, the vast majority of the immigrants. In contrast to the entrepreneurs, there was an inverse relationship between blue-collar status and the longer-settled grooms. In the peak years of immigration, a relatively high proportion of grooms were from the blue-collar class and in years of relatively low immigration there were relatively few blue-collar grooms. Not only was this the most significant indicator, but it also had the highest coefficient. The blue-collar grooms were disproportionately composed of recent arrivals. The blue-collar workers were therefore relatively unassimilated.

This receives some confirmation when the other indicators of assimilation for the blue collars are considered. Neither they nor their brides were likely to sign the register in English, nor were they likely to marry in the more assimilated synagogues. Moreover, the blue-collar immigrants had no status advantage inherited from their fathers or fathers-in-law. They shared therefore almost the exact opposite of the entrepreneurs' characteristics.

Journeymen

Column three focuses on those who were, for our present purposes, the most important group of immigrant grooms, the journeymen. The table shows that they were assimilated like the entrepreneurs, but that, like the blue-collar workers, they enjoyed no parental advantages.

Like the entrepreneurs, journeyman grooms were more likely to marry in those years when there was a relatively high share of the more assimilated, longer-settled immigrants marrying. This, in fact, was the most significant indicator of assimilation and, with the highest coefficient, the strongest. Journeymen were also likely to marry brides with English literacy as well as have the marriages solemnised in the more assimilated synagogues. In contrast to the entrepreneurs, however, they were unlikely to marry English brides and, despite a relatively high 76 per cent of journeymen grooms signing the register in English, the relationship was statistically insignificant. Overall, though, they were relatively assimilated men, considerably more so than the blue-collar workers but not quite as much as the immigrant entrepreneurs. Moreover, whereas the immigrant entrepreneurs benefited from relatively advantaged parental backgrounds, the immigrant journeymen did not. Neither their fathers not their brides' fathers were likely to have held white-collar occupations.

If the immigrant journeymen were assimilating those allegedly anti-entrepreneurial English cultural values, this is what would be expected.

They were not entrepreneurs but, in aping the English Jews, they were more like the entrepreneurs than the blue-collars. Journeymen grooms were more likely to have spent a longer period in Britain between arrival and marriage than the average immigrant and were therefore both less likely to marry in the unassimilated immigrant synagogues and were more likely to be marrying a bride who had also spent sufficient time in Britain since arrival to have acquired basic literacy. While entrepreneurs tended to marry English and journeymen only immigrant brides, the principal difference between them was, nevertheless, not assimilation but parental background. In a word, the entrepreneurs had begun adult life with more advantages, either from their own parental background or from being able to marry into an advantaged parental background. The journeymen, in common with the rest of the blue-collar workers, carried no marks of privilege.

Conclusion

The evidence from the Jewish marriage records suggests that the relatively assimilated immigrants who had arrived in Britain with, or married into, an advantaged parental background were more likely to become entrepreneurs. The assimilated immigrants who had arrived without an advantaged background, and were unable to marry into one, were more likely to become journeymen. Those who were both unassimilated and disadvantaged were more likely to be blue-collar workers.

Entrepreneurship remained both the most remunerative and the highest-status occupation open to the Jewish immigrants in both Britain and the United States. Unlike in New York, however, the assimilated immigrants in London had an alternative route to a higher occupational status. Because entrepreneurship was costly (at the very least in terms of time and responsibility), the less-advantaged assimilated grooms in London were much more likely to avoid it and become journeymen.

Cultural assimilation therefore had an important influence in Jewish immigrant occupational status in New York and London and so played a role in the two immigrant labour markets. The relatively sluggish entrepreneurial response of the Jews in London compared with New York can be interpreted largely as a response to a combination of both the underlying profits and the importance of the acquisition of status in the two immigrant societies, status which was shaped by the two host countries' cultural values.

Part III
Enterprise and Culture in Britain

8
Entrepreneurship, Culture and British 'Declinism'

Turn-of-the-century Jewish immigrant journeymen in London's East End were more assimilated than the average immigrant, whom, in terms of background, they otherwise resembled. Because the two streams of immigration to London and New York were so similar, and because so many more Jewish immigrants went into entrepreneurship in New York despite falling profits, this elementary empirical finding carries quite considerable implications.

First, while it seems safe to conclude that the Jewish immigrant journeymen had assimilated more of the host English culture than most, what is less obvious is exactly what that English culture was. Second, if the immigrant journeymen were more assimilated, this confirms that the Jews assimilated host country cultural values. Third, assimilation influenced their labour market activity and with lasting repercussions. Fourth, this process of assimilation and occupational selection may well highlight a more general phenomenon of economic agents responding to more than simple economic forces, a generalisation that could be an important source for reinterpreting British twentieth-century economic performance.

Working-class craft culture in England

The cultural environments the immigrants found themselves in hardly exposed them to any 'pure' form of English culture, or, for those in New York, American. New York's Lower East Side and London's East End were hardly representative locales of some broader American and British cultures. The immigrants settled into very specific environments and so encountered very particular forms of native culture.

127

In New York, for instance, the Jewish immigrants would scarcely have had any contact with non-Jewish, native-born Americans. To them, American culture was therefore a curious amalgam of stereotypes, from the quaint to the crass, filtered and mediated through the earlier immigrants' eyes and the more established Jewish community. Like a Chinese whisper, the stereotypes of American culture picked up by the Jewish immigrants in New York may well have been crude and peculiar to American eyes, they may even have been wrong. But their legitimacy in immigrant eyes depended on their congruence with some wider and easily recognised ideal of what it meant to be an American.[1] The Jewish immigrants in London's East End were faced with interpreting a different set of values. This form of English culture may have suffered less from successive rounds of immigrant-inspired corruption; the Jewish immigrants in London had, after all, more frequent contact with the native-born working classes around them. Both direct and indirect contact with English cultural values must have presented to the immigrants some notions of the nature of Englishness. And it was to this East End working-class view of the world they began to conform.

While neither of these stereotypes of American and British culture facing the respective immigrant communities can be defined with any completeness, it is surely beyond controversy to suggest that around the world late-nineteenth-century America stood for self-help, individual initiative and entrepreneurship. British, and especially English, culture, by contrast, stood for the elevation of a time-honoured reliability of custom and law, for the importance of yeoman stock, and the dignity of the worker. While the Victorian gentry invented an earlier rural mythology, British workers (like Beatrice Potter's English tailors) were sentimental about pre-industrial autonomy, skill and craft.

This broad and inchoate identification of a sub-set of American and British cultural values is all that can be inferred from the discovery that the more assimilated immigrants became journeymen in London. No more complete definition of cultural values is possible. Yet, this is a start. Through the use of a control population in what is otherwise an unremarkable social science experiment, the conclusion here must be that, compared with America, British culture was relatively anti-entrepreneurial.

For economic historians interested in the merits of the late Victorian entrepreneur, this conclusion is nevertheless somewhat perplexing, because the results indicate little about the values of the entrepreneurial elite but a lot about the strength of a working-class identification with a pre-industrial ideal of skill and autonomy. In the broader debate on the merits of Britain's entrepreneurs, the justification of so detailed a historical scrutiny of such a small proportion of the population has been Britain's relative economic decline. As Britain slipped down the world rankings of economic powers, the search for scapegoats intensified and British business leaders have borne the brunt of a tidal wave of critical comment.

And not without reason. The most obvious proximate cause of British industry's relatively poor performance throughout most of the twentieth century has been under-investment. Explaining why British entrepreneurs elected to invest less in new machinery than their equivalents in USA, Germany, France, Japan and so on, is, however, less straightforward. The most common explanations range from allegations of an under-educated and technologically illiterate management, to a gross disregard of investment in favour of maintaining short-term profitability and dividend payments.[2]

The presence of so many Jewish immigrant journeymen in London's East End before 1914 provides little support for any of the existing cultural schools of 'declinism'. It does suggest, however, that the cultural context in which business decisions were being made needs to be taken more fully into account. Culture did influence labour market choices. Before going on to generalise further about how the strength of a working-class craft culture may have influenced Britain's twentieth-century growth record, two other conclusions need to be raised.

Jewish assimilation and Jewish history

Jewish historians are increasingly interested in how the Jews of the Diaspora related to their host societies – politically, economically and culturally. There were profound differences between the Jewish communities in Europe before 1914. Rubinstein, for example, has recently emphasised how those European economies where the Jews numerically dominated the commercial elite were the nations which fell victim to the grossest forms of twentieth-century anti-Semitism.[3] The Jewish merchants and entrepreneurs in Britain and America were merely isolated exotica by comparison. While Rubinstein has not yet proposed any mechanism linking Jewish commercial over-representation and anti-Semitism, it is a simple matter of historical fact that Britain and America have, on the whole, been relatively peaceful societies for the Jewish immigrants and their descendants over the last century or so.

Had Britain and America retained their 1880 share of world Jewry, this would have been a happy but nevertheless trivial footnote in

Jewish history. The demographic revolution of mass migration and Holocaust has meant, however, that in the space of two generations world Jewry's centre of gravity pitched permanently westwards. It was like the Mosaic Exodus in reverse; rather than the faithless first generation perishing in the sand, those who left when they could lived, while those who remained were slaughtered in the desert of Hitler's Europe.

For Jewish historians, the assimilation of American and British cultural values is central to understanding modern Jewish identity. As the evidence here suggests, this assimilation was both rapid and pronounced. Of greater importance, however, is that its consequences were long-lasting. The occupational advances attained by the Jewish immigrants in New York by 1905 over those in London have been sustained throughout the twentieth century.[4]

Clearly, far more detailed research is required to grasp fully the nature of long-term Jewish social mobility in both nations, but it appears very likely that the assimilation of late-nineteenth-century values by the first immigrants has led to long-term differences in two of the world's largest Jewish population centres. The congruence of modern Jewish identity and middle-class status may therefore be one that is historically contingent on the American background of many. Had turn-of-the-century American conditions been different – had the clothing industry migrated entirely to factories, for example – then late-twentieth-century Jewish social status might have been very different.

Evidence of cultural assimilation has profound consequences for the Jews of today. The state of Israel's commitment to guarantee citizenship to any Jew throughout the world, for example, implies that Jewish identity is paramount, that any identity with other nations is both partial and of a lesser status. While this remains a fundamental tenet of Zionist philosophy, its scientific justification remains unclear. Twentieth-century assimilation into mainstream British and American cultures by Jews has been unrelenting, with concerns rising that the Jewish identity of many has weakened.[5] The evidence here suggests that some assimilation is inevitable, indeed desirable. And while this outsider is wary of overstepping the mark, further research on Jewish and other ethnic assimilation would be a valuable contribution to the understanding of culture in the social sciences.

Culture in economics

Culture matters in economic development. It is the assimilation of British and American cultural values that explains most of the divergence in entrepreneurial outcomes among the Jewish immigrants in London and New York. While the evidence does not stretch as far as to show the lifetime careers of the immigrants in both cities, it is most likely that most of those who chose self-employment and those who preferred craft status continued in their trajectories. The two groups experienced different lifetime earnings, different life experiences. The culturally influenced lower level of entrepreneurship among the Jews in Britain therefore left a long legacy. In sum, culture mattered to the economic welfare of the Jewish communities of America and Britain.

This is challenging not because of the result – many economists now share the same view, that culture is important – but because of the puzzle of how to incorporate culture into mainstream economic thought. In a quantitative discipline, the difficulties of estimating numerical values for what is only a vaguely defined variable are not to be dismissed. Hopefully that task will nevertheless commence. The potential benefits are really very significant. As the débâcle of the post-Soviet economies illustrates, a more nuanced and culturally sensitive policy regime may be able to avoid the excesses of poverty, inequality and gangsterism emerging there from the imposition of facile free market prescriptions.

British culture and 'declinism'

The main purpose of the book has been to discover whether the British culture of *circa* 1914 was in any way anti-entrepreneurial. Despite the general popularity of a culturalist interpretation of British relative decline, most specialists have been wary, disinclined to opt for a hazily defined and poorly specified explanation. Yet the evidence here shows that Britain, or London's East End at the very least, did have cultural values that placed barriers to working-class entrepreneurial advancement.

There are two avenues in which these results might fruitfully be generalised. First, the evidence suggests that working-class entrepreneurship in Britain was less than in America because of the attractions of the existing craft culture. With less bottom-up entrepreneurship, innovation was less than it might have been, and so, ultimately, British economic growth slower. Because British culture valued a more conservative method of work and organisation, the economy missed some of this Schumpeterian type of entrepreneurship that other economies, notably the American, were enjoying. There may be some value in future studies trying to explore this counterfactual. But it must also be emphasised that recent studies of working-class entrepreneurship in the United States have exposed as myth the Horatio Alger ideal.[6]

A far more appealing route for generalising the evidence of craft conservatism is to reinterpret the history of British industrial relations, recasting the story not only as one where the relative political power of the core institutions mattered, but as one where the mindsets of the key participants were seeped in culture. While it is impossible to do justice to such an agenda here, a brief case-study of how craft defensiveness may have influenced one British industry's woes may be illustrative.

For the 'declinists' among British economic historians, the motor car industry is the case of poor British management *par excellence*. Not only has the industry been one of the most important sectors in the economy, but the sheer extent of its fall from grace has appeared impossible to understand without referring to the bloody-minded culpability of workers, managers and owners.[7]

'Declinism' and the British motor car industry

A brief thumbnail sketch of the industry's history would begin with its late-nineteenth-century origins in a multiplicity of small cycle and carriage manufacturers, before rapid expansion in the interwar years, Britain becoming Europe's leading car producer throughout the 1930s. This edge was retained after 1945 when, briefly, Britain became the world's leading exporter of motor vehicles in the early 1950s. While this arose more from American producers' concern with reasserting control of their domestic market than British producers' global competitiveness, it represents a benchmark against which the subsequent decline can be traced.

A newly built German industry overtook British output by 1956, the French industry by the early 1960s, and the Italian by the early 1970s. After nearly thirty years of relatively slow growth, British output peaked in 1972. Hasty mergers and the loss of export markets in the 1960s were succeeded by the collapse in domestic demand in the 1970s, with bankruptcy and *de facto* nationalisation in 1975. Under government tutelage, the industry did not recover its health before ultimately contracting into a constellation of relatively small subsidiaries of the global automobile multinationals.

Considerable gnashing of teeth has accompanied this collapse. Studies of its causes are therefore highly charged and often strongly politicised. Some consensus on the determinants of decline has emerged nevertheless, with postwar government economic policy high on everyone's list. This can only be a partial answer, however, because other nations faced equally difficult macroeconomic environments and yet retained their motor car industries.[8]

Where the British industry appears to have been exceptional is in its degree of underinvestment. The capital intensity of the British car industry fell behind all others, which led to lower productivity and reduced profitability. Even the most optimistic interpretation of this strategy agrees that ultimately it led to a technological cul-de-sac.[9]

While the problem of underinvestment may be readily identifiable, its explanation is less straightforward. Once more the usual candidates step forward: poor management, short-sighted owners and Luddite unions. The links between these explanations of corporate failure and British culture emphasise the influence of overbearing owners and senior managers, their reluctance to embrace new practices, as well as the covert hostility underpinning industrial relations.[10]

Specialists have been reluctant to incorporate culture into their analysis of the motor car industry because of the difficulty in identifying exactly how culture's influence could have been so malign. Discovering that assimilated Jews were more likely to become journeymen in London and entrepreneurs in New York does, however, make a contribution to this notable *cause célèbre* because it acknowledges that working-class culture influenced the British labour market. We might generalise further that the presence of a strongly held craft culture in this, the pre-eminent of mass production industries, may have led to British firms incurring higher costs to retaining managerial control.

Such a hypothesis comes very close to one influential thesis. Lewchuk explained much of the decline of the British car industry by reference to the resistance by workers in British car factories to management control. He emphasised that even before the 1920s worker resistance meant managers were never fully in control of the flow of production. Working practices enshrined this standoff, with managers unwilling to invest in an uncooperative workforce. Technology therefore became dated and, regardless of the skill and flexibility of the workforce, ultimately this proved fatal. When the senior managers finally realised the limits of the low-tech, flexible route of car production, it was too late. The postwar sellers' market collapsed and British producers discovered their lack of competitiveness. After decades of following a particular pattern of work organisation, after years of underinvestment, the British car industry folded quickly in the mid-1970s.[11]

While Lewchuk's thesis has attracted its critics, incorporating the notion of some additional costs arising from a strong craft culture does lend weight to his view of the industry's long-term demise.[12] Craft cultural values were obviously not the whole story, but they may well be an important and hitherto under-emphasised thread.

The obsessive concern with demarcation and individual worker rights seen not only in the British motor car industry but throughout Britain's industrial landscape in much of the postwar period may well have been an inherited yet corrupted version of the craft culture borne in pre-industrial times. Under conditions of government protection, such an inappropriate set of values was allowed to capture the mindset of generations of workers and, especially, their more articulate representatives, contributing to the collapse of much of British industry.[13]

Conclusion

This reinterpretation of Britain's twentieth-century experience has emphasised how the grafting of culture onto an otherwise conventional explanation may aid our understanding of economic decline. It suggests that the cultural environment underpinning British industrial relations was a key factor and needs to be fully incorporated into the study of management–union negotiations. This cultural environment may have been fraught with misunderstanding. For owners and managers, making a profit involved embracing new technology and deskilling work, yet workers wanted to retain an oldfashioned and inappropriate status, which machinery threatened. In the ensuing impasse investment failed to take place, jobs changed little, and ultimately both owners and workers lost out to foreign competition. Such a scenario could be replicated in many industries in Britain.

Future detailed case-study research of specific industries may be able to highlight the mechanisms linking workers' cultural conservatism to under-investment and declining sectoral competitiveness. The purpose of this study was rather to offer an empirical proof of culture's role in labour market activity. Further studies may be able to replicate the methodology here and expand the universe of nations and periods for which some measure of the impact of culture on labour can be derived. The difficulties of identifying relevant control populations, as well as sufficient data, are not to be downplayed, however.

It remains to be seen exactly how culture influences different kinds of economic activity. But economic historians and economists will need to address such mechanisms in their quest to better understand the way the world works.

Notes

1 Culture and Economic Behaviour

1. For classic accounts see, E. Jones *The European Miracle*, and idem, *Growth Recurring*.
2. The 'bounded rationality' school notwithstanding. See H. Simon, 'Rationality as Process and Product of Thought', *American Economic Review*, 68 (1978).
3. G. Hofstede, *Culture's Consequence: International Differences in Work-Related Values*.
4. M. Granovetter, 'Economic Action and Social Structure: the Problem of Embeddedness', *American Journal of Sociology*, 91 (1985); and J. Hall, *Powers and Liberties*.
5. G. Akerloff, 'A Theory of Social Custom, of Which Unemployment May be One Consequence', *Quarterly Journal of Economics*, 95 (1980); A. Atkinson, 'The Distribution of Income in the UK and OECD Countries in the Twentieth Century', *Oxford Review of Economic Policy*, 15 (1999); J. Muellbauer, 'The Assessment: Consumer Expenditure', *Oxford Review of Economic Policy*, 10 (1994); T. Sowell, *Migrations and Cultures: a Worldview*; M. Casson, *The Economics of Business Culture: Game Theory, Transaction Costs, and Economic Performance*.
6. E. Schlicht, *On Custom in the Economy*.
7. K. Polanyi, *The Great Transformation*, first insisted on markets being treated as culturally derived institutions, although was clearly way off the mark in claiming that they were a relatively recent invention. See K. Moore and D. Lewis, *Birth of the Multinational: 2000 Years of Ancient Business History – from Ashur to Augustus*, for an interesting recent contribution.
8. M. Casson and A. Godley (eds), *Cultural Factors in Economic Growth*; M. Casson, 'Culture as an Economic Asset', in A. Godley and O. Westall (eds), *Business History and Business Culture*; and F. Fukuyama, *Trust, The Social Virtues and Creation of Prosperity*.
9. A. Greif, 'Cultural Beliefs and the Organization of Society: a Historical and Theoretical Reflection on Collectivist and Individualist Societies', *Journal of Political Economy*, 102 (1994).
10. The allusion is, of course, to M. Weber, *The Protestant Ethic and the Spirit of Capitalism*.
11. For an excellent treatment of cultural change, see E. Jones, 'Culture and its Relationship to Economic Change', *Journal of Institutional and Theoretical Economics*, 151 (1995).
12. D. McCloskey, 'Bourgeois Virtue and the History of P and S', *Journal of Economic History*, 58 (1998).
13. A. Godley and D. Ross, 'Banks, Networks and Small Firm Finance'; and A. Godley, 'Jewish Soft Loan Societies in New York and London, 1880–1914', both in *Business History*, 38 (1996); T. Corley, 'How Quakers Coped with Business Success: Quaker Industrialists 1860–1914', in

135

D. Jeremy (ed.), *Business and Religion in Britain*; and A. Prior and M. Kirby, 'The Society of Friends and the Family Firm', *Business History*, 35 (1993). More generally, see C. Muldrew, *The Economy of Obligation: the Culture of Credit and Social Relations in Early Modern England*.

14. M. Abramovitz, 'Catching Up, Forging Ahead, and Falling Behind', *Journal of Economic History*, 46 (1986); D. Landes, *The Wealth and Poverty of Nations: Why Are Some So Rich and Others So Poor?*, esp. pp. 215 ff.; McCloskey, 'Bourgeois Virtue'; P. Temin, 'Is It Kosher to Talk about Culture?', *Journal of Economic History*, 57 (1997). These authors are not chosen at random. They are all recent presidents of the American Economic History Association, and the articles are their Presidential addresses.

15. Cited in P. Kennedy, *The Rise and Fall of the Great Powers*, table 16, p. 258.

16. P. Bairoch, 'International Industrialization Levels from 1750 to 1980', *Journal of European Economic History*, 11 (1982); see table 8, p. 292, table 11, p. 299, and table 2, p. 275, table 10, p. 296, table 13, p. 304.

17. D. Aldcroft, 'The Entrepreneur and the British Economy, 1870–1914', *Economic History Review*, XVII (1964), esp. pp. 121–7; A. Levine, *Industrial Retardation in Britain, 1880–1914*, esp. ch. 2, pp. 31–42 and pp. 145–150; H. Habakkuk, *American and British Technology in the Nineteenth Century*, chs V and VI, pp. 132–220.

18. D. Landes, *The Unbound Prometheus: Technological Change and Industrial Development in Western Europe from 1750 to the Present*, p. 337.

19. M. Wiener, *English Culture and the Decline of the Industrial Spirit, 1850–1980*, p. 158.

20. G. Allen, *The British Disease*, pp. 30–50; R. Dahrendorf, *On Britain*, pp. 18–50; S. Brittan, 'How British Is the British Sickness?', *Journal of Law and Economics*, XXI (1978).

21. Keith Joseph, 'Preface', in Samuel Smiles, *Self-Help* (1986 edition), p. 11; also see G. Bannock, *Britain in the 1980s: Enterprise Reborn?*, pp. 16–19. The current government's emphasis on 'modernisation' springs from the same fount.

22. D. Aldcroft, (ed.), *The Development of British Industry and Foreign Competition, 1875–1914*, esp. pp. 11–36; C. Wilson, 'Economy and Society in Late Victorian Britain', *Economic History Review*, XVIII (1965).

23. R. Floud, 'Britain 1860–1914: a Survey', in R. Floud and D. McCloskey (eds), *The Economic History of Britain since 1700*; and S. Pollard, 'Entrepreneurship, 1870–1914', in R. Floud and D. McCloskey (eds), *The Economic History of Britain since 1700*, 2nd edn. J. Williamson, 'Globalization, Convergence and History', *Journal of Economic History*, 56 (1996).

24. J. Williamson, 'Globalization, Convergence and History'.

25. N. Crafts, S. Leybourne, and T. Mills, 'The Climacteric in Late Victorian Britain and France: a Reappraisal of the Evidence', *Journal of Applied Econometrics*, 4 (1989); C. Feinstein, 'What really happened to real wages?: Trends in Wages, Prices, and Productivity in the United Kingdom, 1880–1913', *Economic History Review*, XLIII (1990); and Feinstein, 'New Estimates of Average Earnings in the United Kingdom, 1880–1913', *Economic History Review*, XLIII (1990); S. Broadberry, *The Productivity Race: British Manufacturing in International Perspective, 1850–1990*.

26. S. Broadberry, 'Anglo-German Productivity Differences 1870–1990: a Sectoral Analysis', *European Review of Economic History*, 1 (1997); idem,

'Manufacturing and the Convergence Hypothesis: What the Long Run Data Show', *Journal of Economic History*, 53 (1993). For an optimistic view of specific services see W. Rubinstein, *Capitalism, Culture and Decline in Britain, 1750–1990*; and C. Lee, 'Regional Growth and Structural Change in Victorian Britain', *Economic History Review*, XXXIII (1981).

27. T. Orsagh, 'Progress in Iron and Steel: 1870–1913' *Comparative Studies in Society and History*, III (1961), citation from p. 230. Partly cited in P. Payne, *British Entrepreneurship in the Nineteenth Century*; 2nd edn, p. 43.

28. D. McCloskey (ed.), *Essays on a Mature Economy: Britain after 1840* (London, 1971), esp. the chapter by P. Lindert and K. Trace, 'Yardsticks for Victorian Entrepreneurs'; also L. Sandberg, 'The Entrepreneur and Technological Change', in Floud and McCloskey, *Economic History*.

29. S. Tolliday and J. Zeitlin (eds), *The Power to Manage? Employers and Industrial Relations in Comparative Historical Perspective*.

30. M. Olson, *The Rise and Decline of Nations: Economic Growth, Stagflation and Social Rigidities*; B. Elbaum and W. Lazonick (eds), *The Decline of the British Economy*; M. Kirby, 'Institutional Rigidities and Economic Decline: reflections on the British experience', *Economic History Review*, 45 (1992); and Pollard, 'Entrepreneurship'.

31. Olson, *Rise and Decline*, p. 141; O. Westall, 'The Competitive Environment of British Business, 1850–1914', in M. Kirby and M. Rose (eds), *Business Enterprise in Modern Britain from the Eighteenth to the Twentieth Century*; W. Lazonick and W. Mass, 'The British Cotton Industry and International Competitive Advantage: the State of the Debates', *Business History*, 32 (1990); Lazonick, *Business Organization and the Myth of the Market Economy*; idem, *Competitive Advantage on the Shop Floor*. R. Church, 'Ossified or Dynamic? Structure, Markets and the Competitive Process in the British Business System of the Nineteenth Century', *Business History*, 42 (2000).

32. Kirby, 'Institutional Rigidities', p. 654. For an outstanding recent overview see G.G. Jones, 'Great Britain: Big business, management, and competitiveness in twentieth century Britain', in A.D. Chandler, F. Amatori and T. Hikino (eds), *Big Business and the Wealth of Nations*.

33. I omit capital here simply because entrepreneurship and capital are often conflated.

34. M. Casson, *The Entrepreneur: an Economic Theory*.

35. F. Knight, *Risk, Uncertainty and Profit*, p. 231.

36. J. Schumpeter, *Business Cycles: a Theoretical, Historical and Statistical Analysis of the Capitalist Process*, vol. I, p. 84.

37. J. Cantwell, 'Historical Trends in International Patterns of Technological Innovation', in J. Foreman-Peck (ed.), *New Perspectives on the Late Victorian Economy: Essays in Quantitative Economic History, 1860–1914*.

38. Schumpeter, *Business Cycles*, p. 103.

39. The UK Government measures the level of entrepreneurship in the economy by (a) the number of VAT registrations and (b) the number of self-employed persons in the economy. Jeremy Godfrey, Private Secretary to Lord Young, Department of Trade and Industry, letter to author, dated June 6, 1988.

40. G. Bodanski, *et al.*, 'Evidence for an Environmental Effect in the Aetiology of Insulin Dependent Diabetes in a Transmigratory Population', *British Medical Journal*, 304 (1992), p. 1020.

41. Irish emigration to the USA was of a far more permanent nature. See J. Gould, 'European Inter-Continental Emigration. The Road Home: Return Migration from the USA', *Journal of European Economic History*, 9 (1980), p. 73 n.
42. Gould, 'Return Migration'.
43. Much commented on, of course. See the pernicious W. Sombart, *Jews and Modern Capitalism*; as well as E. Bonacich, 'A Theory of Middlemen Minorities', *American Sociological Review*, 38 (1973); W. Rubinstein, 'Entrepreneurial Minorities: a Typology', in Godley and Casson, *Economic Factors*; H. Pollins, 'Immigrants and Minorities – the Outsiders in Business', *Immigrants and Minorities* 8 (1989); and N. Gross, 'Entrepreneurship of Religious and Ethnic Minorities', *Zeitschrift für Unternehmensgeschichte*, 64 (1992).

2   Jewish History and East European Jewish Mass Migration

1. The eminent Jewish historian Jacob Neusner described this view as emanating from the Judaism of Holocaust and redemption, with therefore a secular rather than a religious motivation.
2. The literature on Jewish history is fairly extensive. I have relied particularly on A. Ruppin, *The Jews in the Modern World*; S. Grayzel *A History of the Jews*; N. Glazer, *American Judaism*; and P. Johnson, *A History of the Jews*.
3. E. Mendelsohn, *The Jews of East Central Europe between the World Wars*.
4. Ruppin, *Jews in the Modern World*, ch. IV, pp. 45–58; V. Lipman, *A History of the Jews in Britain since 1858*, pp. 45–6; Lipman, *Social History of the Jews in England, 1850–1950*, p. 87.
5. N. Barou, *The Jews in Work and Trade: a World Survey*, p. 3.
6. Z. Szajkowski, 'How the Mass Migration to America began', *Jewish Social Studies*, IV (1942), esp. pp. 295–7 and 304–6; idem, 'The European Attitudes to East European Jewish Immigration (1881–93)', *Publications of the American Jewish Historical Society*, XLI (1951–2); L. Gartner, *The Jewish Immigrant in England, 1870–1914*, pp. 41–5; J. Frankel, *Prophecy and Politics: Socialism, Nationalism and the Russian Jews, 1862–1917*, pp. 49–132.
7. C. Russell and H. Lewis, *The Jew in London*, p. 14.
8. H. Adler, 'Jewish Life and Labour in East London', in H. Llewellyn Smith (ed.), *The New Survey of London Life and Labour*, vol. VI, 'Survey of Social Conditions (2), The Western Area (Text)', pp. 268–98, see table V, p. 295. Also for a discussion on relative social mobility in USA and UK see W. Rubinstein, *A History of the Jews in the English Speaking World: Great Britain*, pp. 106–8, 159 and 225–8.
9. Adler, 'Jewish Life and Labour', p. 291. Also see *New Survey*, vol. II, 'The London Industries', ch. V, 'The Clothing Trades', pp. 251–349.
10. Barou, *Jews in Work and Trade*, p. 7. E. Krausz, 'The Economic and Social Structure of Anglo-Jewry', in J. Gould and S. Esh (eds), *Jewish Life in Modern Britain*, suggests that this is the 'lowest estimate', p. 28.
11. Krausz, 'Economic and Social Structure', p. 31.
12. A. Godley, 'Leaving the East End: Regional Mobility among East European Jews in London, 1880–1914', in A. Kershen (ed.), *London: A Promised Land?*

Also see Rubinstein, *History of the Jews*, pp. 106–8 and 159; and I. Feinstein, 'The New Community 1880–1918', in Feinstein (ed.), *Three Centuries of Anglo-Jewish History*, pp. 115–6.

13. Max Cohen, 'The Jew in Business', *American Hebrew*, 22 May, 1891, 47, pp. 50–53. Of course these firms were mostly started by earlier immigrating German Jews.

14. A. Cahan, 'The Russian Jew in the United States', in C. Bernheimer (ed.), *The Russian Jew in the United States*, p. 37. Also see I. Rubinov, 'Economic and Industrial Condition (A) New York', in Bernheimer, *Russian Jew*.

15. T. Kessner, 'The Selective Filter of Ethnicity', in D. Berger (ed.), *The Legacy of Jewish Migration: 1881 and Its Impact*, esp. pp. 172, 178; also idem, *The Golden Door: Italian and Jewish Mobility in New York City, 1880–1915*, pp. 179–80, 195–6.

16. P. Johnson, *A History of the Modern World*, pp. 203–7.

17. B. Hendrik, *The Jews in America*, pp. 108, 169–70, 171.

18. Discussed in H. Feingold, 'Investing in Themselves: the Harvard Case and the Origins of the Third American-Jewish Commercial Elite', *American Jewish Historical Quarterly*, LXXVII (1988).

19. Editors of *Fortune, Jews in America*, p. 20.

20. J. Goldthorpe, *Social Mobility and Class Structure in Modern Britain*, chs 1 and 8; D. Glass (ed.), *Social Mobility in Britain*, ch. 8; T. Kessner, *The Golden Door: Italian and Jewish Immigrant Mobility in New York City, 1880–1915*, p. 171. ch. III S. Thernstrom, *The Other Bostonians: Poverty and Progress in the American Metropolis, 1880–1970*, chs 6 and 7; E. Krausz, 'Occupation and Social Advancement in Anglo-Jewry', *Jewish Journal of Sociology*, IV (1962), pp. 82–90; A. Miles, 'How Open Was Nineteenth Century British Society: Social Mobility and Equality of Opportunity, 1839–1914?', in A. Miles and D. Vincent (eds), *Building European Society: Occupational Change and Social Mobility in Europe, 1860–1940*.

21. N. Reich, 'The Economic Structure of Modern Jewry', in L. Finkelstein (ed.), *The Jews, Their History, Culture and Religion*, vol. II, p. 1251.

22. H. Pollins, *Economic History of the Jews in England*, p. 240.

23. Lipman, *Social History*, ch. 8, pp. 164–84.

24. Examples in S. Aris, *The Jews in Business*, ch. 6–9; Lipman, *Social History*, pp. 172–5; Kessner, *Golden Door*, pp. 86–99; Feingold, 'Investing'.

25. Kessner, *Golden Door*, p. 65.

26. E. Sigsworth, *Montague Burton, A Tailor of Taste*; G. Rees, *St. Michael: A History of Marks and Spencer*; and Aris, *Jews in Business*, for Britain. B. Sarachek, 'Jewish American Entrepreneurs', *Journal of Economic History*, XL (1980).

27. A. Kershen, 'Morris Cohen and the Origins of the Women's Wholesale Clothing Industry in the East End', *Textile History*, 28 (1997); A. Godley, 'Immigrant Entrepreneurs and the Emergence of London's East End as an Industrial District', *London Journal*, 21 (1996); and A. Godley, 'Comparative Labour Productivity in the British and American Clothing Industries, 1850–1950', *Textile History*, 28 (1997).

28. H.S. Goldstein (ed.), *Forty Years of Struggle for a Principle: The Biography of Harry Fischel*.

3   Statistics of Anglo-Jewry and the Synagogue Marriage Records, 1880–1914

1. L.P. Gartner, 'Notes on the Statistics of Jewish Immigration', *Jewish Social Studies*, 22 (1960), citation p. 102; V.D. Lipman, *Social History of the Jews in England, 1850–1950*, esp. pp. 85–100, 141–4 and 160–3; and idem, *a History of the Jews in Britain since 1858*, for a more recent overview.
2. A. Godley, 'Enterprise and Culture: Jewish Immigrants in London and New York, 1880–1914' (unpublished PhD thesis, LSE, 1993), pp. 46–50.
3. See for example the studies in J. Frankel and S. J. Zipperstein (eds), *Assimilation and Community: The Jews in Nineteenth Century Europe*.
4. N. Green, 'A Tale of Three Cities: Immigrant Jews in New York, London and Paris, 1870–1914', in A. Newman and S. Massil (eds), *Patterns of Migration, 1850–1914*, p. 86.
5. E.A. Wrigley (ed.), *Nineteenth Century Society*; and C.H. Lee, *British Regional Employment Statistics*, give good summaries of the general problems when using the population censuses.
6. Gartner, 'Notes'; and J. Garrard, *The English and Immigration 1880–1910*, appendix I, 'Estimating Immigration'.
7. 'Report on the Volume and Effects of Recent Immigration from Eastern Europe into the United Kingdom', P.P. 1894, LXVIII, p. 15.
8. Gartner, 'Notes'; and Lipman, *Social History*, pp. 89–90, citation p. 90.
9. B. Gainer, *The Alien Invasion: The Origins of the Aliens Act of 1905*, ch. 1 on the anti-immigration lobby; S. Rosenbaum, 'A Contribution to the Study of the Vital and Other Statistics of the Jews in the United Kingdom', *Journal of the Royal Statistical Society*, LXVIII (1905), p. 540. Rosenbaum (he later anglicised his name to Rowson) was the first chairman of the Statistical Committee of the Jewish Health Organisation, according to H. Trachtenberg, 'Estimate of the Jewish Population of London in 1929', *Journal of the Royal Statistical Society*, XCVI (1933), p. 96.
10. M. L. King and D. L. Magnuson, 'Perspectives on Historical US census Undercounts', *Social Science History*, 19 (1995).
11. E. J. Thompson, 'The 1991 Census of Population in England and Wales', *Journal of the Royal Statistical Society*, ser. A, 158 (1995), esp. pp. 214–5 on the estimated 9 per cent underenumeration of young men. G. R. Glover, 'Sex Ratio Errors in Census Data', *British Medical Journal*, 307 (1993); M. Leese *et al.*, 'Adjusting for underenumeration in the 1991 census', ibid., 311 (1995), which gives the figure of 30 per cent, p. 394; and F. A. Majeed *et al.*, 'Using data from the 1991 census', ibid., 310 (1995), I am indebted to Dr Sonia Johnson of the Institute of Psychiatry for drawing my attention to this.
12. S. M. Dubnow, *History of the Jews in Russia and Poland*.
13. Cited in Gainer, *Alien Invasion*, ch. 1; also see Garrard, 'Estimating Immigration'.
14. D. Rau, 'The 1891 Census in Spitalfields: a Source for Migration', in Newman and Massil, *Patterns of Migration*, p. 284, on how information was gathered from East End Jews.
15. On the administrative relations between Jews and the state in Russia see M. Stanislawski, *Tsar Nicholas I and the Jews: the Transformation of Jewish*

Society in Russia, 1825–1855, esp. pp. 133–7; and J. D. Klier, *Imperial Russia's Jewish Question, 1855–1881*, esp. pp. 8–9, 222–44.

16. Majeed *et al.*, '1991 census', p. 1513.

17. F. Massarik, 'New Approaches to the Study of the American Jew', *Jewish Journal of Sociology*, 8 (1966); and S. Waterman and B. Kosmin, 'Mapping an Unenumerated Ethnic Population – Jews in London', *Ethnic and Racial Studies*, 10 (1986).

18. S. C. Watkins and A. S. London, 'Personal Names and Cultural Change: a Study of the Naming Patterns of Italians and Jews in the United States in 1910', *Social Science History*, 18 (1994).

19. J. Gjerde and A. McCants, 'Fertility, Marriage and Culture: Demographic Processes among Norwegian Immigrants to the Rural Middle West', *Journal of Economic History*, 55 (1995), find a strong relationship between cultural assimilation and fertility.

20. See, for example, S. Haberman and M. Schmool, 'Estimates of the British Jewish Population 1984–88', *Journal of the Royal Statistical Society*, ser. A, 158 (1995), esp. p. 548. For earlier examples using the burial-statistics-presumed-death-rate methodology see Trachtenberg, 'Estimate'; and M. Kantorowitsch, 'Estimate of the Jewish Population of London in 1929–1933', *Journal of the Royal Statistical Society*, XCIX (1936).

21. J. Jacobs, *Studies in Jewish Statistics. Social, Vital and Anthropometric*, esp. p. 20.

22. *Jewish Year Book*, 1 (1897), Jewish statistics, pp. 27–8; ibid., 8 (1904), citation, p. 237.

23. Rosenbaum, 'Statistics of the Jews', esp. pp. 539–40; also *Jewish Year Book*, 7 (1903), pp. 205–6.

24. C. Booth (ed.), *Life and Labour of the People of London*; D. Feldman, *Englishmen and Jews: Social Relations and Political Culture, 1840–1914*, makes good use of Booth's findings, pp. 163–5. Also see V. D. Lipman, 'The Booth and New London Surveys as Source Material for East London Jewry (1880–1930)', in A. Newman (ed.), *The Jewish East End, 1834–1940*. D. Englander, 'Booth's Jews: the Presentation of Jews and Judaism in *Life and Labour of the People of London*', *Victorian Studies*, 32 (1989), is critical of Booth.

25. In particular the work of the House of Lords Select Committee on the Sweating System (various Reports, P.P. 1888, XX and XXI; P.P. 1889, XIII and XIV; and P.P. 1890, XVII); and the Royal Commission on Alien Immigration, P.P. 1903, IX.

26. Jacobs, *Studies in Jewish Statistics*, p. 13.

27. L. P. Gartner, *The Jewish Immigrant in England, 1870–1914*, lists this data (p. 16) but doesn't make too much of it (pp. 57–8). Green, 'Tale of Three Cities', attempts to use it as the basis of a comparison with New York and Paris, pp. 92–3, 95–6. Feldman, *Englishmen and Jews* reworked the original data but correctly used it as a profile of East European emigrants (pp. 161–2). For South Africa as the eventual destination, see A. Newman, 'Directed Migration: The Poor Jews' Temporary Shelter, 1885–1914' in Newman and Massil, *Patterns of Migration*.

28. *Jewish Chronicle*, 6 October 1899, p. 14. On Jewish marriages generally see A. Benisch, 'How, When and Where did the Present Marriage Ceremony Originate?', ibid., 25 December 1874, pp. 629–30; M. Mielziner, *Jewish Law of Marriage and Divorce in Ancient and Modern Times and Its Relation to the*

Law of the State; H. S. Q. Henriques, *Jewish Marriages and the English Law*; *Encyclopaedia Judaica*, vol. 11, pp. 1025–54; and C. Tucker, 'Jewish Marriages and Divorces in England until 1940: part I', *Genealogists Magazine* 24 (1992).

29. G. Whitehill (ed.), *Bevis Marks Records, part III*, pp. 1–16.
30. G. Alderman, 'The British Chief Rabbinate: A Most Peculiar Practice', *European Judaism* 45 (1990), esp. p. 47; idem, 'Power, Authority and Status in British Jewry: The Chief Rabbinate and Shechita', in idem and C. Holmes (eds.), *Outsiders and Outcasts*; and Tucker, 'Jewish Marriages'. W. R. Rubinstein, *A History of the Jews in the English Speaking World: Great Britain*, is particularly good on the Victorian Anglo-Jewry.
31. Originally the Great Synagogue only, and then from 1855 different synagogues were permitted to be registered for marriage solemnisation; Henriques, *Jews and English Law*, p. 174. I estimate that only 2.2 per cent of all Jewish marriages in Britain were registered with the local registrar rather than at a synagogue, with no differentiation between immigrants and natives. See S. J. Prais and M. Schmool, 'Statistics of Jewish Marriages in Great Britain: 1901–1965', *Jewish Journal of Sociology*, IX (1967); my calculations from tables I and III, pp. 165–8, and confirmed for 1904 in table IV, p. 169.
32. A. Newman, *United Synagogue, 1870–1970*; Whitehill, *Bevis Marks*.
33. G. Alderman, *Federation of Synagogues, 1887–1987*. Since 1914, the Liberal, Reform, and other umbrella groups have opted for similar autonomy.
34. Stanislawski, *Nicholas I*, pp. 36–7 and 133–7; Klier, *Jewish Question*, pp. 8–9, 26, 222–44; S. J. Zipperstein, *The Jews of Odessa: a Cultural History, 1794–1881*, pp. 87–8; and E. Lederhendler, *The Road to Modern Jewish Politics*; pp. 51, 91 and n. 66, p. 182. I am indebted to John Klier for informing me about the 'metric books' and state rabbis.
35. *Jewish Chronicle*, 6 July 1900, p. 21.
36. See letters in *Jewish Chronicle*, 19 December 1890 and 26 December 1890; and Beatrice Potter, 'The Jewish Community', in Booth, *Life and Labour*, 1st ser., p 1, ch. 4, p. 168.
37. Alderman, 'Power, Authority and Status', pp. 13–19; idem, *Federation*, pp. 9–10, 41–6; B. Homa, *A Fortress in Anglo-Jewry, the Story of the Machzike Hadath*, pp. 8–9.
38. After 1904 nearly 2 per cent of all Jewish weddings registered in City and East End synagogues were solemnised at the *Machzike Hadath*; see Table 3.A2, below.
39. Jacobs, *Studies in Jewish Statistics*, pp. 10–21 on the Jewish poor. For 'cheap marriages', see Newman, *United Synagogue*, pp. 90–5; and Report of the Executive Committee of the United Synagogue on Wedding Fees, 13.6.1877, archives of the United Synagogue, and partially reprinted in D. Englander (ed.), *A Documentary History of Jewish Immigrants in Britain, 1840–1920*, pp. 53–4.
40. *Jewish Chronicle*, 7 February 1890. A Russian lawyer (*Jewish Chronicle* 6 July 1900, p. 21) implied that marriage registration was expensive in Poland, because poor Jews sometimes chose not to register their marriages with the State Office, which, if discovered, led occasionally to dire results.
41. Tucker, 'Jewish Marriages', p. 91; and D. Englander, '*Stille Huppah* (Quiet Marriage) among Jewish Immigrants in Britain', *Jewish Journal of Sociology*

XXXIV (1992), assert that *stille huppahs* were relatively common still after 1880, although without much evidence. Analysis of the dataset of marriage records suggests that it is very unlikely that many first-time marriages were missing from the data set. *Stille huppahs* were relatively insignificant. Given the very low rate of remarriage, however, the incidence of non-registration for remarrying divorcees and widowers may have been much higher.

42. U. Engelman, 'Sources of Jewish Statistics', in L. Finkelstein (ed.), *The Jews: Their History, Culture and Religion*, cites evidence of very low intermarriage among American Jews up to the 1940s. Prais and Schmool, 'Jewish Marriages'.

43. M. Anderson, 'The Study of Family Structure', in Wrigley, *Nineteenth Century Society*, esp. pp. 59–61.

44. Gartner, *Jewish Immigrant*, p. 168.

45. Stanislawski, *Nicholas I*, pp. 36–7; the age limits were 18 for men and 16 for women. Kosmin, 'Nuptiality and Fertility'; and Salaman, 'Anglo-Jewish Vital Statistics', part II, on the increasing age at first marriage by the turn of the century, but Herman Adler, the Chief Rabbi, thought that they still married too early, calling it 'a terrible evil' and that there was '[n]o question but that they are too early' in 1897, Booth Collection, BLPES, B197, p. 23.

46. B. Kosmin, 'Nuptiality and Fertility among British Jews', in D. Coleman (ed.), *Demography of Immigrants and Minority Groups in the United Kingdom*, table VII, p. 255, lists mean age of marriage among Jews in Russia for 1880s and 1890s. T. J. Hatton, 'The Immigration Assimilation Puzzle in Late Nineteenth Century America', *Journal of Economic History*, 57 (1997), p. 39, says that the mean age of arrival of foreign born in the USA was 'about 20'. The mean age of first marriage for immigrant grooms in London was 24.3 years, suggesting that most arrived in their early twenties, or at an earlier age than the mean age of marriage among Jews in Russia. M. Freedman, *Leeds Jewry: the First Hundred Years*, p. 27, shows that only 30 per cent of Jewish families in Leeds on census night 1891 with both parents immigrants had children who were immigrants, that is, definitely arrived married. After adjusting for marriages between immigrant and the native-born, the proportion of immigrants who arrived married in Leeds in 1891 drops to around 20 per cent. Until more research is done on the original census manuscripts, there is no way of knowing if this was representative of the wider Jewish immigrant population. Incidentally, Freedman (p. 7) also gives an example of what was an apparently common occurrence, a male immigrant sending to Russia for a bride.

47. H. Southall and D. Gilbert, 'A Good Time to Wed?: Marriage and Economic Distress in England and Wales, 1839–1914', *Economic History Review*, XLIX (1996).

48. On the UK clothing industry and the role of the Jews see A. Godley, 'The Development of the UK Clothing Industry, 1850–1950: Output and Productivity Growth', *Business History*, 37 (1995); 'Jewish Soft Loan Societies in New York and London and Immigrant Entrepreneurship', *Business History*, 38 (1996); 'Immigrant Entrepreneurs and the Emergence of London's East End as an Industrial District', *London Journal*, 21 (1996); 'Singer in Britain: the Diffusion of Sewing Machine Technology and Its Impact on the Clothing Industry in the United Kingdom, 1860–1905', *Textile History*, 27 (1996).

49. Table 3.3 shows that the 'up-to-25' cohort consisted of only 37.9 per cent of the census population but 58.3 per cent of the CRA database, a ratio of 0.65. The 'over-25' cohort consisted of 62.1 per cent of the census population and 41.7 per cent of the CRA database, a ratio of 1.5. The occupational structure of the grooms has therefore been adjusted by reweighting the two age groups according to these two ratios.

50. The ideal method of adjusting for the age-bias would be to know the age-structure of the alien population in every year. However, the census information is limited to only 1901 and 1911. For simplicity's sake 1901 has been chosen. Not only is it considered to be reliable – the 1911 census appears to have undercounted the Jewish immigrant population – but it was the nearest year to the mid-point of the period, and was also the year immediately preceding the median immigrant marriage in the CRA database.

51. Prais and Schmool, 'Jewish Marriages', esp. pp. 162–4 and table III, p. 168, and compared with the Board of Deputies, *Annual Reports* (1881–1915).

52. There were additional synagogues, but not licensed to marry. See V. D. Lipman, 'Rise of Jewish Suburbia', *Transactions of the Jewish Historical Society of England*, XXI (1968), appendix IV, p. 100, census of worship, 1903.

53. Apart from the first book, from 1837, which is in the archives of the United Synagogue.

54. Alderman, *Federation*, pp. 52–4.

55. An estimated 2590 records, from the Board of Deputies returns, which is 8.9 per cent of the estimated total number reported to the Board of Deputies during these years of 29,196 (allowing for estimates for the missing years of 1884 and 1897 to be included, as reported in Table 3.A2).

56. Alderman, *Federation*, pp. 1, 20. 25; Lipman, *Social History*, pp. 72–4, 126.

57. Godley, 'Leaving the East End'.

58. Board of Deputies, *Annual Reports*, for the years 1900 to 1915, appendices.

59. Alderman, *Federation*, p. 24.

60. Ibid., pp. 46–7, 52–4, and 59.

61. Note that there were 50 spoiled or untraced certificates of the Chief Rabbi's authorisation for the grooms and 63 for the brides reducing the totals from which the percentages have been calculated to 1312 and 1299 respectively rather than 1362.

62. Prais and Schmool, 'Statistics', esp. tables V and VI, pp. 169–170. Both 1904 and 1905 were selected as comparator years from the CRA database to give a larger number of records (123).

4 Jewish Immigrant Entrepreneurship in London and New York

1. A. Godley, 'The Development of the UK Clothing Industry, 1850–1950: Output and Productivity Growth', *Business History*, 37 (1995); idem, 'Immigrant Entrepreneurs and the Emergence of London's East End as an Industrial District', *London Journal*, 21 (1996); and idem, 'Singer in Britain: the Diffusion of Sewing Machine Technology and its Impact on the Clothing Industry in the United Kingdom, 1860–1905', *Textile History*, 27 (1996).

2. A. Godley, 'Comparative Labour Productivity in the British and American Clothing Industries, 1850–1950', *Textile History*, **28** (1997); idem, 'Pioneering Foreign Direct Investment in British Manufacturing', *Business History Review, 73*, (1999); and idem, 'The Global Diffusion of the Sewing Machine, 1850–1914', *Research in Economic History*, 20 (2000).

3. A. Godley, 'Selling the Sewing Machine around the World: Singer's International Marketing Strategies, 1850–1914', *Enterprise and Society*, 3 (2002).

4. A. Godley, 'Jewish Soft Loan Societies in New York and London and Immigrant Entrepreneurship' *Business History*, 38 (1996).

5. See Sidney Webb, 'Preface', in B. L. Hutchins and A. L. Harrison, *A History of Factory Legislation*, p. xi. Webb was a pillar of Britain's radical establishment. He went on to found the London School of Economics.

6. W. Besant, *East London*, p. 194.

7. B. Potter, 'The Tailoring Trade', C. Booth, *Life and Labour of the People in London*, 1st ser., vol. 4, ch. 4, pp. 37–68, citation p. 60 (emphasis in original). (Beatrice Potter married Sidney Webb in 1892.)

8. B. Potter, 'The Jewish Community (East London)', Booth, *Life and Labour*, 1st ser., vol. 3, ch. IV, pp. 166–92, citation pp. 185–6, described by Potter as 'typical of the lives of the majority of Polish and Russian Jews from their first appearance at the Port of London', p. 186.

9. Potter, 'Tailoring Trade', p. 60.

10. T. Kessner, *The Golden Door: Italian and Jewish Immigrant Mobility in New York City, 1880–1915*, p. 171.

11. See John Commons' contribution to, 'Foreign-Born Labor in the Clothing Trade,' *Reports of the Industrial Commission on Immigration*, vol. 15, pp. 323–7; I. Rubinov, 'Economic and Industrial Conditions (A) New York', in C. Bernheimer ed., *The Russian Jew in the United States*.

12. D. Englander, 'Booth's Jews: the Presentation of Jews and Judaism in *Life and Labour of the People in London*', *Victorian Studies*, 32 (1989), pp. 551–71, for example.

13. K. Honeyman, 'Gender Divisions and Industrial Divide: the Case of the Leeds Clothing Trade, 1850–1970', *Textile History*, **28** (1997); Jane Humphries, 'Class Struggle and the Persistence of the Working Class Family', *Cambridge Journal of Economics*, 1 (1977); and M. Anderson, 'The Study of Family Structure', in E.A. Wrigley (ed.), *Nineteenth Century Society: Essays in the Use of Quantitative Methods for The Study of Social Data*.

14. E. Krausz, 'The Economic and Social Structure of Anglo-Jewry', in J. Gould and S. Esh (eds), *Jewish Life in Modern Britain*, p. 29.

15. Analysis of bridal occupations in the marriage registers shows that under-recording apparently ceased from 1906. The reason for this remains unknown. Intriguingly, however, US immigration officials also began to record the occupations of female Jews on arrival from then, perhaps suggesting that there may have been a change in customs in the Russian homeland common to both groups of women. See J. Perlmann, 'Selective Migration as a Basis for Upward Mobility?: the Occupations of the Jewish Immigrants to the United States, ca 1900', Jerome Levy Economics Institute working paper no. 172 (1996), esp. p. 7 and Table 3B, p. 15.

16. See, however, A. Godley, 'The Occupational Profile of East European women in Britain, 1880–1914', working paper, forthcoming, for an analysis of the bridal occupational data.

17. S. Thernstrom, *Poverty and Progress in a Nineteenth Century City*; Kessner, *Golden Door*; J. Gurock, *When Harlem was Jewish, 1870–1930*.

18. A. M. Edwards, 'A Social Economic Grouping of the Gainful Workers of the United States', *Journal of the American Statistical Association*, 27 (1933), pp. 377–87, is the originator of the classification system. See S. Thernstrom, *The Other Bostonians: Poverty and Progress in the American Metropolis, 1880–1970*, appendix B, pp. 289–302, for an explanation of the system of socio-economic ranking.

19. White-collar workers were essentially all salary-earning professionals and semi-professionals, along with business owners and managers in the schema; blue-collars were wage-earners (Edwards, 'Social Economic Grouping'). One anomaly arises from adopting the American convention. In the original scheme, peddlers and hawkers were included as entrepreneurs in with the white-collar workers. But by the end of the nineteenth century they were entrepreneurs of only the pettiest kind. The Registrar General from 1911 correctly placed them with the lower social classes (see W. A. Armstrong, 'The Use of Information about Occupation', in Wrigley (ed.), *Nineteenth Century Society*, esp. pp. 198–205 and appendix A, pp. 215–223). This discrepancy may have been a matter of timing. At the beginning of the nineteenth century, Jewish old-clothes men could legitimately claim to be successful businesses, occasionally even developing into significant firms (see S. Chapman, 'The Innovating Entrepreneurs in the British Ready-Made Clothing Industry', *Textile History*, 24 (1993); P. Sharpe, '"Cheapness and Economy": Manufacturing and Retailing Ready-made Clothing in London and Essex 1830–1850', *Textile History*, 26 (1995); and A. Godley, 'The Development of the Clothing Industry: Technology and Fashion', *Textile History*, 28 (1997), p. 6). The spread of fixed retailing and mail order decimated their market, however (see S. Fletcher and A. Godley, 'Foreign Direct Investment in British Retailing, 1850–1962', *Business History*, 42 (2000). By this period hawking was not an attractive route to entrepreneurship among the Jews. Naggar comments that very few were able to move up into shopkeeping (see B. Naggar, *Jewish Pedlars and Hawkers, 1740–1940*, pp. 93–4). In recent years American historians have begun to reclassify peddlers as blue-collar workers. See, for example, the difference between Kessner, *Golden Door*, p. 51 n., and Kessner, 'The Selective Filter of Ethnicity', in D. Berger (ed.), *The Legacy of Jewish Migration: 1881 and Its Impact*, especially pp. 172, 178.

20. N. Barou, *Jews in Work and Trade: a World Survey*, p. 7.

21. Just over half (55 per cent) of the grooms gave no status identifier to their occupations on the marriage registers. Following the census enumerators' practice (see Armstrong, 'Occupation', pp. 216–21), they have been treated as blue-collar tailors, bootmakers, cabinetmakers and so on. This is consistent with other properties of this group. Their mean age of first marriage (24.0 years) was earlier than the machinists, pressers, journeymen, and other firmly identified blue-collar workers (24.2 years), for example, and considerably earlier than the entrepreneurs (25.7 years). Also, they were far less likely to sign the register in English (only 52.5 per cent did) than the entrepreneurs (70.3 per cent) or the firmly identified blue-collar workers (62.2 per cent). Synagogue secretaries, like census

enumerators, would therefore appear to have recorded occupational status consistently.

22. D. Feldman, *Englishmen and Jews: Social Relations and Political Culture, 1840–1914*, pp. 163–165.

23. Thernstrom, *The Other Bostonians*, pp. 49–51, describes the importance of relating ethnic mobility to the underlying, or 'minimum' mobility. Also see A. Godley, 'Enterprise and Culture: Jewish Immigrants in London and New York, 1880–1914' (unpublished PhD thesis, LSE, 1993), pp. 29–32, on the changing structure of the London economy; and G. S. Jones, *Outcast London: a Study in the Relationship between Classes in Victorian Society*.

24. Jones, *Outcast London*, pp. 19–155.

25. J. E. Cairnes, *Some Leading Principles of Political Economy Newly Expounded*; J. H. Goldthorpe, *Social Mobility and Class Structure in Modern Britain*, p. 4.

26. A. H. Halsey, *Change in British Society*, pp. 53, 57.

27. A. Miles, *Social Mobility in Britain, 1837–1914*.

28. Kessner presented results from the only Federal census open to him, the 1880 census, and the 1905 State census. See *Golden Door*, pp. xiv–xv, on failings of the censuses, pp. 44–70 for the results from 1880 and 1905 censuses. In 'Selective Filter', Kessner presented his results from a sample of the 1925 state census, especially pp. 172, 178.

29. Kessner, *Golden Door*, p. 68.

30. Ibid., p. 67.

31. I.G. Wyllie, *The Self Made Man in America: the Myth of Rags to Riches*; M. Rischin (ed.), *The American Gospel of Success*; B. Sarachek, 'American Entrepreneurs and the Horatio Alger Myth', *Journal of Economic History*, XXXVIII (1978).

32. P. Lindert and J. Williamson, 'Growth, Equality and History', *Explorations in Economic History*, 22 (1985).

33. Kessner, *Golden Door*, p. 65.

34. Nor did he list them in his original PhD thesis, 'The Golden Door: Immigrant Mobility in New York City, 1880–1915' (unpublished PhD thesis, Columbia University, 1975).

35. Kessner states that between 1880 and 1905 four-fifths of social class I were businessmen, clothing manufacture and real estate being the most popular (*Golden Door*, p. 64). Only 2 per cent of class II household heads in 1880 were semi-professional or clerks, the remainder being in business (p. 61). By 1905 clerical work had grown, but not by very much. It has been assumed here that the slightly faster growth of some of the non-entrepreneurial occupations led to a share of 3 per cent of the very much larger sample (p. 64). Thus, taking Kessner's white collar class of 21.0 per cent in 1880 and 40.4 per cent in 1905, a recalculation can be made. For 1880 Kessner found that class I consisted of 5.2 per cent and class II 15.8 per cent of the sample (see Table 4.3 here). Therefore, four-fifths of class I and all of class II (less 2 per cent who were clerks) were entrepreneurs, giving a total of 18.0 per cent. In 1905 four-fifths of the 15.3 per cent of the sample that were class I and all of the 25.1 per cent of the sample that were in class II (less 3 per cent who were clerks) would leave a total of 34.3 per cent as the proportion of the workforce that were entrepreneurs. Therefore, while the non-entrepreneurial white-collar class (the clerical and professional workers) had

grown from 3 per cent to 6.1 per cent of the workforce between 1880 and 1905, the entrepreneurs had grown from 18.0 per cent to 34.3 per cent. In 1925 50 per cent of the Russian Jewish immigrants had risen to white-collar status. Kessner gives no exact indication of the share of entrepreneurs among the white-collar class, simply noting that in 1925, '14 per cent of Russian Jewish household heads were in the professions or other white collar occupations that required formal education' – the balance of 36 per cent being presumably all in business as entrepreneurs (Kessner, 'Selective Filter', p. 178). The 1914 level is assumed to be the (rounded) mid-point between the 1905 and the 1925 shares, or 35 per cent.

36. There was little volatility from one year to another in levels of entrepreneurship in London. The comparison of ranges of years with single years is therefore unlikely to distort the results.

37. B. Chiswick, 'The Occupational Attainment and Earnings of American Jewry, 1890–1990', *Contemporary Jewry*, 20 (1999); also see Chiswick, 'The Billings Report and the Occupational Attainment of American Jewry, 1890', *Shofar: An Interdisciplinary Journal of Jewish Studies*, 19 (2001).

5   Jewish Mass Migration and the Choice of Destination

1. *Jewish Chronicle* 24 Feb. 1882, cited in L. Gartner, *The Jewish Immigrant in England, 1870–1914*, p. 42, n. 45.

2. C. Bermant, *Troubled Eden: an Anatomy of British Jewry*, p. 22. Also see Gartner quoting T. Eyges in *Jewish Immigrant*, p. 44; and A. Reutlinger, 'Reflections on the Anglo-American Jewish Experience: Immigrants, Workers, and Entrepreneurs in New York and London, 1870–1914', in *American Jewish Historical Quarterly*, LXVI (1977), esp. pp. 473–6.

3. Reutlinger, 'Reflections', p. 475, n. 5.

4. Jewish Board of Guardians, *Annual Report*, 1897, p. 16. Biographical evidence often emphasises the role of chance – sea-sickness, the loss (or theft) of tickets, and so on – preventing them from going further. The analysis below suggests, however, that these may have been atypical experiences.

5. R. Hebert and A. Link, *The Entrepreneur: Mainstream Views and Radical Critiques*, for a survey.

6. Report of the Royal Commission on Alien Immigration (hereafter RC Aliens), *Minutes of Evidence, Appendix*, (P.P. 1903, IX), table LXII, also see Tables LXIII and LXIIIA, pp. 76–8. This enumeration of Jewish immigrants to the UK cannot be taken too seriously, however. The East European aliens who reported their intention of staying in Britain to ships' captains came to over 70,000 in these eight years. This was far in excess of the actual number of immigrants. For instance, 26.5 per cent of the East-European-born brides and grooms that married in East End synagogue between 1880–1914 were married during these years. If this is taken as a reasonable indicator of the proportion of immigrants arriving between 1895 and 1902, then the 70,000 enumerated 'immigrants' would be 26.5 per cent of the total, giving over 260,000 immigrants that arrived in steerage on German and Dutch steamers at London. It is most unlikely that those arriving in London in steerage on German and Dutch steamers were even half of the total, as many arrived on British steamers and

at other ports. The implication is that if all 70,000 'immigrants' were actually going to settle in the UK, then total immigration over the period would have been around half a million. The best estimates of total East European Jewish immigration to Britain over this period range from 120,000 to 150,000. Perhaps 70,000 to 80,000 therefore at the very most could have arrived in steerage on the continental steamers at London over the entire period; 26.5 per cent of these would total less than 20,000. In other words, less than a third of those who entered London describing themselves as 'immigrants' between 1895 and 1902 actually were. The vast majority were not. No doubt this desire to declare false fealty to Britain was related to the possibility of purchasing the cheaper tickets to the USA available to UK residents and, theoretically, not open to continental transmigrants. For East European Jewish immigration to the UK, Gartner's estimate is 120,000 in L. Gartner, 'Notes on the Statistics of Jewish Immigration to England, 1870–1914', *Jewish Social Studies*, 22 (1960), pp. 97–102; Lipman's is 150,000 in V. Lipman, *A History of the Jews in Britain since 1858*, pp. 45–9, and see his *Social History of the Jews in England, 1850–1950*, p. 89. See note 63 below for the impact of the Atlantic 'rate' war on the classification of immigrants national backgrounds.

7. I. Rubinov, 'Economic and Industrial Condition: (A) New York', in C. Bernheimer (ed.), *The Russian Jew in the United States*, p. 108. Also see A. Kahan, 'Economic Opportunities and Some Pilgrims Progress', in *Journal of Economic History*, 38 (1978), esp. n. 6; US Immigration Commission, *Report*, vol. 1, pp. 102–3. It would appear that the method of calculation was slightly different in London and New York. In London children were included as half adults, in New York everyone was counted. When recalculated on the American basis, London immigrants brought on average 23.9s. or $5.81 over the eight years.

8. RC Aliens, 'Appendix', pp. 76–8 and recalculated on the American basis; and Immigration Commission, ibid., pp. 102–3.

9. US Commissioner General for Immigration, *Annual Reports*, 1903–5. Some Jews arrived rich. Some of the principal sums produced at London, for example, included £4000 in 1896, £850 and £750 in 1899, but these were conspicuous by their very rarity. Nearly 40 per cent arrived with less than 10s.; RC Aliens, 'Appendix', pp. 76–8. Also D. Feldman, *Englishmen and Jews: Social Relations and Political Culture, 1840–1914*, pp. 159–60.

10. Up to a quarter of the Jewish arrivals in London had their passages assisted by relatives already in Britain; RC Aliens, ibid. Assuming that all those who had benefited from the a of relatives stayed, and (following the earlier logic from note 6) that only around a third were actually genuine immigrants, then the vast majority (a quarter divided by a third is three-quarters) had needed financial help in order to get there. See Feldman, *Englishmen and Jews*, pp. 158–9, for evidence of remittances from London. See J. Williamson, 'The Evolution of Global Labor Markets since 1830: Background Evidence and Hypotheses', *Explorations in Economic History*, 32 (1995), T.A3.1, p. 184, for PPP exchange rate of $6.48 to £1 as opposed to the official rate of $4.86, an indicator that living costs were around a third higher in urban America.

11. See, for example, K. O'Rourke and J. Williamson, 'Around the European Periphery 1870–1913: Globalization, Schooling and Growth', *European Review of Economic History*, 1 (1997).

12. S. Kuznets, 'Immigration of Russian Jews to the United States: Background and Structure', in *Perspectives in American History,* 9 (1975), table xiv, p. 115 and discussion pp. 113–6. Note that the greater literacy may have been related more to the differences in age structure, gender and regional background than to any particular bias to the more educated among migrants.

13. S. Stampfer, '*Heder* Study, Knowledge of Torah, and the Maintenance of Social Stratification in Traditional East European Jewish Society', *Studies in Jewish Education,* 3 (1988), esp. pp. 277–9.

14. The records of occupations of those staying at the Poor Jews' Temporary Shelter in London have already been mentioned in Chapter 3. As noted there, this evidence is far from representative of the occupational background of the Jewish immigrants in London. For the occupational information, see Gartner, *Jewish Immigrant,* pp. 57–8. For the ultimate destination of the Shelter's inmates, see A. Newman, 'Directed Migration: The Poor Jews' Temporary Shelter, 1885–1914', in A. Newman and S. Massil (eds), *Patterns of Migration, 1850–1914.* For a recent attempt to use the occupational data, see N. Green, 'A Tale of Three Cities: Immigrant Jews in New York, London and Paris, 1870–1914', in Newman and Massil, *Patterns.*

15. There have been some differences in the way scholars have interpreted these data. Essentially Feldman, Hersch and Kahan believe trade and commercial occupations to be under-represented, while Kuznets believes them to be over-represented. See Feldman, *Englishmen and Jews,* pp. 161–2; L. Hersch, 'International Migration of the Jews', ch. xvi in I. Ferenczi and W. Willcox (eds), *International Migrations,* vol. ii, pp. 471–520, esp. pp. 487–507; A. Kahan, *Essays in Jewish Social and Economic History*; and Kuznets, 'Russian Jews', pp. 102–7.

16. Kuznets, 'Russian Jews', table xb, p. 96; S. Joseph, *Jewish Immigration to the United States from 1881 to 1910,* tables xxxiii and xxxv, pp. 176–177; Hersch, 'International Migration', tables 206 to 209, pp. 483–6; Aliens Act 1905, Part ii, *Annual Report of H.M. Inspector under the Act,* from 1906 to 1913 (hereafter HMI Aliens Act; specific references given below). Also see J. D. Gould, 'European Inter-Continental Emigration The Road Home: Return Migration from the USA', *Journal of European Economic History,* 9 (1980), table 3, p. 60.

17. Kuznets, 'Russian Jews', table xb, p. 96; Joseph, *Jewish Immigration,* tables xxxviii, xxxix, xl, xlii, pp. 179–82.

18. Kuznets, 'Russian Jews', p. 75. Kahan, *Essays,* ch. 1, appendix on regional differences.

19. I. Rubinov, *Economic Conditions of the Jews in Russia,* p. 491; Feldman, *Englishmen and Jews,* p. 153

20. V. Obolensky-Ossinsky, 'Emigration from and Immigration into Russia', in Ferenczi and Willcox, *International Migrations,* vol. ii, p. 546. Obolensky-Ossinsky used a regional breakdown of applications to the Hebrew Emigration Aid Society and the Jewish Colonization Society from 1901 to 1913, which may have been unrepresentative of emigration; see pp. 541–6.

21. S. Stampfer, 'The Geographic Background of East European Jewish Migration to the United States before World War I', in I. Glazier and L. De Rosa (eds), *Migration, Across Time and Nation,* pp. 220–30.

22. Gartner, 'Jewish Migrants En Route from Europe to North America: Traditions and Realities', in *Jewish History,* 1 (1986), pp. 62–3.

23. L. Gartner, 'North Atlantic Jewry', in A. Newman, (ed.), *Migration and Settlement*, pp. 118–125, citation p. 123.
24. The literature is vast and growing. The best traditional works include, P. Taylor, *The Distant Magnet: European Emigration to the USA*; and B. Thomas, *Migration and Economic Growth: a Study of Great Britain and the Atlantic Economy*. The best short survey is D. Baines, *Emigration from Europe 1815–1930*. A summary of the best recent work is T. Hatton and J. Williamson, *The Age of Mass Migration*.
25. Baines, *Emigration*, pp. 21–30. Also see J. Gould, 'European Inter-Continental Emigration 1815–1914: Patterns and Causes', *Journal of European Economic History*, 8 (1979); and T. Hatton and J. Williamson, 'International Migration 1850–1939: an Economic Survey', in Hatton and Williamson (eds), *Migration and the International Labour Market, 1850–1939*.
26. J. Frankel, 'Introduction', in Kahan, *Essays*, pp. xvii–xviii.
27. The literature on the Jews in the Pale is extensive. See S. Dubnow, *The History of the Jews in Russia and Poland*; S. Baron, *Jews under Tsars and Soviets*; J. Frankel, *Prophecy and Politics: Socialism, Nationalism and the Russian Jews, 1862–1917*; L. Greenberg, *The Jews in Russia*; D. Berger (ed.), *The Legacy of Jewish Migration: 1881 and Its Impact*; Kahan, *Essays*; Y. Peled, *Class and Ethnicity in the Pale*; L. Wolf, *The Legal Sufferings of the Jews in Russia*; B. Baskerville, *The Polish Jew*; and E. Mendelsohn, *The Jews of East Central Europe Between the Wars*.
28. Regardless of the debate over the immigrants' occupational background (see note 15 above), a far higher proportion of Jews were middlemen than native Russians. Kahan, *Essays*; Kuznets, 'Russian Jews'.
29. Kuznets, 'Russian Jews', pp. 76–7.
30. M. Falkus, *The Industrialisation of Russia, 1700–1914*; P. Gregory, *Russian National Income, 1885–1913*; Kahan, *Essays*, pp. 1–69.
31. Kahan, ibid., pp. 44, 69 n. 48. Poverty defined by receipt of Passover charity. These general conditions held for those in Galicia and Romania also, although direct political restrictions were fewer. See Mendelsohn, *Jews of East and Central Europe*, pp. 85–130, 171–212.
32. Falkus, *Industrialisation*, p. 55; Taylor, *Distant Magnet*, pp. 45–50. Also see D. Turnock, 'Railway Development in Eastern Europe as a Context for Migration Study', in Newman and Massil, *Patterns*.
33. Frankel, *Prophecy* on the crisis, ch. 2, esp. pp. 68–74; A. Linden (ed.), *Die Jüdenpogrome in Russland* is the best detailed study of anti-Jewish violence. Dubnow, *History*, gives a graphic account of both pogroms and the legislative persecution of the Jews. Also see the map of the areas affected in Z. Gitelman, *A Century of Ambivalence: the Jews of Russia and the Soviet Union, 1881 to the Present*, p. 3.
34. Gartner's apt phrase in *Jewish Immigrant*, p. 41. Also see J. Klier, 'Emigration Mania in Late-Imperial Russia: Legend and Reality', in Massil and Newman, *Patterns*, for important context.
35. Frankel, *Prophecy*, pp. 68–74; idem, 'The Crisis of 1881–82 as a Turning Point in Modern Jewish History', in Berger, *Legacy*, pp. 9–22. also see Z. Szajkowski, 'How the Mass Migration to America began', *Jewish Social Studies*, 4 (1942).
36. T. Hatton and J. Williamson, 'After the Famine: Emigration from Ireland, 1850–1913', *Journal of Economic History*, 53 (1993).

37. A problem with the official immigration series for the United States is that until 1908 there was no differentiation between gross and net immigration. For the earlier years return migration would probably have been lower, when transport costs were higher. See Baines, *Emigration*, p. 39; and A. Keeling, 'The Transportation Revolution and Transatlantic Migration, 1850–1914', *Research in Economic History*, 19 (1999), esp. Table 3.

38. The figures for the Russian Jews in the table have been calculated with a constant return rate. J. Sarna, 'The Myth of No Return: Jewish Return Migration to Eastern Europe, 1881 to 1914', *American Jewish History* (1981), suggests that Jewish return rates were higher for the earlier years, although without supporting evidence. On balance, it is more likely that the Jews followed the general trend to increasing return migration over time. On this, see Gould, 'Return Migration', table 3, p. 60, also pp. 54 n. and 57; Joseph, *Jewish Immigration*, tables XLIII and XLV, pp. 182–3; D. Baines, 'European Labour Markets, Emigration and Internal Migration, 1850–1913', in Hatton and Williamson, *Migration*, p. 47; and Keeling, 'Transportation Revolution'.

39. Estimates of the destinations for the Jewish migration from J. Lestschinsky, 'Jewish Migrations, 1840–1946', in L. Finkelstein (ed.), *The Jews: Their History, Culture and Religion*, table 3A, p. 1216.

40. HMI Aliens Act, *Fourth Annual Report* (P.P. 1910 IX), p. 3.

41. Thomas, *Migration*, pp. 64; HMI Aliens Act, *Fifth Annual Report* (P.P. 1911 X), p. 30; H. Jerome, *Migration and the Business Cycle*; S. Kuznets and E. Rubin, *Immigration and the Foreign Born*. Incidentally, Hersch showed that the Jews behaved in a fashion very similar to US immigration generally; see 'International Migration', p. 475 and diagram 12, p. 476. Kuznets, unsurprisingly, also assumed a relationship between Russian Jewish immigration and the longer economic cycles in 'Russian Jews', pp. 44–45.

42. Real wages from Williamson, 'Global Labor Markets', table A2.1.

43. S. Wegge, 'Chain Migration and Information Networks: Evidence from Nineteenth Century Hesse-Cassel', *Journal of Economic History*, 58 (1998).

44. Baines, 'European Labour Markets', p. 46.

45. Departmental Committee of the Home Office in the *Minutes of Evidence* in the Appendix to the *Report on the Establishment of a Receiving House for Alien Immigrants* (P.P. 1911 X) (hereafter DC Receiving House), q. 734, p. 27. More generally, see M. Antin, *From Plotsk to Boston*.

46. US Bureau of Statistics, *European Emigration*, pp. 278–9.

47. Kuznets, 'Russian Jews', table XIII, p. 113.

48. HMI Aliens Act, *Fifth Annual Report*, p. 38.

49. DC Receiving House, Landau, q. 1364.

50. Wegge, 'Chain Migration'.

51. See T. Hatton and J. Williamson, 'What Drove the Mass Migrations from Europe in the Late Nineteenth Century', *Population and Development Review*, 20 (1994); T. Hatton, 'A Model of UK Emigration, 1870–1913', *Review of Economics and Statistics*, 77 (1995).

52. M. Davis, 'Critique of Official United States Immigration Statistics', in Ferenczi and Willcox, *International Migrations*, Appendix, vol. II, pp. 645–60; Baines, *Emigration*, pp. 17–20. For the Jews, Hersch, 'International Migration', pp. 471–3.

53. US Immigration Commission, *Reports of the Immigration Commission and Abstracts:Abstract of Statistical Revue of Immigration to the United States, 1820–1910*, p. 56.

54. The East European Jews had almost all lived in Poland and Lithuania before these areas were divided up by the Great Powers of Prussia, Austria-Hungary and Russia by 1815. Most of the Jews were then in Russia, some in the Polish provinces of Austria-Hungary (Galicia) and Prussia (Posen). Some subsequently migrated beyond the Carpathian mountains into what became Romania. See Mendelsohn, *Jews of East and Central Europe*, chs 1, 2 and 4.

55. There were some Jews in the Pale of Settlement who were non-Yiddish speakers, but not many. Kahan estimated that they were only around 2 per cent of the total Jewish population, were probably of a higher social status and so were less likely to have emigrated; *Essays*, p. 4.

56. Joseph, *Jewish Immigration*, p. 87.

57. Ibid., pp. 90–1.

58. A second series of estimates was calculated by Mark Wischnitzer, *To Dwell in Safety*, pp. 288–9. These were much higher than Joseph's. He estimated that 944, 688 East European Jewish immigrants arrived in the USA between 1881 to 1898, twice as many as Joseph's 488,358 (see Table 5.3). This is curious to say the least, especially as Wischnitzer gives the impression in his notes that he used the same sources as Joseph – the number of Jews admitted through the three main ports of New York, Philadelphia and Baltimore; Wischnitzer, *To Dwell*, appendix 1, table 1, n. 2, p. 289. However, Wischnitzer appears to have followed an incorrect methodology and double-counted the immigrants met by the welfare societies. This appears to have been similar, and with similar results, to the erroneous methodology reportedly used by the *Jewish Encyclopaedia*; Joseph, *Jewish Immigration* pp. 90–2; and Hersch, 'International Migration', p. 472, n. 1. It is worth noting that the enumerated total of Russian citizens, both Jew and Gentile, that emigrated via the ports of Hamburg and Bremen to the USA between 1881 and 1898 was 575,369, and that the enumerated total of Russian immigrants that arrived in the USA between fiscal years 1881 and 1898 was 549,614 (Ferenczi and Willcox, *International Migrations*, vol. I, p. 808, table VIII; and vol. I, pp. 374–500, especially table II), yet Wischnitzer states that 526, 120 Jews arrived in the USA from Russia during this period, when the Jewish share of Russian migration was only just over half (Wischnitzer, *To Dwell*, p. 288; Joseph, *Jewish Immigration*, table XII, p. 164). It would seem that Wischnitzer's estimates can safely be dismissed.

59. Kuznets, 'Russian Jews', table I, pp. 39–41 and discussion pp. 36–42.

60. A. Ruppin, *Jews in the Modern World*, p. 51.

61. For example, in 1909, 118,221 transmigrants passed through the UK; in 1910 140,353. HMI Aliens Act, *Fifth Annual Report*, pp. 29–30.

62. Thomas says that 'some of the returns were just guesswork'; *Migration*, pp. 44–5.

63. L. Gartner, 'Eastern European Jewish Immigrants in England: a Quarter-Century's View', in *Transactions of the Jewish Historical Society*, XXIX (1982–6), esp. pp. 302–3; Taylor, *Distant Magnet*, on the Atlantic Shipping Ring, pp. 145–67. M. Rischin, *The Promised City: New York's Jews, 1870–1914*,

p. 33; and DC Receiving House, *Minutes of Evidence*, Landau, qq. 1359, 1403–4, 1410, on relative prices (it was £2 cheaper to buy a ticket from the UK than from the continental ports). US Department for Commerce and Labor, *Report* (1904), pp. 44–5; US Commissioner General for Immigration, *Report* (1904), pp. 844–5, on how large numbers of apparently English emigrants were not English at all but had their nationalities erroneously reported because of the rate war. The shipping cartel rules stipulated that immigrants had to remain in the UK for five weeks before being able to take advantage of the lower fares, however, UK agents widely flouted these rules; see A. Keeling, 'Transatlantic Shipping Cartels and Migration between Europe and America, 1880–1914', *Essays in Economic and Business History* 17 (1999). Reutlinger appeared to think that the Aliens Act, which came into force on 1 January 1906, was the cause of the increase in Jews arriving in the USA notionally from the UK during fiscal year 1905, that is 1 July 1904 to 30 June 1905. He is clearly wrong. 'Reflections', pp. 479–80.

64. Thomas, *Migration*, deals with the problems of officialdom, pp. 44–5.
65. For any years when the total of Jewish immigration from 'other' countries summed to more then 2 per cent of the total; Kuznets, 'Russian Jews', table 1, pp. 39–41.
66. Wischnitzer, *To Dwell*, p. 292; Ruppin, *Jews*, pp. 52–54; H. Trooper, Jews and Canadian Immigration Policy, 1900–1950', in M. Rischin (ed.), *The Jews of North America*, pp. 44–56; and generally G. Tulchinsky, *Taking Root: the Origins of the Canadian Jewish Community*.
67. For East European Jewish migration to Canada, see Ferenczi and Willcox, *International Migrations*, table VI, pp. 364–5. Jewish immigration to Canada subsequently exceeded the 1905/6 peak in 1913/14. Thomas, *Migration*, pp. 45–48 on Canada–USA migration.
68. Kuznets, 'Russian Jews', notes to table I, p. 41.
69. Kuznets assumed that the port of New York was the dominant entry point, but increasingly less so as time went on, and so he used a variable multiplier of the New York totals to estimate total arrivals. The multiplier started at 1.25 in 1886 and grew by annual increments to 1.32 in 1893. The result of this is that Kuznets's estimates are considerably higher than Joseph's, giving over a quarter more immigrants arriving in the 1880s, for example. The major problem with this revision appears to derive from Kuznets having overlooked Joseph's sources, which were from all three ports and beginning not in 1894, as Kuznets's sources did, but in 1886 (Joseph, *Jewish Immigration*, table II, p. 159, shows figures for New York and Philadelphia ports from 1886 and Baltimore from 1891). These three ports accounted for almost all Jewish immigration during this period, and, from Joseph's' data, it is apparent that New York was a much more dominant entry-point at this time than Kuznets had allowed.
70. The multiplier starts at 1.02 in 1890 and rises by annual increments of 0.02 to 1.08 in 1893. Kuznets also assumed that Joseph's enumeration of all non-East-European Jews were in actual fact East European in origin and so also needed to be redistributed in the same manner as for the period 1899–1914. This is unlikely to have been the case, however, because, as Table 5.3 shows, this was clearly a phenomenon of German Jewish immigration and, as such, was unlikely to be East European in origin. German Jewish migration did include some from the eastern province of Posen, part

of Prussian Poland, but the greater part by part by far was of German west-ernised Jews. See A. Barkai, 'German Jewish Migration in the Nineteenth Century, 1830–1910', in Glazier and De Rosa, *Migration Across Time and Nations*. Also see in the same volume W. Kamphoefner, 'At the Crossroads of Economic Development: Background Factors Affecting Emigration from Nineteenth-Century Germany', especially fig. 9.1, p. 176 showing regional relative intensity of emigration from Germany to USA and the low intensity from Posen. German-Polish Jews who left Posen typically migrated to Berlin, not New York or London. See Kahan, 'The Urbanization Process of the Jews in Nineteenth Century Europe', in *Essays*, pp. 70–81.

71. There was also a slight readjustment arising out of some immigrants in the US official series classified as originating from Poland (which was not then a sovereign state) that Joseph omitted. However, it was only a very small number of immigrants and can safely be ignored; Kuznets, 'Russian Jews', p. 41.

72. Kuznets (p. 41) only gives totals for 1881–9. If the overestimate from his multiplier is subtracted then his total for the 1880s falls from 200.2 thou-sand to 176.6 thousand; Joseph's estimate is 164.4 thousand.

73. Joseph, *Jewish Immigration*, n. 3, pp. 90–1.

74. Joseph's 'correct' Austria-Hungarian calculations are contained in ibid., n. 3, pp. 90–1. The annual ratios of Russian Jewish to all Jewish immigration are given in table XII, p. 164. This ratio fluctuated quite widely, from 0.92 in the next crisis year of 1891 to 0.32 of the much larger and wider migration movement in 1910. The 1886 ratio was 0.79. Kuznets used a ratio of 0.7 (notes to table I, p. 41 in Kuznets, 'Russian Jews'). Joseph's estimate for the Romanian Jews has been left unaltered.

75. *Whitaker's Almanac* claimed in 1892 that Jews were pouring into the coun-try at the rate of 140,000 per year! Cited in Bermant, *Point of Arrival*. Also see B. Gainer, *The Alien Invasion: The Origins of the Aliens Act of 1905*; Gartner, 'Notes'; Lipman, *Social History*, pp. 87–90 and 142–3; J. A. Garrard, *The English and Immigration, 1880–1910*, appendix I, pp. 213–16; RC Aliens, *Report*, pp. 87–8; HMI Aliens Act, *First Annual Report* (P.P. 1907, LXVI), p. 3. On the enumeration of immigrants under the Aliens Act see the evidence of the Inspector, W. Haldane Porter, DC Receiving House, pp. 3–11.

76. HMI Aliens Act, *Reports*, for the years 1906–14. See especially the *Second Annual Report* (P.P. 1908, LXXXVII), p. 5, for the 1906 estimate and problems of classification, also Lipman, *Social History*, p. 142; the *Fifth Annual Report*, (P.P. 1911, X) which contains a useful five-year summary with valuable fig-ures, for example, p. 38; the *Sixth Annual Report*, (P.P. 1912–13, XII) for 1911 figures; the *Eighth Annual Report* (P.P. 1914, XIV) for 1912 and 1913.

77. The *Ninth Annual Report* (P. P. 1915, VII), p. 21.

78. The Inspector under the Aliens Act calculated that 20.7 per cent of 1907 returns for alien arrivals (not including transmigrants) were residents returning. *Second Annual Report*, p. 5. If this proportion is subtracted from the total of Russian arrivals of 12,481 in 1906 then the estimated total of immigrants is 9897, giving an eighth observation.

79. Gartner, 'Notes'.

80. Bearing in mind that the trends were non-linear in both series (see Table 5.1 below), this is a remarkably high coefficient.

81. The US figures, as they stand in Tables 5.4 and 5.5, are not strictly comparable with those of the UK because of the difference in the reporting periods
between the USA, using the American fiscal year (running from July 1 of
the previous to June 30 of the current year), and the UK, using calendar
years. This means that the UK series has a time-lag of six months. For the
official series for 1906–13 this evidently makes little sense. However, no
adjustment has been made to the UK series primarily because for the majority
of observations the series is not immigrant arrivals but marriages. It has been
assumed that six months is a reasonable estimate of the median time-
lag between arrival and marriage in the UK.

82. For calculating the permanent Jewish immigrant population in Britain, some
account has to be made of those who subsequently moved on to other destinations, overwhelmingly the United States. Gartner guessed (his word) that
this group might be as many as 400,000 to 500,000 Jews who had 'passed
two or more years in the British Isles' ('North Atlantic Jewry', p. 121).
Despite his guess, no clear evidence exists of the rate of stage migration.
But the 1709 notionally British Yiddish-speaking Jews that arrived in the
USA from 1899 to 1904 (see table 5.4) represented 0.4 per cent of all East
European Jewish immigrants. If these were actually stage migrants and
their share was consistent throughout the period, then total East European
stage migration from Britain to the USA would have been around 8000, or
just over 5 per cent of the estimated total stock of Jews in Britain. The underlying statistical series for table 5.6 assume that stage migration was 5.5 per
cent from Britain, accounting also therefore for those who went to destinations other than the USA. It follows that the stock of permanent settlers in
Britain was closer to 135,000 than 145,000 (94.5 per cent of 143,450 is
135,560).

83. Feldman, *Englishmen and Jews*, pp. 157–9, links the high share of women
Jewish immigrants to low rates of return migration. It is not unreasonable
to infer that temporary immigrants were less likely to marry in situ.

84. Feldman, *Englishmen and Jews*, pp. 302–4, on the activities of British Jewish
charities, although he earlier (p. 157) suggests that return rates were similar
for both the USA and UK Jewish immigration.

85. Older historiography assumed that the Aliens Act stopped immigrants
choosing Britain, for example, Lipman, *Social History*, chapter v (although
see his *History of the Jews*, p. 73, for his later more nuanced view). More
recent work also follows the standard restrictionist view, see Feldman,
Englishmen and Jews, p. 179, for example. On inadequate policing, see
J. Pellew, 'The Home Office and the Aliens Act, 1905', *Historical Journal*,
32 (1989). This, incidentally, has the intriguing implication that the most
profound but unintended consequence of the Act was the loss of much of
the valuable transmigrant trade to British shipowners and railway companies. See Landau's evidence to the Departmental Committee on the
Receiving House, *Minutes of Evidence*, qq. 1324 and 1398; and Garrard,
English and Immigration, pp. 46–7, on shipowners' concerns.

86. In part this is explained by the higher uncertainty of prospects of employment in the destination country; see Hatton, 'Model', pp. 6–7.

87. See W. Arthur, 'Competing Technologies: an Overview', in G. Dosi,
C. Freeman, *et al.* (eds), *Technical Change and Economic Theory*, pp. 590–607.

6 Entrepreneurship and Profits in the Jewish Immigrant Economies of London and New York

1. I. Kirzner, *Competition and Entrepreneurship*, p. 35 and passim.
2. Specialists will insist that the relevant 'profit' is the rate of return on capital, less the return from its next best alternative (typically assumed to be the base rate). Given the very low entry barriers, however, I have emphasised wages as the relevant opportunity cost here. See J. Foreman-Peck, E. Boccaletti and T. Nicholas, 'Entrepreneurs and business performance in nineteenth century France', *European Review of Economic History*, 2 (1998), esp. pp. 239–42 for a similar discussion.
3. The standard texts on the economics of entrepreneurship cover these and other required attributes. M. Casson, *The Entrepreneur: An Economic Theory*, especially ch. 17; J. Schumpeter, *Business Cycles: A Theoretical, Historical and Statistical Analysis of the Capitalist Process*, pp. 103–4; H. Leibenstein, *General X-efficiency Theory and Economic Development*; and Kirzner, *Competition*.
4. S. Tenenbaum, 'Culture and Context: The Emergence of Hebrew Free Loan Societies in the United States', *Social Science History*, 13 (1989), p. 221. J. Chapman, *Commercial Banks and Consumer Instalment Credit*, p. 28. US Industrial Commission, *Report on Immigration* (1901–2, hereafter Industrial Commission) gives the example of a contractor with a capital of $500 to $600 getting lines of credit from banks, vol. 15, p. 322.
5. A. Godley, 'Jewish Soft Loan Societies in New York and London and Immigrant Entrepreneurship, 1880–1914', *Business History*, 38 (1996); and Godley, 'Credit Rationing in the New York and London Garment Industries', in A. Grandori and M. Neri (eds), *The Games of Networks* (1999).
6. The New York Kehillah [Jewish Community], *The Jewish Communal Register of New York, 1917–1918*, p. 689.
7. V. Lipman, *A Century of Social Service, 1859–1959, The History of the Jewish Board of Guardians*, pp. 39, 60, 67, 107 and 163, also table 1, pp. 276–89. Loans proved to be so successful that the Charity Organisation Society imitated the Board's policy. See H. Bosanquet, *Social Work in London*, p. 43.
8. Booth Collection, British Library of Politics and Economic Sciences, LSE (hereafter BLPES), A19, 'Interview with Simon Ansell', fo. 58–62. This led to public criticism of the Board's loans policy; Charles Booth, for example, claimed that '[m]oney lent or given for trade purposes fosters the artificial multiplication of small masters, and is one of the direct causes of the sweating system', C. Booth, *Labour and Life of the People*, vol. 1, p. 574.
9. S. Tenenbaum, *A Credit to Their Community: Jewish Loan Societies in the United States, 1880–1945*; Tenenbaum, 'Immigrants and Capital: Jewish Loan Societies in the United States, 1880–1945', *American Jewish History*, LXXVI (1986), pp. 67–77; The New York Hebrew Free Loan Society, *The Poor Man's Bank*. The New York Society figures in all the standard histories of the New York Jewry, for example M. Rischin, *the Promised City: New York's Jews, 1870–1914*, p. 106, and A. Goren, *New York Jews and the Quest for Community: The Kehillah Experiment, 1908–1922*, p. 199.
10. New York Hebrew Free Loan Society, *11th Annual Report*, January 1903, p. 6.
11. There were no other comparable sources of small loans in the two cities in this period. In New York by 1917 the New York Hebrew Free Loan Society

accounted for 77 per cent of all soft loans, but its share was close to 100 per cent in 1905, Godley, 'Soft Loan Societies', p. 107.

12. See table 3.2 above. For general descriptions see H. Pollins, *The Economic History of the Jews in England*, ch. 9; and L. Gartner, *The Jewish Immigrant in England, 1870–1914*.

13. Godley, 'Soft Loan Societies', pp. 102–5. Note that some historians accept an East European birthplace as a Jewish identifier in the US census records. See E. Rosenthal, 'The Equivalence of United States Census Data for Persons of Russian Stock or Descent with American Jews', *Demography*, 14 (1975). The extent of non-Jewish Russian immigration will, however, always make such projections problematical.

14. Gartner, *Jewish Immigrant*, pp. 57–62; Rischin, *Promised City*, pp. 54–75. For specific examples see, W. Besant, *East London*, p. 200; G. Rees, *St. Michael: A History of Marks and Spencer*, pp. 27–31; RC Aliens *Minutes* on Jewish undertakers, see q. 8756 ff., and q. 9610 ff.; milksellers from q. 8883 ff., and q. 9645 ff.; haberdashers and postmasters from q. 8812 ff.

15. T. Kessner, *The Golden Door: Italian and Jewish Immigrant mobility in New York City, 1880–1915*, p. 64.

16. I. Howe, *The World of Our Fathers*, p. 164. Also see B. Hendrik, 'The Great Jewish Invasion', *McClure's*, January 1907, p. 307; J. Gurock, *When Harlem Was Jewish, 1870–1930*, pp. 30–34 and 44–46; H. Goldstein (ed.), *Forty Years of Struggle for a Principle: The Biography of Harry Fischel*; Leo Grebler, *Housing Market Behaviour in a Declining Area: Long Term Changes in Inventory and Utilization of Housing in New York's Lower East Side*, ch. 1.

17. Report of the Royal Commission on Alien Immigration (hereafter RC Aliens) (P.P. 1903, IX), p. 6; *Minutes of Evidence*, see Thomas, qq. 5661–5, Silver, qq. 2659–69, Belder, q. 4300, and *Appendix*, tables XXXVIII to XLVIII, pp. 44–51, and tables LIV and LXXVI to LXXVII, pp. 61, 91–2, for the enormous amount of detail showing Jewish immigrant investment and subsequent rent rises in the East End property market. Also D. Feldman, *Englishmen and Jews: Social Relations and Political Culture, 1840–1914*, pp. 172–84. The involvement of the Jewish immigrants as real estate entrepreneurs in London has not received the research attention it deserves, this despite the ample evidence of the second-generation immigrant property entrepreneurs in London. Max Rayne, Jack Cotton, Harry Hyams, Jack Rose, Charles Clore and Harold Samuel transformed the property sector in post-1945 Britain. See S. Aris, *The Jews in Business*, ch. 9; O. Marriot, *The Property Boom*; and P. Scott, *The Property Masters: a History of the British Commercial Property Sector*.

18. H. Llewellyn Smith, 'Influx of the Population (East London)', in C. Booth, *Life and Labour of the People in London*, 1st ser., vol. 3, ch. II, pp. 58–119; E. Aves, 'The Furniture Trade', in Booth, *Life and Labour*, 1st ser., vol. 4, ch. VI, pp. 157–218. W. Massil, *Immigrant Furniture Workers in London, 1881–1939*, esp. pp. 11–57, is a source of interesting anecdotes.

19. D. Schloss, 'Bootmaking', in Booth, *Life and Labour*, 1st ser., vol. 4, ch. IV, pp. 69–137; also see ch. V, 'Tailoring and Bootmaking – East End and West End', by Booth, J. MacDonald and Clara Collet, pp. 138–156. Feldman, *Englishmen and Jews*, pp. 141–65 and 185–214.

20. J. Perlman, 'Selective Migration as a Basis for Upward Mobility? The occupations of the Jewish Immigrants to the United States ca. 1900', Jerome Levy Economics Institute, working paper, no. 172 (1996).
21. A. Kahan, 'The Impact of Industrialization in Tsarist Russia on the Socioeconomic Conditions of the Jewish Population', in Kahan, *Essays in Jewish Social and Economic History*; F. Carstensen, *American Enterprise in Foreign Markets*, on sewing machine sales in Russia.
22. Booth Collection, A19, 'Interview with Abraham Rosenthal', fo. 76.
23. Booth Collection, A19, 'Interview with Simon Ansell' on 'tipping foremen', fo. 59; 'Interview with Mr Cohen', fo. 66; 'Interview with Morris Marks', on the difficulty of getting work from the warehouses, fo. 69; also see Beatrice Webb's (née Potter) interview with the foreman of Samuel's Wholesalers on the question of bribery, Passfield Papers, BLPES, s. vii.1, pt. 8 '"Wholesale clothing trade 1887" notes of interviews', folios 45–46.
24. Industrial Commission, *Report*, p. 321.
25. J. Buckman, *Immigrants and the Class Struggle: the Jewish Immigrants in Leeds, 1880–1914*, pp. 17–19.
26. See Sidney Webb's 'Preface' to B. Hutchins and A. Harrison, *A History of Factory Legislation*, p. xi.
27. Feldman, *Englishmen and Jews*, pp. 185–257, contains the best summary of the Jewish economy in London (and is especially good on misperception of the Jewish trades, for example, pp. 185–204). Also see R. Wechsler, 'The Jewish Garment Trade in East London, 1875–1914: a Study of Conditions and Responses' (unpublished PhD dissertation, Columbia University, 1979); and A. Godley, 'Immigrant Entrepreneurs and the Emergence of London's East End as an Industrial District', *London Journal*, 21 (1996). For New York, J. Pope, *The Clothing Industry in New York*; Industrial Commission; and US Immigration Commission, *Reports, Immigrants in Industries* (1911; hereafter Immigration Commission), pt 6, ch. ii, 'Clothing Manufacture in New York City', remain unsurpassed.
28. Pope, *Clothing Industry*, pp. 6–7. Also see W. Browning, 'The Clothing and Furnishing Trades', in C. Depew (ed.), *One Hundred Years of American Commerce*, pp. 561–5; New York Clothing Manufacturers' Exchange, *The New York Story: A History of the New York Clothing Industry', 1924–1949*; S. Fraser, 'Combined and Uneven Development in the Men's Clothing Industry', *Business History Review*, 57 (1983); Immigration Commission, esp. pp. 369–73.
29. Pope, *New York*, pp. 8–9, 12–13; Fraser, 'Men's Clothing', p. 527; NY Exchange, *New York Story*, pp. 66–7.
30. Pope, *New York*, p. 25; and Browning, 'Clothing', pp. 561–3, citation p. 563. A. Godley, 'Singer in Britain: the Diffusion of Sewing Machine Technology and Its Impact on the Clothing Industry in the United Kingdom, 1860–1905', *Textile History*, 27 (1996), for the development of the technology and a bibliography.
31. A. Godley, 'Pioneering Foreign Direct Investment in British Manufacturing', *Business History Review*, 73 (1999); Godley, 'Selling the Sewing Machine around the world: Singer's International Marketing Strategies, 1850–1914', *Enterprise and Society*, 3 (2002); and R. Davies, *Peacefully Working to Conquer the World; Singer Sewing Machines in Foreign Markets, 1854–1920*, on Singer.

Godley, 'The Global Diffusion of the Sewing Machine, 1850–1914', *Research in Economic History*, 20 (2000), on sewing machines generally.

32. Godley, 'The Global Diffusion of the Sewing Machine', table 1, although most of this increase was from family rather than industrial demand.
33. Cited in Pope, *New York*, p. 26.
34. A. Godley, 'Comparative Labour Productivity in the British and American Clothing Industries, 1850–1950', *Textile History*, 28 (1997).
35. Pope, *New York*, p.303; P. Scranton, 'The Transition from Custom to Ready-to-wear clothing in Philadelphia, 1890–1930', *Textile History*, 25 (1994).
36. A. Godley, 'The Development of the Clothing Industry: Technology and Fashion', *Textile History*, 28 (1997).
37. Browning, 'Clothing', pp. 563–4.
38. On seventeenth-century origins see B. Lemire, *Fashion's Favourite*. On regional centres in England and Wales see A. Godley, 'The Development of the UK Clothing Industry, 1850–1950: Output and Productivity Growth', *Business History*, 37 (1995); Godley, 'Immigrant Entrepreneurs'; and Godley, 'The Emergence of Mass Production in the UK Clothing Industry', in I. Taplin and J. Winterton (eds), *Restructuring Within a Labour Intensive Industry*.
39. S. Levitt, 'Cheap Mass-Produced Men's Clothing in the Nineteenth and Early Twentieth Centuries', *Textile History*, 22 (1991); J. Styles, 'Clothing the North: the Supply of Non-Elite Clothing in the Eighteenth Century North of England', *Textile History*, 25 (1994).
40. S. Chapman, 'The Innovating Entrepreneurs in the British Ready Made Clothing Industry' *Textile History*, 24 (1993); P. Sharpe, "Cheapness and Economy": Manufacturing and Retailing Ready-Made Clothing in London and Essex 1830–50', *Textile History*, 26 (1995); D. Green, 'The Nineteenth Century Metropolitan Economy; a Revisionist Interpretation', *London Journal*, 21 (1996), p. 18.
41. *Quarterly Review*, 97 (June 1855), pp. 211–12. This made Moses the second biggest advertising spenders in Britain (after Holloway's pills) and Nichols the sixth. I am indebted to Tony Corley for this reference.
42. Chapman, 'Innovating Entrepreneurs', p. 5.
43. J. Schmiechen, *Sweated Industries and Sweated Labour: The London Clothing Trades, 1860–1914*, ch. 1. The lower grade work in pre-machine days, the early ready-made industry, was the source of such appalling conditions that it prompted Tom Hood's *Song of the Shirt* (published in *Punch*, December 1843) and Charles Kingsley's *Alton Locke* (1850), from where the term 'sweating' probably originated. On the sweating debate generally see J. Morris, 'The Characteristics of Sweating: the Late Nineteenth Century London and Leeds Tailoring Trade', in A. John (ed.), *Unequal Opportunities: Women's Employment in England, 1800–1918*; and D. Bythell, *The Sweated Trades: Outwork in Nineteenth Century Britain*. The sewing machine's introduction improved working conditions substantially. A. Kershen, *Uniting the Tailors: Trade Unionism Amongst the Tailors of London and Leeds, 1870–1939*, gives some examples of early mechanisation in the 1860s, pp. 13–15.
44. Godley, 'Comparative Labour Productivity'.
45. John Burnett, *Report to the Board of Trade on Alien Immigration to the United States*, (P.P. 1893–94, LXXI), 'Miscellaneous', pp. 183–383, citation p. 233.

46. J. Jefferys, *Retail Trading in Britain, 1850–1950.* Also see A. Godley and S. Fletcher, 'Foreign Direct Investment in British Retailing, 1850–1962', *Business History*, 42 (2000).

47. Cited in Wechsler, 'Jewish Garment Trade', p. 55.

48. B. Potter, 'The Tailoring Trade', in Booth, *Life and Labour*, 1st ser., vol. 4, ch. III, p. 55.

49. Feldman, *Englishmen and Jews*, pp. 191–2 and 210. Mark Moses, in defence to the accusations levelled by the Burnett Report (*Report to the Board of Trade on the Sweating System at the East End of London*, P.P. 1887, LXXXIX), refers to the trade having grown and states that exports had exceeded £4m by 1888, two-thirds of which, he said, was produced in London. Booth Collection, A19, 'Interview with Mark Moses', folio 87. Also see W. Fishman, *East End Jewish Radicals, 1875–1914*, pp. 84–5. A. Briggs, *Friends of the People*, p. 128, refers to the doubling in the share of income spent on clothing from 6 per cent in 1845, although I have not been able to trace his unsourced 1845 figure. Bowley estimated that clothing's share of working-class expenditure remained constant from 1860, implying that price and income elasticity of demand were close to unitary. See Godley, 'Development', for a fuller discussion.

50. Pope, *New York*, pp. 27–60, esp. pp. 45 ff.; Potter, 'Tailoring Trade', esp. p. 47.

51. R. Waldinger, *Through the Eye of the Needle*, pp. 51–2; Industrial Commission, pp. 345, 383–7; Pope, *New York*, pp. 51–3, 66–78.

52. Booth Collection, A19, 'Interview with Mark Moses esq.', folio 89.

53. Booth Collection, A19, 'Interview with Mr Myers', on employing Christians, fos. 122–3.

54. See Morris Cohen's testimony to RCAliens, *Minutes*, qq. 18967–19045. Also Godley, 'Immigrant Entrepreneurs'; and A. Kershen, 'Morris Cohen and the Origins of the Women's Wholesale Clothing Industry in the East End', *Textile History*, 28 (1997).

55. Booth Collection, A19, 'Interview with P. Woolf esq.', folio 70, 'prices given by warehouses were very low'; boys' overcoats were apparently reduced by nearly 30 per cent in the mid-1880s, 'Interview with Woolf Cohen', folio 73. Other examples in fo. 79, 80, 89, 94 and 104. Also see Feldman, *Englishmen and Jews*, pp. 199–201.

56. Pope, *New York*, p. 91.

57. *Cost of Living of the Working Classes: Report of an Enquiry by the Board of Trade into Working Class Rents and Retail Prices* (P.P. 1913 LXVI), pp. xlviii-xlix and p. 307. From the base year of 1905 (equal to 100) the wholesale price of suits increased to 103.9 by 1910, and to 107.5 by 1912. Overcoats increased in price from 103.7 in 1909, and to 111.1 in 1912, p. xlix.

58. *Select Committee on Homework* (P.P. 1908, VII), 'Minutes of Evidence' (hereafter SC Homework), qq. 1179–96, 1271 and 1289; Buckman, *Immigrants and the Class Struggle*, p. 92; and Feldman, *Englishmen and Jews*, p. 239.

59. Industrial Commission, p. 345.

60. Industrial Commission, p. 337.

61. L. Gartner, 'The Jews of New York's East Side, 1890–93', *American Jewish Historical Quarterly*, LIII (1964). They were mostly clothing industry workers.

62. Burnett, *Alien Immigration*, pp. 238, 244, 234 and 240–2. His earlier report was the *Report on the Sweating System*, 1887. Industrial Commission, p. 347 on the four-and-a-half day week.

63. Industrial Commission, pp. 337 and 347 (profit); and assuming the 1893 average profit was in the middle of Burnett's range. S. Fraser, *Labor Will Rule: Sidney Hillman and the Rise of American Labor*, p. 27 for 1899.

64. Immigration Commission, p. 370, table 102, pp. 376–7. Also see B. Chiswick, 'Jewish Immigrant Wages in America in 1909: an Analysis of the Dillingham Commission Data', *Explorations in Economic History*, 29 (1992).

65. Burnett, *Alien Immigration*, p. 241; Industrial Commission, p. 346.

66. Booth Collection, A19, 'Interview with Mr Cohen': 'wholesale work did not pay', folio 66; also see 'Interview with Mr Jacobs', folio 65.

67. Passfield Papers, folio 45. Booth Collection, A19, 'Interview with Mr Goldstein', 'With regard to wages, there had been a great change', at least partly because of machinery, 'but did not account for all the difference. Most of his people he had to train into his way of working', fo. 71. Also see 'Interview with Harris Garfinkle', fo. 93.

68. The data on wages in the Jewish workshops in 1887–8 is extensive. See Booth Collection, tables with weekly expenditures and wages, A19, fos. 153–61. Potter, 'The Tailoring Trade', esp. pp. 44 ff. Also see Feldman, *Englishmen and Jews*, pp. 199–201.

69. C. Collet, 'Foreign Immigration in Relation to Women's Labour', *Report to the Board of Trade on the Volume and Effects of Recent Immigration from Eastern Europe into the United Kingdom* (P.P. 1894, LXVIII) part III, pp. 108–9 (wages), 114 (Leeds competition and days per week), and p. 112 (on relative conditions).

70. Board of Trade (Labour Department), *Report on Changes in Rates of Wages and Hours of Labour in the United Kingdom in 1908* (P.P. 1909, LXXX), p. 27 on the quality of data, rates of change calculated from tables vib and vii, pp. 62–5 and 72–3.

71. *Report of an Enquiry by the Board of Trade into the Earnings and Hours of the Workpeople of the United Kingdom*, II 'Clothing Trades in 1906' (P.P. 1909, LXXX) p. 109 on wages (Men 20 years and older, tailoring (ready-made [i.e. East End]) in London); and pp. 94–7 on seasonality (for London, November was 94 per cent and May 108 per cent of the mean employment level in 1906, but the next most seasonal months were December, 98 per cent and April, 102 per cent).

72. SC Homework, qq. 1166–1172; esp. qq. 1284 (on improvements in the last five years), 1179–84 (on rates of pay), and 1340–44 (on days per week).

73. SC Homework, q. 1245.

74. SC Homework, qq. 1190–1; Industrial Commission, p. 337.

75. R. Tawney, *The Establishment of Minimum Rates in the Tailoring Industry under the Trade Boards Act of 1909*, p. 19 also p. 6.

76. Tawney, *Minimum Rates*, p. 21.

77. Tawney, *Minimum Rates*, p. 104

78. Godley, 'Immigrant Entrepreneurs'; and Kershen, 'Morris Cohen'.

79. Feldman, *Englishmen and Jews*, includes some contradictory evidence on wages (e.g. p. 206), but concludes that overall wages increased over the period.

80. 1910 was in fact the turning-point for the New York industry because it heralded the advent of collective bargaining. Conditions (along with increased prices) improved dramatically. See R. Greenwald, '"More than a Strike": Ethnicity, Labor Relations and the Origins of the Protocols of Peace in the New York Ladies' Garment Industry', *Business and Economic History*, 27 (1998); N. Green, *Ready-to-Wear and Ready-to-Work: a Century of Industry and Immigrants in Paris and New York*; and Fraser, *Labor will Rule*.

81. Immigration Commission, pp. 372–3.

82. Immigration Commission, pp. 372–3. Green, *Ready-to-Wear*, esp. chs 6–7 on immigration.

83. M. Piore, *Birds of Passage: Migrant Labor and Industrial Societies*, is the standard work on how immigrant labour markets become detached and segmented from the wider labour markets with few routes for exiting from over-populated immigrant sectors.

84. A. Reutlinger, 'Reflections on the Anglo-American Jewish Experience', *American Jewish Historical Quarterly*, LXVI (1977), esp. p. 473.

85. *Jewish Chronicle*, 'Jewish Labour Conditions: Tailoring', 29 January 1937, pp. 20–1.

86. Pope, *New York*, p. 114; Tawney, *Minimum Rates*, p. 19.

7 Cultural Assimilation among Jewish Immigrants in London and New York

1. Booth Collection, British Library of Political and Economic Science, LSE, B B197, 'Interview with Herman Adler, the Chief Rabbi', p. 23.

2. M. Rischin, *The Promised City: New York's Jews, 1870–1914*, pp. 98–103; I. Howe, *World of our Fathers*, pp. 127–9 and 229–35; and A. Karp, 'The Making of Americans: German-Russian Jewish Confrontation in the Process of Americanization', in G. Wigoder (ed.), *Contemporary Jewry: Studies in Honor of Moshe Davis*. S. Tananbaum, 'Making Good Little English Children: Infant Welfare and Anglicization among the Jewish Immigrants in London, 1880–1939', *Immigrants and Minorities*, 12 (1993); and D. Feldman, 'Jews in London, 1880–1914', in R. Samuel (ed.), *Patriotism: The Making and Unmaking of British National Identity*, vol. 2.

3. Howe, *World of their Fathers*, p. 128.

4. Rischin, *Promised City*, p. 117; and Howe, *World of their Fathers*, p. 128.

5. C. Russell and H. Lewis, *The Jew in London: a Study of Racial Character and Present-Day Conditions*, p. 104.

6. Russell and Lewis, *Jew in London*, pp. 35–6. Also see I. Feinstein, 'The New Community 1880–1918', in Feinstein (ed.), *Three Centuries of Anglo-Jewish History*, esp. pp. 115–6.

7. It was notable that there were otherwise very few skilled blue-collars among the immigrants, just seven tailors' cutters, for example.

8. Author's interview with Mr Mick Mindel, May 1993. Mindel, a Jewish immigrant tailor, was an officer of the London Ladies' Tailors' Trade Union for many years from the early 1930s onwards and had experience of the Jewish tailoring trade dating back to the First World War. A. Kahan, 'The Impact of

Industrialization in Tsarist Russia on the Socioeconomic Conditions of the Jewish Population', in A. Kahan, *Essays in Jewish Social and Economic History*, p. 27.

9. Mindel said that 'it was impossible for Yiddish tailors to be journeymen'; Mindel interview.

10. The Jewish Journeymen Boot Finishers Union was active in the 1880s and 1890s, with 300 members in 1890; see D. Feldman, *Englishmen and Jews: Social Relations and Political Culture, 1840–1914*, p. 235; V. Lipman, *Social History of the Jews in England, 1850–1950*, p. 116; and W. Fishman, *East End Jewish Radicals, 1875–1914*, pp. 183 and 188. There was also the International Journeymen Tailors Machiners and Pressers Union, which amalgamated with the larger International Tailors Machiners and Pressers Union in 1898, Lipman, *Social History*, p. 116. More generally on Jewish unions see A. Kershen, *Uniting the Tailors*.

11. Feldman, *Englishmen and Jews*, p. 210 ff.

12. Kershen, *Uniting*, pp. 5–15. Also see B. Lemire, *Fashion's Favourite*, p. 102 on early developments. *National Board for Prices and Incomes*, Report 110, 'Pay and Conditions in the Clothing Industries' (P.P. 1968–9, XLII), appendix H, pp. 56–8, on the term's synonymity with craft status.

13. *Report by the Board of Trade into the Earnings ad Hours of Labour of the Workpeople of the United Kingdom. II. The Clothing Trades in 1906* (P.P. 1909, LXXX), pp. xxxvi ff.

14. C. Collet, 'Foreign Immigration in Relation to Women's Labour', Board of Trade, *Report into the Volume and Effects of Recent Immigration from Eastern Europe into the United Kingdom* (P.P. 1894, LXVIII), p. 116. Mindel also suggested that the immigrant Jewish tailors were reluctant to work further than a five-minute walk from their homes, because of the universal custom of returning home for lunch. Mindel interview. The immigrant journeymen in the CRA database were all East End residents.

15. *Select Committee on Homework* (P.P. 1908, VIII), qq. 1179–85 and 1222–3.

16. Ibid., qq. 1179–85 and 1222–3.

17. Feldman, *Englishmen and Jews*, p. 225.

18. Anne Kershen kindly asked the subjects of an oral history research project (inhabitants of Jewish old age pensioners' homes) whether they recalled the meaning of a journeyman in the East End trade. The consensus was that it was only for those who made the garments all the way through, a redundant feature of the East End trade in this period. By the 1930s, and especially after 1945, the journeyman function grew as West End bespoke houses increasingly used Jewish East End tailors. I am indebted to Dr Kershen for this assistance.

19. M. Rose, 'Family Firm, Community and Business Culture: a Comparative Perspective on the British and American Cotton Industries', in A. Godley and O. Westall (eds), *Business History and Business Culture*, on the importance of craft culture in the Philadelphia textile industry compared with that of New England.

20. I. Rosenwaike, *A Population History of New York City*, pp. 55–130.

21. Professional, clerical and other non-entrepreneurial white collar occupations were extremely rare among the Russian Jews in New York. See T. Kessner, *The Golden Door: Italian and Jewish Immigrant Mobility in New York*

City, 1880–1915; and B. Chiswick, 'The Occupational Attainment and Earnings of American Jewry, 1890–1990', *Contemporary Jewry*, 20 (1999).

22. S. Cott Watkins and A. London, 'Personal Names and Cultural Change: A Study of the Naming Patterns of Italians and Jews in the United States in 1910', *Social Science History*, 18 (1994); J. Gjerde and A. McCants, 'Fertility, Marriage, and Culture: Demographic Processes Among Norwegian Immigrants to the Rural Middle West', *Journal of Economic History*, 55 (1995).

23. See Chapter 5, p. 87, above.

24. Fitting immigration to a straight-line trend produced the following equation: Jewish immigration to $UK = 9.54 + 2.34y$ ($R^2 = 0.69$), and significant to the 0.1 per cent confidence level.

25. The actual method was to subtract the year of median marriage from the mean year across the full range of time-spans. Thus, for the time-span from 1880 to 1914 (35 years), the mean year was year 18, 1897, but the year of median marriage was 1902 (year 23), thus giving a value of -5 for 1914.

26. The Yiddish alphabet uses Hebrew script. Some immigrant Jews may have had knowledge of other alphabets; Russian uses the Cyrillic alphabet and Polish the Latin. While literacy in Yiddish was reasonable common in the Pale, knowledge of non-Yiddish languages was slight and disproportionately among the wealthier classes, who tended not to emigrate. Kahan, 'Impact', p. 4 on non-Yiddish-speaking Jews and emigration. Moreover, there was no bias to Polish background among the journeymen.

27. The fact that literacy among the brides of English grooms was much higher, both absolutely and relative to male literacy, than among the brides of immigrant grooms suggests that Jewish women gained disproportionately from education in the UK. Primary education in the Pale tended to be restricted to males. See S. Stampfer, 'Heder Study, Knowledge of Torah, and the Maintenance of Social Stratification in East European Jewish Society', *Studies in Jewish Education*, 3 (1988).

28. T. Heaton and S. Albrecht, 'The Changing Patterns of Interracial Marriage', *Social Biology*, 43 (1996).

29. Russell and Lewis, *Jew in London*, p. 24; also see J. Jacobs, *Studies in Jewish Statistics*, pp. 20–1 on the 'New English'.

30. See Howe, *World of our Fathers*, pp. 195–200, for New York, and Feldman, *Englishmen and Jews*, ch. 12, for London and references in each.

31. B. Potter, 'The Jewish Community (East London)', in C. Booth, *Life and Labour of the People in London*, 1st ser., vol. 3, pp. 185–6, for example. For analysis of immigrant income over time in the United States, see T. Hatton, 'The Immigration Assimilation Puzzle in Late Nineteenth-Century America', *Journal of Economic History*, 57 (1997); B. Chiswick, 'Jewish Immigrant Skill and Occupational Attainment at the Turn of the Century', *Explorations in Economic History* 28 (1991); and Chiswick, 'Jewish Immigrant Wages in America in 1909: An Analysis of the Dillingham Commission Data', *Explorations in Economic History* 29 (1992).

32. All variables are discreet except the modified time trend, although this was rebased to range from 0 to 1 for ease of comparability. When the modified time trend was recalculated as a discrete variable, the resulting logistic regression produced very similar results.

8 Entrepreneurship, Culture and British 'Declinism'

1. Not that this was itself straightforward. See E. Jones, 'Regional Cultures and Immigration', in S. Engerman and R. Gallaman (eds), *Cambridge Economic History of the United States* (Cambridge, 1996), for an impressive attempt to tie down the relationship between immigration and American culture.
2. These are covered in most textbooks. See M. Dintenfass, *The Decline of Industrial Britain, 1870–1980*; S. Pollard, *Britain's Prime and Britain's Decline*; R. Middleton, *The British Economy Since 1945*.
3. W. Rubinstein, 'Jewish Participation in National Economic Elites and Anti-Semitism', in D. Jeremy, (ed.), *Religion, Business and Wealth in Modern Britain*.
4. B. Chiswick, 'The Occupational Attainment and Earnings of American Jewry, 1890–1990', *Contemporary Jewry*, 20 (1999).
5. Kosmin estimated the rate of Jewish exogamy in 1982 as 25 per cent. B. Kosmin, 'Nuptiality and Fertility among British Jews', in D. Coleman (ed.), *Demography of Immigrants and Minority Groups in the United Kingdom*, esp. pp. 256–7.
6. B. Sarachek, 'American Entrepreneurs and the Horatio Alger Myth', *Journal of Economic History*, XXXVIII (1978).
7. R. Church, *The Rise and Decline of the British Motor Industry*, is the best summary.
8. J. Foreman-Peck, S. Bowden, and A. McKinlay, *The British Motor Industry*.
9. J. Zeitlin, 'Reconciling Automation and Flexibility? Technology and Production in the Postwar British Motor Vehicle Industry', *Enterprise and Society*, 1 (2000).
10. R. Church, 'Historical Foundations of Corporate Culture: British Leyland, Its Predecessors and Ford', in A. Godley and O. Westall (eds), *Business History and Business Culture*.
11. W. Lewchuk, *American Technology and the British Vehicle Industry*; and Lewchuk, 'The Motor Vehicle Industry', in B. Elbaum and W. Lazonick (eds), *The Decline of the British Economy*. The Lewchuk thesis also emphasises high dividend payments, but this isn't relevant here, and also has been effectively disproved by Church, *Motor Industry*, pp. 26–30. Lewchuk's labour control thesis nevertheless remains influential. See Church, ibid.; and A. Chandler, *Scale and Scope*, pp. 345–8.
12. Notably, S. Tolliday, 'The Failure of Mass Production unionism in the Motor Industry, 1914–1939', in C. Wrigley (ed.), *A History of British Industrial Relations*; and idem, 'Management and Labour, 1896–1939', in Tolliday and J. Zeitlin (eds), *The Automobile Industry and its Workers*.
13. S. Broadberry and N. Crafts, 'British Economic Policy and Industrial Performance in the Early Postwar Period', *Business History*, 38 (1996).

Bibliography

(Unless otherwise stated, place of publication for books is London.)

Abramovitz, M., 'Catching Up, Forging Ahead, and Falling Behind', *Journal of Economic History*, 46 (1986).

Adler, H., 'Jewish Life and Labour in East London', in H. Llewellyn Smith (ed.), *The New Survey of London Life and Labour* (1930–35).

Akerloff, G., 'A Theory of Social Custom, of which Unemployment may be one Consequence', *Quarterly Journal of Economics*, 95 (1980).

Aldcroft, D., 'The Entrepreneur and the British Economy, 1870–1914', *Economic History Review*, XVII (1964).

Aldcroft, D. (ed.), *The Development of British Industry and Foreign Competition, 1875–1914* (1968).

Alderman, G., 'The British Chief Rabbinate: a Most Peculiar Practice', *European Judaism*, 45 (1990).

Alderman, G., 'Power, Authority and Status in British Jewry: the Chief Rabbinate and Shechita', in G. Alderman and C. Holmes (eds), *Outsiders and Outcasts* (1993).

Alderman, G., *Federation of Synagogues, 1887–1987* (1987).

Allen, G., *The British Disease* (1976).

Anderson, M., 'The Study of Family Structure', in E.A. Wrigley (ed.), *Nineteenth Century Society: Essays in the Use of Quantitative Methods for the Study of Social Data* (Cambridge, 1972).

Antin, M., *From Plotsk to Boston* (Philadelphia, 1907).

Aris, S., *The Jews in Business* (1970).

Armstrong, W.A., 'The use of information about occupation', in E.A. Wrigley (ed.), *Nineteenth Century Society*.

Arthur, W., 'Competing Technologies: an Overview' in G. Dosi, C. Freeman *et al.* (eds), *Technical Change and Economic Theory* (1988).

Atkinson, A., 'The Distribution of Income in the UK and OECD Countries in the Twentieth Century', *Oxford Review of Economic Policy*, 15 (1999).

Aves, E., 'The Furniture Trade', in C. Booth (ed.), *Life and Labour of the People of London*, 1st ser. vol. 4 ch. VI (17 vols, 1902–3).

Baines, D., *Emigration from Europe 1815–1930* (1990).

Baines, D., 'European Labour Markets, Emigration and Internal Migration, 1850–1913', in T. Hatton and J. Williamson (eds), *Migration and the International Labour Market, 1850–1939* (1994).

Bairoch, P., 'International Industrialization Levels from 1750 to 1980', *Journal of European Economic History*, 11 (1982).

Bannock, G., *Britain in the 1980s: Enterprise Reborn?* (1987).

Barkai, A., 'German Jewish Migration in the Nineteenth Century, 1830–1910', in I. Glazier and L. De Rosa (eds), *Migration Across Time and Nations* (New York, 1986).

Baron, S., *Jews under Tsars and Soviets* (New York, 1976).

Barou, N., *The Jews in Work and Trade: A World Survey* (1946).

Baskerville, B., *The Polish Jew: His Social and Economic Value* (1906).

Benisch, A., 'How, When and Where did the Present Marriage Ceremony Originate?', *Jewish Chronicle*, 25 December 1874.

Berger, D (ed.), *The Legacy of Jewish Migration: 1881 and Its Impact* (New York, 1983).

Bermant, C., *Troubled Eden: an Anatomy of British Jewry* (1969).

Bernheimer, C. (ed.), *The Russian Jew in the United States* (New York, 1905).

Besant, W., *East London* (1903).

Board of Deputies of British Jews, *Annual Reports* (1881–1915).

Bodanski, G. *et al.*, 'Evidence for an Environmental Effect in the Aetiology of Insulin Dependent Diabetes in a Transmigratory Population', *British Medical Journal*, 304 (1992).

Bonacich, E., 'A Theory of Middlemen Minorities', *American Sociological Review*, 38 (1973).

Booth, C. (ed.), *Labour and Life of the People* (2 vols, 1889–91).

Booth, C. (ed.), *Life and Labour of the People of London* (17 vols, 1902–3).

Booth Collection, British Library of Politics and Economic Sciences.

Booth, C., J. MacDonald and C. Collet, 'Tailoring and Bootmaking – East End and West End', in Booth, *Life and Labour*, 1st ser. vol. 4, ch. III.

Bosanquet, H., *Social Work in London* (1914).

Briggs, A., *Friends of the People* (1956).

British Parliamentary Papers:

    Report to the Board of Trade on the Sweating System at the East End of London, P.P. 1887, LXXXIX.

    House of Lords Select Committee on the Sweating System, various Reports, P.P. 1888, XX and XXI; P.P. 1889, XIII and XIV; and P.P. 1890, XVII.

    Report on the Volume and Effects of Recent Immigration from Eastern Europe into the United Kingdom, P.P. 1894, LXVIII.

    Report to the Board of Trade on Alien Immigration to the United States, P.P. 1893–94, LXXI.

    Royal Commission on Alien Immigration, Report, P.P. 1903, IX.

    Select Committee on Homework, Report, P.P. 1908, VIII.

    Board of Trade (Labour Department), Report on Changes in Rates of Wages and hours of Labour in the United Kingdom in 1908, P.P. 1909, LXXX.

    Report of an Enquiry by the Board of Trade into the Earnings and Hours of the Workpeople of the United Kingdom, II, 'Clothing Trades in 1906', P.P. 1909, LXXX.

    H.M. Inspector under the Act, Annual Reports of 1907 to 1915.

    Departmental Committee of the Home Office, Report on the Establishment of a Receiving House for Alien Immigrants, P.P. 1911, X.

    Cost of Living of the Working Classes: Report of an Enquiry by the Board of Trade into Working Class Rents and Retail Prices, P.P. 1913, LXVI.

    National Board for Prices and Incomes, Report 110, 'Pay and Conditions in the Clothing Industries', P.P. 1968–9, XLII.

Brittan, S., 'How British is the British Sickness?', *Journal of Law and Economics*, XXI (1978).

Broadberry, S., 'Manufacturing and the Convergence Hypothesis: What the Long Run Data Show', *Journal of Economic History*, 53 (1993).

Broadberry, S., *The Productivity Race: British Manufacturing in International Perspective, 1850–1990* (Cambridge, 1997).

Broadberry, S., 'Anglo-German Productivity Differences 1870–1990: a Sectoral analysis', *European Review of Economic History*, 1 (1997).

Broadberry, S. and N. Crafts, 'British Economic Policy and Industrial Performance in the Early Postwar Period', *Business History*, 38 (1996).

Browning, W., 'The Clothing and Furnishing Trades', in C. Depew (ed.), *One Hundred Years of American Commerce* (New York, 1885).

Buckman, J., *Immigrants and the Class Struggle: the Jewish Immigrants in Leeds, 1880–1914* (Manchester, 1983).

Bythell, D., *The Sweated Trades: Outwork in Nineteenth Century Britain* (1971).

Cahan, A. 'The Russian Jew in the United States', in C. Bernheimer (ed.), *The Russian Jew in the United States*.

Cairnes, J.E., *Some Leading Principles of Political Economy Newly Expounded* (1874).

Cantwell, J., 'Historical Trends in International Patterns of Technological Innovation', in J. Foreman-Peck (ed.), *New Perspectives on the Late Victorian Economy: Essays in Quantitative Economic History, 1860–1914* (Cambridge, 1991).

Carstensen, F., *American Enterprise in Foreign Markets* (Chapel Hill, NC, 1984).

Casson, M., *The Entrepreneur: an Economic Theory* (Oxford, 1982).

Casson, M., *The Economics of Business Culture: Game Theory, Transaction Costs, and Economic Performance* (Oxford, 1991).

Casson, M., 'Culture as an Economic Asset', in A. Godley and O. Westall (eds), *Business History and Business Culture* (Manchester, 1996).

Casson, M. and A. Godley (eds), *Cultural Factors in Economic Growth* (Berlin, 2000).

Chandler, A., *Scale and Scope: The Dynamics of Industrial Capitalism* (Cambridge MA, 1990).

Chapman, J., *Commercial Banks and Consumer Instalment Credit* (New York, 1940).

Chapman, S., 'The Innovating Entrepreneurs in the British Ready-Made Clothing Industry', *Textile History*, 24 (1993).

Chiswick, B., 'Jewish Immigrant Skill and Occupational Attainment at the Turn of the Century', *Explorations in Economic History*, 28 (1991).

Chiswick, B., 'Jewish Immigrant Wages in America in 1909: an Analysis of the Dillingham Commission Data', *Explorations in Economic History*, 29 (1992).

Chiswick, B., 'The Occupational Attainment and Earnings of American Jewry, 1890–1990', *Contemporary Jewry*, 20 (1999).

Chiswick, B., 'The Billings Report and the Occupational Attainment of American Jewry, 1890', *Shofar: an Interdisciplinary Journal of Jewish Studies*, 19 (2001).

Church, R., *The Rise and Decline of the British Motor Industry* (Basingstoke, 1994).

Church, R., 'Historical Foundations of Corporate Culture: British Leyland, Its Predecessors and Ford', in A. Godley and O. Westall (eds), *Business History and Business Culture*.

Church, R., 'Ossified or Dynamic? Structure, Markets and the Competitive Process in the British Business System of the Nineteenth Century', *Business History*, 42 (2000).

Cohen Max, 'The Jew in Business', *American Hebrew*, 22, May 1891.

Corley, T., 'How Quakers Coped with Business Success: Quaker Industrialists 1860–1914', in D. Jeremy (ed.), *Business and Religion in Britain* (Aldershot, 1988).

Crafts, N., S. Leybourne, and T. Mills, 'The Climacteric in Late Victorian Britain and France: a Reappraisal of the Evidence', *Journal of Applied Econometrics*, 4 (1989).

Dahrendorf, R., *On Britain* (1982).

Davies, R., *Peacefully Working to Conquer the World; Singer Sewing Machines in Foreign Markets, 1854–1920* (New York, 1976).

Davis, M., 'Critique of Official United States Immigration Statistics', in I. Ferenczi and W. Willcox (eds), *International Migrations* (Washington, DC, 2 vols, 1929–31).

Dintenfass, M., *The Decline of Industrial Britain, 1870–1980* (1992).

Dubnow, S. M., *History of the Jews in Russia and Poland* (Philadelphia, 3 vols, 1918–19).

Edwards, A.M., 'A Social Economic Grouping of the Gainful Workers of the United States', *Journal of the American Statistical Association*, 27 (1933).

Elbaum, B. and W. Lazonick (eds), *The Decline of the British Economy* (Oxford, 1986).

Encyclopaedia Judaica (Jerusalem, 1964).

Engelman, U., 'Sources of Jewish Statistics', in L. Finkelstein (ed.), *The Jews: Their History, Culture and Religion* (New York, 1949).

Englander, D., 'Booth's Jews: the Presentation of Jews and Judaism in *Life and Labour of the People of London*', *Victorian Studies*, 32 (1989).

Englander, D., '*Stille Huppah* (Quiet Marriage) among Jewish Immigrants in Britain', *Jewish Journal of Sociology*, xxxiv (1992).

Englander, D. (ed.), *A Documentary History of Jewish Immigrants in Britain, 1840–1920* (Leicester, 1994).

Falkus, M., *The Industrialisation of Russia, 1700–1914* (1972).

Feingold, H., 'Investing in Themselves: the Harvard Case and the Origins of the Third American-Jewish Commercial Elite', *American Jewish Historical Quarterly*, lxxvii (1988).

Feinstein, C., 'What Really Happened to Real Wages?: Trends in Wages, Prices, and Productivity in the United Kingdom, 1880–1913', *Economic History Review*, xliii (1990).

Feinstein, C., 'New Estimates of Average Earnings in the United Kingdom, 1880–1913' *Economic History Review*, xliii (1990).

Feinstein, I., 'The New Community 1880–1918', in V. Lipman (ed.), *Three Centuries of Anglo-Jewish History* (1961).

Feldman, D., 'Jews in London, 1880–1914', in R. Samuel (ed.), *Patriotism: The Making and Unmaking of British National Identity* (1989).

Feldman, D., *Englishmen and Jews: Social Relations and Political Culture, 1840–1914* (New Haven, CT, 1994).

Ferenczi, I. and W. Willcox (eds), *International Migrations* (Washington, DC, 2 vols, 1929–31).

Finkelstein, L. (ed.), *The Jews: Their History, Culture and Religion* (2 vols, New York, 1949).

Fishman, W., *East End Jewish Radicals, 1875–1914* (1975).

Fletcher, S. and A. Godley, 'Foreign Direct Investment in British Retailing, 1850–1962', *Business History*, 42 (2000).

Floud, R., 'Britain 1860–1914: a survey', in R. Floud and D. McCloskey (eds), *The Economic History of Britain since 1700* (Cambridge, 1981).

Foreman-Peck, J., S. Bowden and A. McKinlay, *The British Motor Industry* (Manchester, 1995).

Foreman-Peck, J., E. Boccaletti and T. Nicholas, 'Entrepreneurs and business Performance in Nineteenth Century France', *European Review of Economic History*, 2 (1998).

Fortune, *Jews in America* (New York, 1936).

Frankel J., *Prophecy and Politics: Socialism, Nationalism and the Russian Jews, 1862–1917* (Cambridge, 1981).

Frankel, J., 'Introduction', in A. Kahan, *Essays in Jewish Social and Economic History* (1986).

Frankel, J., 'The Crisis of 1881–82 as a Turning Point in Modern Jewish History', in Berger (ed.), *The Legacy of Jewish Migration: 1881 and Its Impact*.

Frankel, J. and S.J. Zipperstein (eds), *Assimilation and Community: the Jews in Nineteenth Century Europe* (Cambridge, 1992).

Fraser, S., 'Combined and Uneven Development in the Men's Clothing Industry', *Business History Review*, 57 (1983).

Fraser, S., *Labor Will Rule: Sidney Hillman and the Rise of American Labor* (New York, 1991).

Freedman, M., *Leeds Jewry: the First Hundred Years* (Leeds, 1992).

Fukuyama, F., *Trust, the Social Virtues and Creation of Prosperity* (New York, 1995).

Gainer, B., *The Alien Invasion: The Origins of the Aliens Act of 1905* (1972).

Garrard, J., *The English and Immigration 1880–1910* (Oxford, 1971).

Gartner, L., 'Notes on the Statistics of Jewish Immigration to England, 1870–1914', *Jewish Social Studies*, 22 (1960).

Gartner, L., *The Jewish Immigrant in England, 1870–1914* (1960).

Gartner, L., 'The Jews of New York's East Side, 1890–93', *American Jewish Historical Quarterly*, LIII (1964).

Gartner, L., 'North Atlantic Jewry', in A. Newman (ed.), *Migration and Settlement* (1971).

Gartner, L., 'Eastern European Jewish Immigrants in England: a Quarter-Century's View', in *Transactions of the Jewish Historical Society*, XXIX (1982–6).

Gartner, L., 'Jewish Migrants En Route from Europe to North America: Traditions and Realities', in *Jewish History*, 1 (1986).

Gitelman, Z., *A Century of Ambivalence: the Jews of Russia and the Soviet Union, 1881 to the Present* (1988).

Gjerde, J. and A. McCants, 'Fertility, Marriage and Culture: Demographic Processes among Norwegian Immigrants to the Rural Middle West', *Journal of Economic History*, 55 (1995).

Glass, D. (ed.), *Social Mobility in Britain* (1954).

Glazer, N., *American Judaism* (Chicago, 1972).

Glazier, I., and L. De Rosa (eds), *Migration Across Time and Nations* (New York, 1986).

Glover, G.R., 'Sex Ratio Errors in Census Data', *British Medical Journal*, 307 (1993).

Godley, A., 'Enterprise and Culture: Jewish Immigrants in London and New York, 1880–1914' (unpublished PhD thesis, LSE, 1993).

Godley, A., 'The Development of the UK Clothing Industry, 1850–1950: Output and Productivity Growth', *Business History*, 37 (1995).

Godley, A., 'Immigrant Entrepreneurs and the Emergence of London's East End as an Industrial District', *London Journal*, 21 (1996).

Godley, A., 'Singer in Britain: the Diffusion of Sewing Machine Technology and its Impact on the Clothing Industry in the United Kingdom, 1860–1905', *Textile History*, 27 (1996).

Godley, A., 'The Emergence of Mass Production in the UK Clothing Industry', in I. Taplin and J. Winterton (eds), *Restructuring within a Labour Intensive Industry* (Aldershot, 1996).

Godley, A., 'Jewish Soft Loan Societies in New York and London and Immigrant Entrepreneurship', *Business History*, 38 (1996).

Godley, A., 'Comparative Labour Productivity in the British and American Clothing Industries, 1850–1950', *Textile History*, 28 (1997).

Godley, A., 'The Development of the Clothing Industry: Technology and Fashion', *Textile History*, 28 (1997).

Godley, A., 'Leaving the East End: Regional mobility among East European Jews in London, 1880–1914', in A. Kershen (ed.), *London: A Promised Land?* (Aldershot, 1997).

Godley, A., 'Pioneering Foreign Direct Investment in British Manufacturing', *Business History Review*, 73 (1999).

Godley, A., 'Credit Rationing in the New York and London Garment Industries', in A. Grandori and M. Neri (eds), *The Games of Networks* (1999).

Godley, A., 'The Global Diffusion of the Sewing Machine, 1850–1914', *Research in Economic History*, 20 (2000).

Godley, A., 'Selling the Sewing Machine Around the World: Singer's International Marketing Strategies, 1850–1914', *Enterprise and Society*, 3 (2002).

Godley, A., 'The Occupational Profile of East European Women in Britain, 1880–1914', University of Reading, Discussion Paper in Economics (2001).

Godley, A. and D. Ross, 'Banks, Networks and Small Firm Finance', *Business History* (1996).

Godley, A. and O. Westall (eds), *Business History and Business Culture* (Manchester, 1996).

Goldsmith, R., 'The Economic Growth of Tsarist Russia, 1860–1913', *Economic Development and Cultural Change*, 9 (1961).

Goldstein, Herbert S. (ed.), *Forty Years of Struggle for a Principle: the Biography of Harry Fischel* (New York, 1928).

Goldthorpe, J.H., *Social Mobility and Class Structure in Modern Britain* (Oxford, 1980).

Goren, A., *New York Jews and the Quest for Community: the Kehillah Experiment, 1908–1922* (New York, 1970).

Gould, J., 'European Inter-Continental Emigration 1815–1914: Patterns and Causes', *Journal of European Economic History*, 8 (1979).

Gould, J., 'European Inter-Continental Emigration, the Road Home: Return Migration from the USA', *Journal of European Economic History*, 9 (1980).

Granovetter, M., 'Economic Action and Social Structure: the Problem of Embeddedness', *American Journal of Sociology*, 91 (1985).

Grayzel, S., *A History of the Jews* (New York, 1968).

Grebler, L., *Housing Market Behaviour in a Declining Area: Long Term Changes in Inventory and Utilization of Housing in New York's Lower East Side* (New York, 1952).

Green, D., 'The Nineteenth Century Metropolitan Economy; a Revisionist Interpretation', *London Journal*, 21 (1996).

Green, N., 'A Tale of Three Cities: Immigrant Jews in New York, London and Paris, 1870–1914', in A. Newman and S. Massil (eds), *Patterns of Migration, 1850–1914* (1996).

Green, N., *Ready-to-Wear and Ready-to-Work: a Century of Industry and Immigrants in Paris and New York* (Durham, NC, 1997).

Greenberg, L., *The Jews in Russia* (2 vols, New Haven, CT, 1951).

Greenwald, R., '"More than a Strike": Ethnicity, Labor Relations and the Origins of the Protocols of Peace in the New York Ladies' Garment Industry', *Business and Economic History*, 27 (1998).

Gregory, P., *Russian National Income, 1885–1913* (Cambridge, 1982).

Greif, A., 'Cultural Beliefs and the Organization of Society: a Historical and Theoretical Reflection on Collectivist and Individualist Societies', *Journal of Political Economy*, 102 (1994).

Gross, N., 'Entrepreneurship of Religious and Ethnic Minorities', *Zeitschrift für Unternehmensgeschichte*, 64 (1992).

Gurock, J., *When Harlem was Jewish, 1870–1930* (New York, 1979).

Habakkuk, H., *American and British Technology in the Nineteenth Century* (1967).

Haberman, S. and M. Schmool, 'Estimates of the British Jewish Population 1984–88', *Journal of the Royal Statistical Society*, ser. A, 158 (1995)

Hall, J., *Powers and Liberties* (Harmondsworth, 1986).

Halsey, A. H., *Change in British Society*, 3rd edn (Oxford, 1986).

Hatton, T., 'A Model of UK Emigration, 1870–1913', *Review of Economics and Statistics*, 77 (1995).

Hatton, T., 'The Immigration Assimilation Puzzle in Late Nineteenth Century America', *Journal of Economic History*, 57 (1997).

Hatton, T. and J. Williamson, 'After the Famine: Emigration from Ireland, 1850–1913', *Journal of Economic History*, 53 (1993).

Hatton, T. and J. Williamson, 'What Drove the Mass Migrations from Europe in the Late Nineteenth Century', *Population and Development Review*, 20 (1994).

Hatton, T. and J. Williamson, 'International Migration 1850–1939: an Economic Survey', in Hatton and Williamson (eds), *Migration and the International Labour Market, 1850–1939* (1994).

Hatton, T. and J. Williamson (eds), *Migration and the International Labour Market, 1850–1939* (1994).

Hatton, T. and J. Williamson, *The Age of Mass Migration: Causes and Economic Impact* (Oxford, 1998).

Heaton, T. and S. Albrecht, 'The Changing Patterns of Interracial Marriage', *Social Biology*, 43 (1996).

Hebert, R. and A. Link, *The Entrepreneur: Mainstream Views and Radical Critiques* (New York, 1982).

Hendrik, B., 'The Great Jewish Invasion', *McClure's*, January 1907.

Hendrik, B., *The Jews in America* (New York, 1922).

Henriques, B. S. Q., *The Jews and English Law* (Oxford, 1908).

Henriques, B. S. Q., *Jewish Marriages and the English Law* (Oxford, 1909).

Hersch, L., 'International Migration of the Jews', in I. Ferenczi and W. Willcox (eds), *International Migrations*.

Hofstede, G., *Culture's Consequence: International Differences in Work-Related Values* (Beverley Hills, CA, 1980).

Homa, B., *A Fortress in Anglo-Jewry, the Story of the Machzike Hadath* (1953).

Honeyman, K., 'Gender Divisions and Industrial Divide: the Case of the Leeds Clothing Trade, 1850–1970', *Textile History*, 28 (1997).

Howe, I., *The World of Our Fathers* (New York, 1976).

Humphries, J., 'Class Struggle and the Persistence of the Working Class Family', *Cambridge Journal of Economics*, 1 (1977).

Jacobs, J., *Studies in Jewish Statistics. Social, Vital and Anthropometric* (1884).

Jefferys, J., *Retail Trading in Britain, 1850–1950* (Cambridge, 1954).

Jerome, H., *Migration and the Business Cycle* (New York, 1926).

Jewish Board of Guardians, *Annual Reports* (1870–1914).

Jewish Chronicle (various dates).

Jewish Year Book (1897–1915).

Johnson, P., *A History of the Jews* (1987).

Jones, E., *The European Miracle* 2nd edn (Cambridge, 1987).

Jones, E., *Growth Recurring* (Oxford, 1988).

Jones, E., 'Culture and its Relationship to Economic Change', *Journal of Institutional and Theoretical Economics*, 151 (1995).

Jones, E., 'Regional Cultures and Immigration' in S. Engerman and R. Gallman (eds), *Cambridge Economic History of the United States* (Cambridge, 1996). Jones,

Jones, G.G. 'Great Britain: Big business, management, and competitiveness in twentieth century Britain', in A. D. Chandler, F. Amatori and T. Hikino (eds), *Big Business and the Wealth of Nations* (Cambridge, 1997).

Joseph, K., 'Preface', in Samuel Smiles, *Self-Help* (1986 edition).

Joseph, S., *Jewish Immigration to the United States from 1881 to 1910* (New York, 1914).

Kahan, A., 'Economic Opportunities and Some Pilgrims Progress', in *Journal of Economic History*, 38 (1978).

Kahan, A., *Essays in Jewish Social and Economic History* (1986).

Kamphoefner, W., 'At the Crossroads of Economic Development: Background Factors Affecting Emigration from Nineteenth-Century Germany', in I. Glazier and L. De Rosa (eds), *Migration Across Time and Nations*.

Kantorowitsch, M., 'Estimate of the Jewish Population of London in 1929–1933', *Journal of the Royal Statistical Society*, XCIX (1936).

Karp, A., 'The Making of Americans: German-Russian Jewish Confrontation in the Process of Americanization', in G. Wigoder (ed.), *Contemporary Jewry: Studies in Honor of Moshe Davis* (Jerusalem, 1984).

Keeling, A., 'Transatlantic Shipping Cartels and Migration between Europe and America, 1880–1914', *Essays in Economic and Business History*, 17 (1999).

Keeling, A., 'The Transportation Revolution and Transatlantic Migration, 1850–1914', *Research in Economic History*, 19 (1999).

Kennedy, P., *The Rise and Fall of the Great Powers, 1500–2000* (1988).

Kershen, A., *Uniting the Tailors: Trade Unionism Amongst the Tailors of London and Leeds, 1870–1939* (1995).

Kershen, A., 'Morris Cohen and the Origins of the Women's Wholesale Clothing Industry in the East End', *Textile History*, 28 (1997).

Kessner, T., 'The Golden Door: Immigrant Mobility in New York City, 1880–1915' (unpublished PhD thesis, Columbia University, 1975).

Kessner, T., *The Golden Door: Italian and Jewish Immigrant Mobility in New York City, 1880–1915* (New York, 1977).

Kessner, T., 'The Selective Filter of Ethnicity', in D. Berger (ed.), *The Legacy of Jewish Migration: 1881 and Its Impact*.

King, M. L. and D. L. Magnuson, 'Perspectives on Historical US Census Undercounts', *Social Science History*, 19 (1995).

Kingsley, C., *Alton Locke* (1850).

Kirby, M., 'Institutional Rigidities and Economic Decline: Reflections on the British Experience', *Economic History Review*, 45 (1992).

Kirzner, I., *Competition and Entrepreneurship* (1973).

Klier, J., *Imperial Russia's Jewish Question, 1855–1881* (Cambridge, 1995).

Klier, J., 'Emigration Mania in Late-Imperial Russia: Legend and Reality', in Massil and Newman, *Patterns of Migration*.

Knight, F., *Risk, Uncertainty and Profit* (1921).

Kosmin, B., 'Nuptiality and Fertility among British Jews', in D. Coleman (ed.), *Demography of Immigrants and Minority Groups in the United Kingdom* (1982).

Krausz, E., 'Occupation and Social Advancement in Anglo-Jewry', *Jewish Journal of Sociology*, IV (1962).

Krausz, E., 'The Economic and Social Structure of Anglo-Jewry', in J. Gould and S. Esh (eds), *Jewish Life in Modern Britain* (1964).

Kuznets, S. and E. Rubin, *Immigration and the Foreign Born* (New York, 1954).

Kuznets, S., 'Immigration of Russian Jews to the United States: Background and Structure', *Perspectives in American History*, 9 (1975).

Landes, D., *The Unbound Prometheus: Technological Change and Industrial Development in Western Europe from 1750 to the Present* (Cambridge, 1969).

Landes, D., *The Wealth and Poverty of Nations: Why Are Some So Rich and Others So Poor?* (New York, 1998).

Lazonick, W. and W. Mass, 'The British Cotton Industry and International Competitive Advantage: the State of the Debates', *Business History*, 32 (1990).

Lazonick, W., *Competitive Advantage on the Shop Floor* (Cambridge, MA, 1990).

Lazonick, W., *Business Organization and the Myth of the Market Economy* (Cambridge, MA, 1991).

Lederhendler, E., *The Road to Modern Jewish Politics* (Oxford, 1989).

Lee, C., *British Regional Employment Statistics* (Cambridge, 1979).

Lee, C., 'Regional Growth and Structural Change in Victorian Britain', *Economic History Review*, XXXIII (1981).

Leese, M. *et al.*, 'Adjusting for Underenumeration in the 1991 Census', *British Medical Journal*, 311 (1995).

Leibenstein, H., *General X-Efficiency Theory and Economic Development* (New York, 1978).

Lemire, B., *Fashion's Favourite: the Cotton Trade and the Consumer in Britain, 1660–1800* (Basingstoke, 1991).

Lestschinsky, J., 'Jewish Migrations, 1840–1946', in L. Finkelstein (ed.), *The Jews: Their History, Culture and Religion* (New York, 1949).

Levine, A., *Industrial Retardation in Britain, 1880–1914* (1967).

Levitt, S., 'Cheap Mass-Produced Men's Clothing in the Nineteenth and Early Twentieth Centuries', *Textile History*, 22 (1991).

Lewchuk, W., *American Technology and the British Vehicle Industry* (Cambridge, 1987).

Lewchuk, W., 'The Motor Vehicle Industry', in B. Elbaum and W. Lazonick (eds), *The Decline of the British Economy*.

Linden, A. (ed.), *Die Judenpogrome in Russland* (2 vols, Cologne and Leipzig, 1910).

Lindert, P. and K. Trace, 'Yardsticks for Victorian Entrepreneurs', in D. McCloskey (ed.), *Essays on a Mature Economy: Britain after 1840* (1971).

Lindert, P. and J. Williamson, 'Growth, Equality and History', *Explorations in Economic History*, 22 (1985).

Lipman, V., *Social History of the Jews in England, 1850–1950* (1954).

Lipman, V., *A Century of Social Service, 1859–1959, the History of the Jewish Board of Guardians* (1959).

Lipman, V., 'Rise of Jewish Suburbia', *Transactions of the Jewish Historical Society of England*, xxi (1968).

Lipman, V., 'The Booth and New London Surveys as Source Material for East London Jewry (1880–1930)', in A. Newman (ed.), *The Jewish East End, 1834–1940* (1980).

Lipman, V., *A History of the Jews in Britain since 1858* (Leicester, 1990).

Llewellyn Smith, H., 'Influx of the Population (East London)', in C. Booth, *Life and Labour of the People in London*.

Llewellyn Smith, H. (ed.), *The New Survey of London Life and Labour* (9 vols, 1930–35).

McCloskey, D., 'Bourgeois Virtue and the History of P and S', *Journal of Economic History*, 58 (1998).

Majeed, F. A. *et al.*, 'Using Data from the 1991 Census', *British Medical Journal*, 310 (1995).

Marriot, Oliver, *The Property Boom* (1967).

Massarik, F., 'New Approaches to the Study of the American Jew', *Jewish Journal of Sociology*, 8 (1966).

Massil, W., *Immigrant Furniture Workers in London, 1881–1939* (1997).

Mendelsohn, E., *The Jews of East Central Europe Between the World Wars* (Bloomington IN, 1983).

Middleton, R., *The British Economy since 1945* (Basingstoke, 2000).

Mielziner, M., *Jewish Law of Marriage and Divorce in Ancient and Modern Times and its Relation to the Law of the State* (New York, 1901).

Miles, A., 'How Open Was Nineteenth Century British Society: Social Mobility and Equality of Opportunity, 1839–1914?', in A. Miles and D. Vincent (eds), *Building European Society: Occupational Change and Social Mobility in Europe, 1860–1940* (Manchester, 1993).

Miles, A., *Social Mobility in Britain, 1837–1914* (Basingstoke, 1999).

Moore, K. and D. Lewis, *Birth of the Multinational: 2000 years of Ancient Business History – from Ashur to Augustus* (Copenhagen, 1999).

Morris, J., 'The Characteristics of Sweating: the Late Nineteenth Century London and Leeds Tailoring Trade', in A. John (ed.), *Unequal Opportunities: Women's Employment in England, 1800–1918* (Oxford, 1986).

Muellbauer, J., 'The Assessment: Consumer Expenditure', *Oxford Review of Economic Policy*, 10 (1994).

Muldrew, C., *The Economy of Obligation: the Culture of Credit and Social Relations in Early Modern England* (New York, 1998).

Naggar, B., *Jewish Pedlars and Hawkers, 1740–1940* (Camberley, 1992).

Newman, A., *United Synagogue, 1870–1970* (1977).

Newman, A. and S. Massil (eds), *Patterns of Migration, 1850–1914* (1996).

Newman, A., 'Directed Migration: the Poor Jews' Temporary Shelter, 1885–1914', in Newman and Massil, *Patterns of Migration*.

New York Clothing Manufacturers' Exchange, *The New York Story: A History of the New York Clothing Industry, 1924–1949* (New York, n.d. (1949?)).

New York Hebrew Free Loan Society, *Annual Reports* (1894–1940).

New York Hebrew Free Loan Society, *The Poor Man's Bank* (New York, 1942).

New York Kehillah [Jewish Community], *The Jewish Communal Register of New York, 1917–1918* (New York, 1918).

Obolensky-Ossinsky, V., 'Emigration from and Immigration into Russia', in Ferenczi and Willcox, *International Migrations*.

Olson, M., *The Rise and Decline of Nations: Economic Growth, Stagflation and Social Rigidities* (New Haven CT, 1982).

O'Rourke, K. and J. Williamson, 'Around the European Periphery 1870–1913: Globalization, Schooling and Growth', *European Review of Economic History*, 1 (1997).

Orsagh, T., 'Progress in Iron and Steel: 1870–1913', *Comparative Studies in Society and History*, III (1961).

Passfield Papers, British Library of Political and Economic Science.

Payne, P., *British Entrepreneurship in the Nineteenth Century*, 2 edn (1988).

Peled, Y., *Class and Ethnicity in the Pale* (1987).

Pellew, J., 'The Home Office and the Aliens Act, 1905', *Historical Journal*, 32 (1989).

Perlmann, J., 'Selective Migration as a Basis for Upward Mobility?: The Occupations of the Jewish Immigrants to the United States, ca 1900', Jerome Levy Economics Institute, working paper no. 172 (1996).

Piore, M., *Birds of Passage: Migrant Labor and Industrial Societies* (Cambridge, 1979).

Polanyi, K., *The Great Transformation* (Boston, MA, 1944).

Pollard, S., *Britain's Prime and Britain's Decline* (1989).

Pollard, S., 'Entrepreneurship, 1870–1914', in R. Floud and D. McCloskey (eds), *The Economic History of Britain Since 1700*, 2nd edn (Cambridge, 1994).

Pollins, H., *Economic History of the Jews in England* (1982).

Pollins, H., 'Immigrants and Minorities – the Outsiders in Business', *Immigrants and Minorities*, 8 (1989).

Pope, J., *The Clothing Industry in New York* (New York, 1905).

Potter, B., 'The Jewish Community (East London)', in Booth, *Life and Labour*, 1st ser. vol. 3, ch. IV

Potter, B., 'The Tailoring Trade', in Booth, *Life and Labour*, 1st ser. vol. 4, ch. IV.

Prais, S. J. and M. Schmool, 'Statistics of Jewish Marriages in Great Britain: 1901–1965', *Jewish Journal of Sociology*, IX (1967).

Prior, A. and M. Kirby, 'The Society of Friends and the Family Firm', *Business History*, 35 (1993).

Punch (various issues).

Quarterly Review (1855).

Rau, D., 'The 1891 Census in Spitalfields: a Source for Migration', in A. Newman and S. Massil, *Patterns of Migration*.

Rees, G., *St. Michael: a History of Marks and Spencer* (1969).

Reich, N., 'The Economic Structure of Modern Jewry', in L. Finkelstein (ed.), *The Jews, Their History, Culture and Religion*.

Reutlinger, A., 'Reflections on the Anglo-American Jewish Experience: Immigrants, Workers, and Entrepreneurs in New York and London, 1870–1914', *American Jewish Historical Quarterly*, LXVI (1977).

Rischin, M., *The Promised City: New York's Jews, 1870–1914* (New York, 1962).

Rischin, M. (ed.), *The American Gospel of Success* (Chicago, IL, 1965).

Rose, M., 'Family Firm, Community and Business Culture: a Comparative Perspective on the British and American Cotton Industries', in A. Godley and O. Westall (eds), *Business History and Business Culture*.

Rosenbaum, S., 'A Contribution to the Study of the Vital and Other Statistics of the Jews in the United Kingdom', *Journal of the Royal Statistical Society*, LXVIII (1905).

Rosenthal, E., 'The Equivalence of United States Census Data for Persons of Russian Stock or Descent with American Jews', *Demography*, 14 (1975).

Rosenwaike, I., *A Population History of New York City* (Syracuse, NY, 1972).

Rubinov, I., 'Economic and Industrial Conditions (A) New York', in C. Bernheimer (ed.), *The Russian Jew in the United States*.

Rubinov, I., *Economic Conditions of the Jews in Russia* (Washington, DC, 1907).

Rubinstein, W., *Capitalism, Culture and Decline in Britain, 1750–1990* (1993).

Rubinstein, W., *A History of the Jews in the English Speaking World: Great Britain* (Basingstoke, 1996).

Rubinstein, W., 'The Weber Thesis, Ethnic Minoroties and British Entrepreneurship', in D. Jeremy (ed.), *Religion, Business and Wealth in Modern Britain* (1998).

Rubinstein, W., 'Entrepreneurial Minorities: A Typology', in Godley and Casson, *Economic Factors*.

Ruppin, A., *The Jews in the Modern World* (1934).

Russell, C. and H. Lewis, *The Jew in London: a Study of Racial Character and Present-day Conditions* (1900).

Sandberg, L., 'The Entrepreneur and Technological Change', in Floud and McCloskey, *Economic History*.

Sarachek, B., 'American Entrepreneurs and the Horatio Alger Myth', *Journal of Economic History*, XXXVIII (1978).

Sarachek, B., 'Jewish American Entrepreneurs', *Journal of Economic History*, XL (1980).

Sarna, J., 'The Myth of No Return: Jewish Return Migration to Eastern Europe, 1881 to 1914,' *American Jewish History* (1981).

Schlicht, E., *On Custom in the Economy* (Oxford, 1998).

Schloss, D., 'Bootmaking', in Booth, *Life and Labour*, 1st ser. vol. 4, ch. iv.

Schmiechen, J., *Sweated Industries and Sweated Labour: the London Clothing Trades, 1860–1914* (1984).

Schumpeter, J., *Business Cycles: a Theoretical, Historical and Statistical Analysis of the Capitalist Process* (2 vols, New York, 1939).

Scott, P., *The Property Masters: a History of the British Commercial Property Sector* (1996).

Scranton, P., 'The Transition from Custom to Ready-to-wear Clothing in Philadelphia, 1890–1930', *Textile History*, 25 (1994).

Sharpe, P., '"Cheapness and Economy": Manufacturing and Retailing Ready-Made Clothing in London and Essex 1830–1850', *Textile History*, 26 (1995).

Sigsworth, E., *Montague Burton, a Tailor of Taste* (1989).

Simon, H., 'Rationality as Process and Product of Thought', *American Economic Review*, 68 (1978).

Sombart, W., *Jews and Modern Capitalism* (New York, 1951).

Southall, H. and D. Gilbert, 'A Good Time to Wed?: Marriage and Economic Distress in England and Wales, 1839–1914', *Economic History Review*, XLIX (1996).

Sowell, T., *Migrations and Cultures: a Worldview* (New York, 1996).

Stampfer, S., '*Heder* Study, Knowledge of Torah, and the Maintenance of Social Stratification in Traditional East European Jewish Society', *Studies in Jewish Education*, 3 (1988).

Stampfer, S., 'The Geographic Background of East European Jewish Migration to the United States before World War I', in Glazier and De Rosa, *Migration in Time and Place*.

Stanislawski, M., *Tsar Nicholas I and the Jews: the Transformation of Jewish Society in Russia, 1825–1855* (Philadelphia, PA, 1983).

Styles, J., 'Clothing the North: the Supply of Non-elite Clothing in the Eighteenth Century North of England', *Textile History*, 25 (1994).

Szajkowski, Z., 'How the Mass Migration to America Began', *Jewish Social Studies*, IV (1942).

Szajkowski, Z., 'The European Attitudes to East European Jewish Immigration (1881–93)', *Publications of the American Jewish Historical Society*, XLI (1951–2).

Tananbaum, S., 'Making Good Little English Children: Infant Welfare and Anglicization among the Jewish Immigrants in London, 1880–1939', *Immigrants and Minorities*, 12 (1993).

Tawney, R., *The Establishment of Minimum Rates in the Tailoring Industry under the Trade Boards Act of 1909* (1915).

Taylor, P., *The Distant Magnet: European Emigration to the USA* (1971).

Temin, P., 'Is it Kosher to Talk about Culture?', *Journal of Economic History*, 57 (1997).

Tenenbaum, S., 'Immigrants and Capital: Jewish Loan Societies in the United States, 1880–1945', *American Jewish History*, LXXVI (1986).

Tenenbaum, S., 'Culture and Context: the Emergence of Hebrew Free Loan Societies in the United States', *Social Science History*, 13 (1989).

Tenenbaum, S., *A Credit to their Community: Jewish Loan Societies in the United States, 1880–1945* (Detroit, MI, 1993).

Thernstrom, S., *Poverty and Progress in a Nineteenth Century City* (Cambridge, MA, 1964).

Thernstrom, S., *The Other Bostonians: Poverty and Progress in the American Metropolis, 1880–1970* (Cambridge, MA, 1973).

Thomas, B., *Migration and Economic Growth: a Study of Great Britain and the Atlantic Economy* (Cambridge, 1954).

Thompson, E. J., 'The 1991 Census of Population in England and Wales', *Journal of the Royal Statistical Society*, ser. A, 158 (1995).

Tolliday, S., 'Management and Labour, 1896–1939', in Tolliday and J. Zeitlin (eds), *The Automobile Industry and Its Workers* (New York, 1986).

Tolliday, S., 'The Failure of Mass Production Unionism in the Motor Industry, 1914–1939', in C. Wrigley (ed.), *A History of British Industrial Relations* (1987).

Tolliday, S. and J. Zeitlin (eds) *The Power to Manage? Employers and Industrial Relations in Comparative Historical Perspective* (1991).

Trachtenberg, H., 'Estimate of the Jewish Population of London in 1929', *Journal of the Royal Statistical Society*, xcvi (1933).

Trooper, Harold, 'Jews and Canadian Immigration Policy, 1900–1950', in M. Rischin (ed.), *The Jews of North America* (Detroit, MI, 1987).

Tucker, C., 'Jewish Marriages and Divorces in England until 1940: Part I', *Genealogists Magazine*, 24 (1992).

Tulchinsky, G., *Taking Root: the Origins of the Canadian Jewish Community* (Toronto, 1992).

Turnock, D., 'Railway Development in Eastern Europe as a Context for Migration Study', in Newman and Massil, *Patterns of Migration*.

United States Congressional Papers:

    Bureau of Statistics, *European Emigration* (Washington, DC, 1890).

    Commissioner General for Immigration, *Annual Reports*, 1903–1905 (Washington, DC, 1904–06).

    Department for Commerce and Labor, *Report* (Washington, DC, 1904).

    Immigration Commission, *Reports of the Immigration Commission and Abstracts: Abstract of Statistical Revue of Immigration to the United States, 1820–1910* (Washington, DC, 1911).

    Immigration Commission, *Reports, Immigrants in Industries* (Washington, DC, 41 vols, 1911).

    Industrial Commission on Immigration, 'Foreign-Born Labor in the Clothing Trade,' *Reports of the Industrial Commission on Immigration*, vol. 15 (Washington, DC, 1901).

Waldinger, R., *Through the Eye of the Needle* (New York, 1986).

Waterman, S. and B. Kosmin, 'Mapping an Unenumerated Ethnic Population – Jews in London', *Ethnic and Racial Studies*, 10 (1986).

Watkins, S. C. and A. S. London, 'Personal Names and Cultural Change: a Study of the Naming Patterns of Italians and Jews in the United States in 1910', *Social Science History*, 18 (1994).

Webb, S., 'Preface', in B. L. Hutchins and A. L. Harrison, *A History of Factory Legislation* (1911).

Weber, M., *The Protestant Ethic and the Spirit of Capitalism* (trans. Talcott Parsons, 2nd edn, 1976).

Wechsler, R., 'The Jewish Garment Trade in East London, 1875–1914: a Study of Conditions and Responses' (unpublished PhD dissertation, Columbia University, 1979).

Wegge, S., 'Chain Migration and Information Networks: Evidence from Nineteenth Century Hesse-Cassel', *Journal of Economic History*, 58 (1998).

Westall, O., 'The Competitive Environment of British Business, 1850–1914', in M. Kirby and M. Rose (eds), *Business Enterprise in Modern Britain from the Eighteenth to the Twentieth Century* (1994).

Whitaker's Almanac (1903).

Whitehill, G. (ed.), *Bevis Marks Records*, Pt III (1973).

Wiener, M., *English Culture and the Decline of the Industrial Spirit, 1850–1980* (1981).

Williamson, J., 'The Evolution of Global Labor Markets since 1830: Background Evidence and Hypotheses', *Explorations in Economic History*, 32 (1995).

Williamson, J., 'Globalization, Convergence and History', *Journal of Economic History*, 56 (1996).

Wilson, C., 'Economy and Society in Late Victorian Britain', *Economic History Review*, XVIII (1965).

Wischnitzer, Mark, *To Dwell in Safety* (Philadelphia, PA, 1948).

Wolf, L., *The Legal Sufferings of the Jews in Russia* (1912).

Wrigley, E. A. (ed.), *Nineteenth-Century Society: Essays in the Use of Quantitative Methods for the Study of Social Data* (Cambridge, 1972).

Wyllie, I. G., *The Self Made Man in America: The Myth of Rags to Riches* (New Brunswick, NJ, 1954).

Zeitlin, J., 'Reconciling Automation and Flexibility? Technology and Production in the Postwar British Motor Vehicle Industry', *Enterprise and Society*, 1 (2000).

Zipperstein, S. J., *The Jews of Odessa: a Cultural History, 1794–1881* (Stanford, CA, 1985).

Index